Harrie Marsman B-Book
First Edition

B-Book

How to reply to an official communication and pass Paper B of the European Qualifying Examination

written and edited by

Harrie Marsman, European representative and tutor at CEIPI, Strasbourg

First Edition

Carl Heymanns Verlag 2021

Citation: Marsman, B-Book, 1st edition, para 35

Bibliographic information published by the Deutsche Nationalbibliothek
the Deutsche Nationalbibliothek lists this publication in the Deutsche Nationalbibliografie; detailed bibliographic data are available in the internet at http://dnb.d-nb.de

ISBN 978-3-452-27994-1

www.wolterskluwer.de

© 2021 Wolters Kluwer Deutschland GmbH, Wolters-Kluwer-Straße 1, 50354 Hürth, Germany.

All rights reserved. No part of this publication may be reproduced or transmitted in any form or by any means, or stored in any retrieval system of any nature without prior written permission, except for permitted fair dealing under the Copyright Act, or in accordance with the terms of a license issued in respect of photocopying and/or reprographic reproduction. Application for permission for other use of copyright material including permission to reproduce extracts in other published works shall be made to the publishers. Full acknowledgment of author, publisher and source must be given.

The publisher and the authors can accept no liability for errors in the content or for printing errors.

Cover: Martina Busch, Grafik-Design, Homburg Kirrberg, Germany
Typesetting: Datagroup-Int SRL, Timisoara, Romania
Printed by Wydawnictwo Diecezjalne i Drukarnia w Sandomierzu, Sandomierz, Polen

Printed on non-acid and aging resistant paper.

Foreword to the first edition

To pass the European qualifying examination (EQE) is a major challenge. Candidates have to demonstrate that they possess comprehensive legal and technical knowledge enabling them to represent applicants before the European Patent Office (EPO). Therefore, a thorough preparation is a key factor to success.

From the outset, when the first examination was held in 1979, the Centre for International Intellectual Property Studies (CEIPI) at the University of Strasbourg (France) was entrusted with the organisation of training courses and seminars for candidates preparing for the EQE. Over the past decades, CEIPI has gained widespread experience and an outstanding reputation based on excellence and efficiency. With its teaching staff comprising about 80 tutors coming from both the circle of professional representatives and the staff of the EPO, CEIPI provides courses and seminars covering both the Pre-examination and the four papers of the main examination.

Various tutors developed teaching concepts and materials over a period of many years. This work led to the publication of the "C-book" edited by Bill Chandler and Hugo Meinders in 2005. In the meantime, the "C-Book" has become a standard tool for the preparation of paper C of the EQE.

Early in 2014 Andrew Rudge prepared the "D-Book", which offers advice and support for candidates preparing for paper D dealing with legal questions.

The "A-Book" edited by Erich and Michael Wäckerlin followed quickly thereafter, in 2015. This A-Book teaches candidates how to draft claims and the introductory part of a patent application. It was intended by these editors that the B-Book would soon thereafter be published to complete the series of books to prepare for all four main exam papers. This was however delayed, because it became clear that the format of papers A and B would change in 2017. It would make sense to wait until it was clear how the single papers A and B would look like. And, then, unfortunately, early 2018, Erich passed away.

With this publication of the "B-Book" edited by Harrie Marsman the series of textbooks for preparing the main examination is finally complete. The new format of paper B introduced in 2017 was taken into account. CEIPI is pleased to provide comprehensive information and advice to help candidates prepare all four papers from A to D.

When sitting the EQE, candidates have to know what they are supposed to do, which strategy they are going to apply, and how the difficulties of each individual paper can be overcome. No seminar and no textbook will ever replace their judgment and release them from the burden of finding their own solutions to the papers.

Nevertheless, proper training material can reduce the time and efforts needed for the preparation, thus turning the learning process into an exciting experience.

We at CEIPI are confident that the "B-Book" will serve its purpose and become a useful tool for candidates, who need nothing more than sound preparation, chances of success at passing the EQE, and a bit of luck.

On behalf of CEIPI, I would like to express my thanks to the author. His commitment, dedication and long-time loyalty to CEIPI is striking.

Strasbourg, June 2021

Thierry Debled
Director of the International Section

Preface

The "B-Book" completes the series of CEIPI textbooks relating to papers A to D of the EQE. It is intended to be a practical guide for candidates preparing for paper B and complements volumes of the series, in particular the "A-Book" as set up and edited by my dear friend and master tutor Erich Wäckerlin, who unfortunately passed away far too young in 2018, and the widely used "C-Book" edited by fellow tutors Bill Chandler and Hugo Meinders.

But why a "*B-Book*"?

Is there really a need for a textbook dealing with replying to an official communication by an Examiner of the European Patent Office? Defending the claims of a European patent application, optionally after amending these, is a task that most candidates preparing for the European Qualifying Examination (EQE) know quite well from their day-to-day job. When sitting the main examination of the EQE, candidates have usually a proven record of performance in a wide range of activities pertaining to the procedures before the European Patent Office, including the responding to communications and amending claims. Moreover, by passing the Pre-examination they have demonstrated their ability to answer legal questions and questions dealing with claim analysis. Yet, the pass rate of first-time sitters of paper B is often below 60 %. How is this possible?

Experience gained in the preparatory courses and seminars of CEIPI shows that an overwhelming majority of candidates are well prepared and knowledgeable. Apart from having a sound basis of patent law, they possess the analytical skills required for problem solving and decision-making. If anything is lacking, it is the ability to apply the rather academic knowledge to the facts of the case presented in paper B. Obviously the need to apply abstract principles of patent law to concrete facts and circumstances described in the examination paper is for many candidates a major difficulty.

As said, this "*B-Book*" is intended to be a practical guide for candidates preparing for paper B. When writing the "*B-Book*", I have tried to keep in mind candidates who have passed the Pre-examination and are now preparing for the main examination. I suppose that the students know how claims may be amended under the European Patent Convention (EPC), and which requirements are laid down in the EPC, in particular with regard to support in the application as originally filed, novelty, inventive step, clarity, unity-of-invention and the requirements of Rule 43(2) EPC. There is no doubt that all students are also well acquainted with the Guidelines for Examination in the EPO.

I have chosen to follow the structural approaches that were earlier developed by Bill and Hugo in their C-Book and by Erich and Michael in their A-Book, and I cannot thank these guys enough for their good work! The following order of presentation is used.

Chapter 1 gives an introduction to the fundamental concept of paper B. It is designed to make candidates aware of the specific requirements of the paper.

Chapter 2 is devoted to a methodology for solving paper B. It includes a section regarding a strategy for solving paper B, as well as a section containing a number of practical tips. I consider this chapter the core of this book, because therein I elaborated step-by-step a method that works very well for me.

I believe that candidates who complete Chapter 2 will know the principles and basic considerations of paper B. My method, however, does not need to be their method. They should be able to develop their own strategy and method for solving paper B.

Chapter 3 relates to the principles of interpretation and analysis of disclosures, as far as these are relevant to paper B.

Chapters 4-8 deal with the following topics, which are essential for solving paper B:

Chapter 4: State of the Art.

Chapter 5: Patentable and non-patentable inventions.

Chapter 6: Novelty.

Chapter 7: Inventive Step

Chapter 8: Claims and Clarity
Chapter 9: Amendments and Correction.
Chapter 10, finally, deals with the drafting of the letter to the EPO.
Following the chapters of this book, there are three appendices.
Appendix 1 contains paper B 2017.
Appendix 2 contains the Examiners' Report of paper B 2017.
Appendix 3 contains the CEIPI solution of paper 2017.

I could only write this book, because of the many years of in-depth discussions among the CEIPI tutors for papers A and B in Strasbourg, of the insights coming from the Examiners' Reports of, especially, the 2017-2019 papers B, and of the fruitful annual meetings of EQE tutors and members of the EQE Committees at the EPO in Munich.

Special thanks go to Steef Polderdijk, coordinator of the CEIPI A- and B-seminars, for providing his useful comments on my draft for my methodology and for his work on the CEIPI solutions of papers B 2017, 2018 and 2019; to Wim van der Poel, Member of the EQE Examination Board and coordinator of Committee I, for his willingness to discuss some general issues with paper B; to Thierry Debled, Director of the International Section of CEIPI; to Bill Chandler and Hugo Meinders, the editors of the C-Book; and of course to Christiane Melz, the Administrative Manager of the International Section of CEIPI for her continuous support and enthusiasm.

Further, I am grateful to Margaretha Pirzer of Wolters Kluwer Deutschland GmbH for her assistance in the production of the book.

Although the present volume forms part of the CEIPI series of books on papers A to D, the responsibility for writing and editing the "B-Book" is mine and mine alone. The views expressed in this volume do not necessarily represent those of the EQE Examination Board, the Examination Secretariat or the Examination Committee I, which is in charge of paper B. The citations in this book do not substitute in any manner the official publications issued by these competent bodies or the EPO.

I am certain that mistakes and errors are present in this book and would welcome any amendments, comments, criticism and suggestions regarding this "*B-Book*" on my email address harrie@marsmanoctrooi.nl.

Haaren, The Netherlands, June 2021 *Harrie Marsman*

Contents

Foreword to the first edition	V
Preface	VII
Abbreviations used	XV
1 Introduction	1
2 Methodology	11
3 Interpretation and analysis of disclosures	57
4 State of the Art	61
5 Patentable and non-patentable inventions	65
6 Novelty	71
7 Inventive Step	79
8 Claims and Clarity	87
9 Amendments and correction	103
10 Drafting the letter in response to the communication	111
Appendix 1 – Paper B 2017	115
Appendix 2 – Examiners' Report Paper B 2017	125
Appendix 3 – CEIPI Model Solution Paper B 2017	141
Index	145

Detailed Contents

Foreword to the first edition		V
Preface		VII
Abbreviations used		XV
1	**Introduction**	1
1.1	Object of this book	1
1.2	Replying to official communications under Art. 94(3) EPC in the prosecution of European patent applications	1
1.3	Description of paper B	2
1.4	Study materials for the preparation for paper B	4
1.4.1	European Patent Convention (EPC)	4
1.4.2	Official Journal of the EPO	4
1.4.3	Guidelines for Examination in the European Patent Office	5
1.4.4	Case law of the EPO Boards of Appeal	5
1.4.5	Regulation on the European qualifying examination for professional representatives	6
1.4.6	Examination Compendium	6
1.4.7	Recommended commentaries in English, French and German	7
1.4.8	Selected guides for the preparation of the EQE	7
1.4.9	EQE online support by the EPO	8
1.5	Overall method for solving paper B	8
1.6	How to use this book?	9
2	**Methodology**	11
2.1	Objective	11
2.2	Preliminary steps	11
2.2.1	Regulation on the EQE	12
2.2.2	Implementing provisions to the Regulation on the EQE (IPREE)	14
2.2.3	Instructions to candidates concerning the conduct of the European qualifying examination and Instructions to candidates concerning the conduct of the European qualifying examination 2021	17
2.3	Detailed methodology for solving paper B	18
2.3.1	Step 1: Getting an overview of the components of your paper B	19
2.3.2	Step 2: Performing a preliminary analysis of the subject-matter of paper B	19
2.3.3	Step 3: Finding the objections	22
2.3.4	Step 4: Performing a preliminary analysis of the prior art	30
2.3.5	Step 5: Performing an in-depth analysis of the patent application	32
2.3.6	Step 6: Drafting the set of amended claims	37
2.3.7	Step 7: Determining for the draft set of amended claims whether the material requirements (Art. 52-57 EPC) have been met, and optionally adapting the draft set of amended claims	42
2.3.8	Step 8: Drafting the supplementary note, if any	46
2.3.9	Step 9: Drafting the letter in response to the communication	49
2.3.10	Step 10: Final check	53
2.4	Strategy for solving paper B	54
3	**Interpretation and analysis of disclosures**	57
3.1	Legal basis	57
3.2	Relevance to paper B	57

3.3	Interpreting features	57
3.3.1	Interpreting technical terms and expressions	58
3.3.2	Non-limiting features	58
3.3.3	Identical features	58
3.3.4	Generic versus specific features	59
3.3.5	Features incorporated by reference	59
3.3.6	Implicit features	59
4	**State of the Art**	**61**
4.1	Legal basis	61
4.2	Relevance to paper B	62
4.3	State of the art	62
4.4	Examples from past papers	63
5	**Patentable and non-patentable inventions**	**65**
5.1	Legal basis	65
5.2	Relevance to paper B	66
5.3	Patentable inventions	67
5.4	Non-inventions according to Art. 52(2), (3) EPC	68
5.5	Exceptions to patentability under Art. 53 EPC	68
5.6	Non-technical features	69
5.7	Industrial application	70
5.8	Examples from past papers	70
6	**Novelty**	**71**
6.1	Legal basis	71
6.2	Relevance to Paper B	73
6.3	Analysis of novelty	73
6.4	Parameters	74
6.5	Novelty of selection inventions	75
6.5.1	Selection of chemical substances or groups of substances from generic formulae comprised in the state of the art	75
6.5.2	Selection of sub-ranges from broader ranges comprised in the state of the art	76
6.5.3	Overlapping ranges	76
6.5.4	Multiple selections	77
6.6	Novelty test	77
6.7	Examples from past papers	77
7	**Inventive Step**	**79**
7.1	Legal basis	79
7.2	Relevance to Paper B	80
7.3	Outlines of the problem and solution approach	80
7.4	The meaning of the requirement of inventive step in Paper B	83
7.5	Examples from past papers	84
8	**Claims and Clarity**	**87**
8.1	Legal basis	87
8.2	Requirements according to Art. 84 EPC	87
8.3	Provisions regarding the form and content of claims	88
8.4	Kinds of claims	89
8.5	Clarity and interpretation of claims	90
8.6	Support of the claims by the description	90
8.7	Independent claims	90
8.7.1	General principles	90
8.7.2	Things to avoid when drafting independent claims	92
8.8	Combinations of independent claims in different categories	92
8.9	More than one independent claim in the same category	93
8.10	Relevance to Paper B	93

8.11	Dependent claims	93
8.11.1	General principles applicable to dependent claims	93
8.12	Relevance to Paper B	95
8.13	Examples from past papers	95
9	**Amendments and correction**	**103**
9.1	Legal basis	103
9.2	Relevance to paper B	105
9.3	Judging added subject-matter	106
9.3.1	The gold standard	106
9.3.2	The "Novelty test" and the "Modified novelty test" or "Disclosure test"	106
9.3.3	Removing or replacing features (Essentiality test or Three-Point test)	106
9.3.4	Unallowable intermediate generalisation	107
9.4	Disclaimers	107
9.4.1	Undisclosed disclaimers	107
9.4.2	Disclosed disclaimers	108
9.5	Corrections of errors	108
9.6	Examples from previous papers	108
10	**Drafting the letter in response to the communication**	**111**

Appendix 1 – Paper B 2017 115

Appendix 2 – Examiners' Report Paper B 2017 125

Appendix 3 – CEIPI Model Solution Paper B 2017 141

Index 145

Abbreviations used

Art./R.	Article/Rule
A-Book	A-Book – How to draft claims and the introductory part of a European patent application and pass paper A of the European Qualifying Examination. Second edition, Köln; Carl Heymanns Verlag, July 2019
Case Law Book	Case Law of the Boards of Appeal of the European Patent Office. 9th Edition, July 2019, Munich: EPO, 2019.
C-Book	C-Book – How to write a successful opposition and pass paper C of the European Qualifying Examination. Sixth edition, Köln; Carl Heymanns Verlag, July 2019.
Compendium	Collection of past examination papers and examiners´ reports published by the EPO.
EPC	European Patent Convention and its Implementing Regulations.
epi	Institute of Professional Representatives before the EPO.
EPO	European Patent Office.
EQE	European qualifying examination.
Guidelines, GL	Guidelines for Examination in the EPO. Revised edition of March 2021, Munich: EPO, 2021.
Instructions Instr.	Instructions to candidates concerning the conduct of the European qualifying examination.
IPREE	Implementing provisions to the Regulation on the European qualifying examination.
l.	Line
OJ EPO	Official Journal of the EPO.
p.	Page
REE	Regulation on the European qualifying examination for professional representatives.
"White Book"	see Case Law Book.

1 Introduction

1.1 Object of this book

The European qualifying examination (EQE) is designed to establish whether a candidate is qualified to practise as a professional representative before the European Patent Office. Passing the examination requires quite a bit of technical and legal knowledge, as well as the ability to analyse complex patent-related issues within a very short time. A clear strategy and efficient methods for solving the papers are crucial for success.

The first object of this book is to provide a qualitative introduction to the basic concepts of paper B. Chapter 1 is designed to make you aware of the characteristic features of paper B, and to give you some hints regarding the working tools. This chapter should not absorb too much of your time, but it is not recommended to skip it completely.

The presentation of my approach or my methodology for solving paper B focuses on the key issues. To say it clearly: there is not just one way of performing the various tasks within the framework of the paper, and no particular method can claim to be perfect. Many roads lead to Rome, but, irrespective of this, it is essential to know at least one viable path which leads you to the goal. Once you have studied Chapter 2 of this book, you should not only have a fairly good understanding of the problems, but also a sound idea how these problems can be overcome. This will enable you to adapt the method to your own needs and preferences.

There exists extensive literature dealing with the fundamental concepts of patent law, such as patentable and non-patentable inventions, the state of the art, novelty and inventive step, clarity of claims and support in the application as originally filed. Since these concepts are well known, there is hardly any need to repeat them, thus reinventing the wheel. It is essential, however, to be aware of the relevance of the concepts to paper B. These topics are elaborated in Chapters 3 to 9.

The last chapter, chapter 10, of the book gives a practical guide to drafting the response to the communication.

You may wish to study a model solution of paper B. For this purpose, a model solution of Paper B 2017, drawn up and used by CEIPI tutors, has been included as Appendix 3. This model solution corresponds to the expectations of the Examination Committee and illustrates the format of the answer paper.

The preceding remarks should make clear that active participation is required to benefit from the content of this book. Simply reading or learning the topics by heart brings practically nothing. Treat every topic of the book as if you were trying to discover it yourself, using the text merely as a guide that you should leave behind. Remember that the best method of learning new things is to practice them. With this in mind, you will hopefully enjoy what is presented in this book.

1.2 Replying to official communications under Art. 94(3) EPC in the prosecution of European patent applications

The grant procedure for European patent applications comprises two stages. In the first stage an examination on filing and a formalities examination of the application are carried out (Art. 90 EPC). Subsequently, an extended European search report in the form of a European search report, normally accompanied by a non-binding opinion on patentability is drawn up (Art. 92 EPC; Rule 62 EPC). After receiving the search report and before receiving the first communication from the Examining Division, the applicant has to submit substantive observations on any objections raised in the extended search report. He may also amend the description, claims and drawings of his own volition (Rule 137(1), (2) EPC).

The second stage comprises the substantive examination (Art. 94 EPC). Whenever the examination reveals that the application does not meet the requirements of the EPC, the Examining Division issues a reasoned first communication inviting the applicant to file observations and, if necessary, to submit amendments to the description, claims and drawings (Art. 94(3) EPC; Rule 71(1), (2) EPC). All objections raised by the Examining Division should be considered, so that the examination procedure can be completed after as few actions as possible. If, after examining the response from the applicant, the application is still not ready for grant, the examination is continued. Further written communications are issued as often as necessary (Art. 94(3) EPC), but no further amendments are possible without the consent of the Examining Division (Rule 137(3) EPC). **It is this second stage, the substantive examination, that is tested in paper B of the EQE.**

10 The examination procedure leads to the decision to grant the patent, or to refuse the application (Art. 97(1), (2) EPC), depending on whether the application is in conformity with the requirements of the EPC, or not.

11 After validation, filings of European patent applications take effect in all designated contracting states to the EPC. The centralised grant procedure in one language is an effective alternative to separate national filings in each of the concerned states.

1.3 Description of paper B

12 The framework of paper B is laid down in Art. 1(4) of the Regulation on the European qualifying examination for professional representatives (REE) and Rule 24 of the Implementing provisions to the Regulation on the European qualifying examination (IPREE). In addition, the Regulation on the European qualifying examination for professional representatives in Supplementary publication 2 of OJ EPO 2019 comprises instructions to candidates.

13 Paper B tests the candidates´ ability to prepare a reply to an official letter in which prior art has been cited.

14 Paper B used to be drafted for two technical fields, namely Electricity/Mechanics and Chemistry, and candidates were free to choose between the two alternatives. However, as of 2017, a single paper B is presented at the EQE in a technical field that is or at least should be accessible to everyone.

15 According to Rule 24(1) IPREE, the duration of paper B is three hours; yet as from 2017, candidates sitting paper B are granted an additional thirty minutes (Decision of the Supervisory Board, 17 November 2016 (Supplementary publication 2 – OJ EPO 2017, 43)). At first sight this seems like a lot of time, but what is said in the "*C-Book*" on paper C applies also to paper B; *"the many pieces of information to be considered, the number of decisions to be taken and the parts of the solution to be written mean that good time management is essential"* (p. 3–4).

16 The general scenario of paper B is that the candidates receive the text of a European patent application that has been filed designating all the contacting states of the EPC, together with an official EPO communication. In addition, a client's letter is included containing instructions about the way the client wishes to proceed with the European patent application and a draft set of amended claims to be filed with the candidates' response to the official communication.

17 In practice, the official communication will refer to attached prior art documents. Paper B 2021 also included anonymous third party observations referring to a public prior use.

18 The number of parts that make up paper B may vary from one year to another.

19 Single paper B in the 2017, 2018 and 2019 EQEs each comprised the description of the application accompanied by drawings of the application, and three documents representing the state of the art. The Mock paper B provided in 2016 as example for the first single paper B also comprised the description of the application accompanied by drawings of the application, yet contained two pieces of prior art.

20 In 2020, the EQE was cancelled by Decision of the Supervisory Board dated 20 April 2020, because of the COVID-19 pandemic in Europe.

21 For 2021, the Supervisory Board announced on 23 July 2020 that the EQE was planned to be conducted online and that "the syllabus and the structure of the various examination papers will be as outlined in the REE and IPREE and in line with previous years' examination paper". See in this light also the "Information on the schedule for the EQE 2021 examination papers" dated 2 December 2020 (http://documents.epo.org/projects/babylon/eponot.nsf/0/66EB601464EC7BECC12586320050164F/$FILE/ExamPapers%20EQE%202021_EN.pdf).

22 Single paper B 2021 also comprised the description of the application accompanied by drawings of the application, and three documents representing the state of the art;

moreover anonymous third party observations including information on a public prior use formed part of this paper. Candidates were allowed to print the prior-art documents and the drawing(s), but none of the following: the description and claims of the application, the EPO communication, the client's letter and the amended claims. The documents allowed for printing were made available at least ten minutes before the start of the examination.

As said, Paper B used to be drafted in two technical fields, namely Electricity/Mechanics and Chemistry, and candidates were free to choose between the two alternatives. In the years 2013–2016, the formats of papers B Chemistry and Electricity/Mechanics were quite similar to the current single papers B. An application as originally filed, optionally with accompanying drawings, was included, together with an official communication, two or three documents representing the state of the art, a client's letter and a draft set of claims. Before 2013, there was less guidance on what the set of claims needed to protect.

The main tasks of paper B are to respond to all points raised in the official and to amend the claims supplied by the client so that these meet the requirements of the EPC. The description need not be amended.

In order to collect marks in paper B, it is essential to follow the instructions in the client's letter "about the way the client wishes to proceed with the European patent application". This includes the draft set of claims provided by the client. As appears from the Examiners' Reports for Paper B, not the claim set as a whole as prepared by the candidate but **the amendments carried out to the draft set of claims provided by the client received marks**. These amendments are in line with the client's wishes, yet must meet the requirements of the EPC. In other words, the client indicates in which direction the answer is to be found, yet that client is not an expert on the provisions of the EPC.

For the amendments carried out to the draft set of claims provided by the clients, 30 marks are reserved. At least, that was the case in the single papers B of 2017–2019, of 2021 and also in the years before 2017. With some practice, it should be doable to collect easily some 20 marks. These are important marks, not only because you only need 50 marks to pass, but also because starting from a set of claims that is expected by the Examination Committee, simply makes it easier to collect marks for the argumentation and motivation part (the letter in response to the communication), as well.

It is also essential to respond to all points raised in the official communication. The candidates shall further identify clearly all amendments made in the claims and their basis in the application as filed and provide additional explanations where necessary. In paper B 2021, it was also required to give a reaction to the third party observations and the alleged public prior use, for example while pointing to the relevant passages in the Guidelines.

In practice, the set of claims must meet the requirements of the EPC and the letter to the Examiner must elaborate why this is the case. The claims must be directed to subject-matter that is novel and involves an inventive step. In addition, the subject-matter of the claims must relate to an invention in the sense of Art. 52 EPC and may not violate Art. 53 EPC. Further, the requirements of Art. 123(2) EPC need to be met. The claims *per se* and the set of claims as a whole must meet the requirement of clarity under Art. 84 EPC and must meet the requirements of unity-of-invention and of R. 43(2) EPC.

Although the tasks involved in paper B reflect to a certain extent the daily work of a professional representative before the EPO, candidates should bear in mind that, unavoidably, the scenario of the paper is a bit artificial. Other than in real-life situations, when sitting the examination, it is for example impossible to ask the applicant any questions. Moreover, candidates have only very limited control over the time which is available for performing the individual tasks. What makes things worse: both the set of claims and the letter to the Examiner have to result in a communication under R 71(3) EPC (apart from maybe the amendment of the description). There is no opportunity to enter into a dialogue with the Examining Division and to effect any subsequent amendments. Candidates who consider these circumstances and their implications have an advantage, whereas candidates who disrespect these circumstances and implications may face a failure.

When enrolling for the examination, candidates may request to submit their answer in an official language of a contracting state which is not an official language of the EPO. In this case, the Secretariat arranges for a translation into one of the EPO official languages (Art. 12(3) REE; Rule 5 (1) IPREE). It is important to note, however, that the examination papers are drawn up only in the three official languages of the EPO, namely English,

French and German. All candidates receive them in all three languages (Art. 12(1) REE). These copies are the basis for elaborating the answer paper.

1.4 Study materials for the preparation for paper B

31   The following list gives an overview of legal sources, commentaries and other materials for the preparation of the examination.

Legal texts

1.4.1   European Patent Convention (EPC)

32   The 17th printed edition published in November 2020 is available in English, French and German. It contains the following texts:
- European Patent Convention (EPC)
- Implementing Regulations to the EPC (usually also abbreviated EPC)
- The Rules relating to Fees (as last amended on 27 March 2020)
- Various protocols, including the Protocol on the Interpretation of Art. 69 EPC
- An extract from the EPC Revision Act of 29 November 2000
- The Administrative Council´s decision of 28 June 2001 on the transitional provisions under Art. 7 of the Revision Act.

33   The publication contains also an index of decisions and opinions of the Enlarged Board of Appeal (Annex I), a cross-reference list of EPC 1973/EPC 2000 (Annex II) and an alphabetical keyword index.

34   Apart from the printed version the EPC is also available in HTML and PDF format at the EPO website. The HTML version is updated on a regular basis and contains internal links between the articles and rules of the EPC. In contrast the PDF file reflects the latest printed edition, *i.e.* without amendments adopted by the Administrative Council since its publication:

www.epo.org/law-practice/legal-texts/epc.html

35   At the examination the printed version (also known as *"The Grey Book"*) should preferably be used. According to point 20 of the Instructions to candidates concerning the conduct of the European qualifying examination 2021, other than the computer system required for the examination (PC or laptop, monitor, keyboard, mouse, *etc.*) and routers and printers, no other electronic equipment (calculators, digital watches, tablets, smartphones, smart watches, *etc.*) are permitted during the examination unless expressly authorised in advance by the Examination Secretariat (http://documents.epo.org/projects/babylon/eponot.nsf/0/0EBC9DA304DF20A4C125868100424C67/$FILE/Instructions_Candidates_EQE2021.pdf).

36   The current version of the EPC entered into force on 13 December 2007. Any references in this book to Articles of the EPC and Rules of the Implementing Regulations refer to the EPC as amended by the Act revising the EPC of 29 November 2000, unless it is expressly stated that the previous version of the EPC from 1973 is meant. It is unlikely that the EPC 1973 has any impact on paper B, because the object of the paper is the filing of a new European application and not the prosecution of an application eventually filed before 13 December 2007.

1.4.2   Official Journal of the EPO

37   Previously published in printed form, the Official Journal of the EPO became an electronic-only publication in January 2014. All articles are available in HTML format to facilitate on-screen reading, and include links to material cited in them. In addition, the Office publishes an officially certified PDF file of each issue. The online Official Journal no longer uses page numbers as a way of referencing articles. Instead, each article carries a reference number starting with "A1" for the first article in the first issue of the year and continues sequentially throughout the year. Page numbers are included in the PDF file for convenience but should not be used for citations.

www.epo.org/law-practice/legal-texts/official-journal.html

38   For the purpose of the examination print-outs of the relevant articles have to be prepared.

1.4.3 Guidelines for Examination in the European Patent Office

The revised 2021 edition of the Guidelines for Examination in the European Patent Office (*"Guidelines"* or *"GL"*) entered into force on 1 March 2021. It supersedes all previous editions, in particular the edition of November 2019 that was to be used for the EQE 2021. The revised 2021 edition is the only valid official version of the Guidelines.

The Guidelines are available online on the EPO website in the three official languages in HTML and PDF format. There no longer exists a printed version of the Guidelines. For the purpose of the examination, print-outs of the relevant parts have to be prepared by the individual candidates.

www.epo.org/law-practice/legal-texts/guidelines.html

In the course of restructuring the Guidelines in 2012, the EPO decided to allow for annual revisions in order to keep the Guidelines in line with legal and procedural developments.

The Guidelines contain a wealth of information on how to apply the provisions laid down in the EPC and other relevant legal sources. The following parts are particularly important for preparing paper B:

Part C: Guidelines for Procedural Aspects of Substantive Examination.

Part F: The European Patent Application. This part deals with the requirements which applications must fulfil other than patentability, including unity of invention (Art. 82 EPC) and clarity (Art. 84 EPC).

Part G: Patentability. This part deals with the requirements of patentability provided for in Art. 52–57 EPC, including exclusions from patentability (Art. 52(2) EPC and Art. 53 EPC), novelty (Art. 54 EPC) and inventive step (Art. 56 EPC).

Part H: Amendments and Corrections. This part deals with the requirements to amend or correct a European patent application or European patent in examination, opposition and limitation proceedings.

The Guidelines give general instructions about the practice and procedure to be followed in accordance with the EPC and its Implementing Regulations. It should be noted, however, that they do not constitute legal provisions in the strict sense. Since they are intended to cover normal occurrences, it may become necessary to depart from the Guidelines in exceptional cases. Nevertheless, candidates sitting the examination can rely on the content of the Guidelines until such time as they – or the relevant legal provisions – are amended. Relevant in this respect is the Decision of the Supervisory Board amending Rules 2, 22 and 27 IPREE of 29 September 2017, amending (*inter alia*) Rule 22 IPREE to read "Candidates are expected to be familiar with at least the following documents in the versions valid as at 31 October of the year prior to (…) the examination: (…) (m) the Guidelines for Examination in the EPO".

In-depth knowledge of the Guidelines is indispensable for passing paper B of the examination.

During the preparation, and even more so during the examination itself, it is essential to be able to retrieve the information from the Guidelines as quickly as possible. For the convenience of the users of the Guidelines, an alphabetical keyword index has been published by the EPO in the three official languages (see, *e.g.*, https://www.epo.org/law-practice/legal-texts/html/guidelines/e/k.htm) . It can be downloaded in PDF format from the website of the EPO. The keyword index does not form part of the Guidelines, however.

1.4.4 Case law of the EPO Boards of Appeal

The latest version is the 9th edition published in July 2019. See also Supplementary publication 4, OJ EPO 2020, EPO Boards of Appeal Case Law 2018 and 2019; and Supplementary publication 2, Official Journal 2021, EPO Boards of Appeal Case Law 2020.

This source of information is available in printed form (also known as *"The White Book"*), as well as online at the EPO website in HTML format and PDF format. Both the HTML and the PDF version include full-text search functionality.

The publication covers the case law under the EPC developed since the first decision of a Board of Appeal was handed down in 1979. The 9th edition of the book takes account of decisions made available in writing by the end of 2018, as well as a number of particularly important decisions rendered at the beginning of 2019 and the questions of law referred to the Enlarged Board of Appeal under Art. 112 EPC in cases G 1/19, G2/19 and G 3/19.

53   In contrast to the Guidelines, the case law book contains summaries of decisions handed down in individual cases rather than explanations of the general principles governing the practice and procedure of the EPO. Thus, it is only wise to verify in critical cases, whether and to which extent a specific decision can be generalised. For the rest, all decisions which appear to be relevant to a particular issue should be consulted in full and not just on the basis of summaries.

1.4.5 Regulation on the European qualifying examination for professional representatives

54   This Regulation is available online at the EPO website as Supplementary publication 2 OJ EPO 2019 in HTML format and as a certified PDF file.

55   The supplementary publication 2 of OJ EPO 2019 is the latest version of the collection of relevant legal provisions governing the EQE. It includes in particular the following texts:
- Decision of the Administrative Council of 10 December 2008 amending the Regulation on the European qualifying examination for professional representatives before the European Patent Office (CA/D 26/08) (p. 1).
- Regulation on the European qualifying examination for professional representatives (REE) (p. 2–17).
- Implementing provisions to the Regulation on the European qualifying examination (IPREE) (p. 18–35).
- Instructions to candidates concerning the conduct of the European qualifying examination (Instr.) (p. 36–40).
- Decision of the Supervisory Board of 17 November 2016 (p. 41).

56   Thorough knowledge of the Regulation on the EQE is crucial, since it contains essential information on the conditions and the conduct of the examination. Reference is further and again made to the Decision of the Supervisory Board amending Rules 2, 22 and 27 IPREE of 29 September 2017 (http://documents.epo.org/projects/babylon/eponot.nsf/0/F77998C59D5CBF8DC12581AA003E3AA2/$File/Final_Decision_SB_amendment_IPREE_webpublication.pdf).

57   Because of the fact that there was, for the first time, an online EQE in 2021, specific Instructions to candidates concerning the conduct of the European qualifying examination 2021 were published based on the decision of the Examination Secretariat with effect from 1 March 2021: http://documents.epo.org/projects/babylon/eponot.nsf/0/0EBC9DA304DF20A4C125868100424C67/$FILE/Instructions_Candidates_EQE2021.pdf

1.4.6 Examination Compendium

58   After the examination, the Examination Committee prepares each year an *"Examiners' report"* on paper B, together with the outlines of a model solution. For the single paper B, only the reports for the years 2017, 2018, 2019 and 2021 are available, in addition to such a report for a Mock paper B issued in 2016. At the moment of publication of this book, the report for 2021 will be available, as well. Yet, separate reports are drawn up for the older papers B Electricity/Mechanics and papers B Chemistry. These documents are available in English, French and German on the website of the EPO under the title *"Compendium"*. They can be downloaded together with the text of the concerned papers from the website of the EPO. Quite regularly samples of answer papers drafted by candidates at the examination are also published on the Compendium site. These answers are real answer papers illustrating how candidates have coped with the difficulties of the papers. On no account they represent perfect solutions free from any shortcomings. The latter is not only relevant to bear in mind for the published candidates' answers, but also applies to the Examiners' reports on paper B Electricity/Mechanics and paper B Chemistry, since these are of a different structure, although as of 2013, it seems that these papers B already anticipated on the single paper B as introduced in 2017. This has to be kept in mind when evaluating them.

59   Although not legal texts in the strict sense, the *"Examiners' reports"* and the model solutions are important sources of information. They illustrate the thinking of the Examination Committee I and make plain what candidates are expected to do.

Commentaries on the EPC

1.4.7 Recommended commentaries in English, French and German

Visser, Derk; Lai, Laurence; De Lange, Peter; Suominen, Kaisa: Visser's Annotated Patent Convention; 2021 edition; Wolters Kluwer.
ISBN: 9789403532035

There is no need to introduce the *"Annotated Visser"* here. It is perhaps the most widely used commentary on the EPC. Apart from the text of the EPC it contains extensive comments and a detailed overview of the PCT with cross-references to the EPC.

Hoekstra, Jelle: References to the European Patent Convention.
Eindhoven: Delta Patents, July 2020.

Baque, Grégory: CBE – PCT.
Mise à jour au 1er Mai 2020. Paris: CLGB Editions, 2020.
ISBN: 9782954468167.

The *"Baque"* is the leading commentary on the EPC and PCT in French. The work is updated nearly every year.

Singer/Stauder/Luginbühl: Europäisches Patentübereinkommen. Kommentar.
8. Auflage, Köln: Carl Heymanns Verlag, 2018.
Heymanns Taschenkommentare; ISBN 978-3-452-29232-2

The *'Singer-Stauder'* is a comprehensive commentary on the EPC. It explains the principles of the law and addresses many questions on the application of the EPC and the PCT.

Kley, Hansjörg; Gundlach, Harald: Kommentar zum EPÜ 2000; 4. Auflage.
Loseblattwerk mit Aktualisierungen Januar 2020, Hirschberg:
mfh-Verlag ISBN 9783981214147.

Published in loose-leaf format, the work is divided into two ring binders. It is available in printed and electronic form. The work is regularly updated and provides a quick and comprehensive overview of the law. It contains references to the OJ EPO, the Guidelines, the case law of the Boards of Appeal and various other sources. A number of key topics are presented in the form of multi-coloured mindmaps.

1.4.8 Selected guides for the preparation of the EQE

Study guides and reference materials relating to the EQE

An enormous mass of literature on the EQE has been published since the first examination, which was held in 1979. During the past decades the format and content of the examination was the subject of major changes. Many of the older publications are outdated and should be used with caution.

European qualifying examination. Guide for preparation.
9th edition. Munich: EPO, 2019.

Published and edited by the European Academy of the EPO in co-operation with epi and CEIPI. The brochure, usually called *"Study Guide"*, is available in printed form and as a PDF file. It can be downloaded from the EPO website. (http://documents.epo.org/projects/babylon/eponet.nsf/0/AD1DEB5847E771FEC125764E0056D80B/$File/eqe_preparation_guide_9th_edition_2019_en.pdf).

Chandler, William E.; Meinders, Hugo: C-Book. How to write a successful opposition and pass paper C of the European Qualifying Examination.
Sixth Edition. Cologne: Carl Heymanns Verlag, 2019. ISBN 978-3-452-29200-1.

Although devoted primarily to paper C, the book offers a lot of useful information which is relevant to paper B as well. Separate chapters provide essential insights into critical issues such as interpretation and analysis, the state of the art, inventive step, and ranges.

EQE Paper A&B Methodology Course.
Eindhoven: Delta Patents, 2021.

1.4.9 EQE online support by the EPO

75 The online support is provided by the European Patent Academy and can be found at the following address:
http://www.epo.org/learning-events/eqe/eqe-training.html

1.5 Overall method for solving paper B

76 Paper B involves quite a number of (sometimes complex) tasks which have to be performed within a minimum of time and without major errors or misconceptions. Unless you have natural talent in all required areas, you need a systematic and structured approach for solving the paper and elaborating your answer. Splitting the overall task into separate subtasks is an effective way to reduce the complexity and to cope with the wealth of information which has to be processed.

77 The following sequence of steps appear to be effective, both in terms of accelerating the decision making and, at the same time, improving the quality of the decisions:

78 **Step (1): Get an overview of the components of your paper B**
- Determine the components of the paper
- Check whether there are any particularities

79 **Step (2): Perform a preliminary analysis of the subject-matter of paper B**
- Read the introductory paragraphs of the patent application up to and including the definition of the problem underlying the invention
- Mark or write down the technical field of the invention
- Mark or write down the problem underlying the invention
- Read the claims

80 **Step (3): Find the objections**
- Read the communication
- Mark or write down the objections raised in the communication
- Read the client's letter
- Mark or write down the suggestions of the client and re-phrase these into objections
- Read the draft set of claims
- Study and check each suggested amendment and re-phrase this into one or more objections

81 **Step (4) Perform a preliminary analysis of the prior art**
- Read each prior art document
- Mark or write down for each prior art document what its technical field is
- Mark or write down for each prior art document any advantages and disadvantages and technical effects
- Indicate any other remarkable aspect

82 **Step (5): Perform an in-depth analysis of the patent application**
- Read the description in detail
- Couple each potential solution to the observed objections
- Trace down technical effects and couple these to technical features

83 **Step (6): Draft the set of amended claims**
- Restudy the draft set of claims
- Amend the claims based on the description and bearing in mind the wishes of the client
- Check the dependency of the dependent claims
- Check the requirements of unity of invention and of Rule 43(2) EPC

84 **Step (7): Determine for the draft set of amended claims whether the material requirements (Art. 52-57 EPC) have been met, and optionally adapt the draft set of amended claims**
- Check whether the independent claim(s) is (are) novel over each prior art document
- For each prior art document, write down the difference(s) using the words of the independent claim(s)
- Check whether the independent claim(s) involve(s) an inventive step using the problem-solution approach

- Determine the closest prior art
- Link the difference(s) of each independent claim to technical effects
- Determine the objective problem
- Determine whether the problem is solved in non-obvious way
- Check whether other grounds under Art. 52–57 EPC exist, and if so whether objections based on these grounds are overcome

Step (8): Draft a supplementary note, if any
- Check whether a supplementary note is required
- If yes, determine the contents of the supplementary note
- Draft the supplementary note

Step (9): Draft the letter in response to the communication
- Start a letter to the EPO and request the grant of a patent based on the attached set of amended claims
- Per claim, provide all arguments as to why the requirements of Art. 123(2) EPC have been met
- Per clarity objection, indicate how and why this objection is overcome
- Discuss novelty of the independent claim(s). Use for each document a separate paragraph
- Check whether these novelty arguments also apply for the dependent claims
- Discuss inventive step using the problem-solution approach
  - Indicate what the closest prior art is
  - Motivate why this is the closest prior art
  - Provide arguments why the other available prior art is not the closest
  - Mention the difference(s) in technical terms between the independent claim and the closest prior art
  - Determine the technical effect(s) of the difference(s)
  - Formulate the objective technical problem
  - Check whether this objective problem is solved (over the full scope of the claim by the technical terms that form the difference(s))
  - Give arguments why the closest prior art document *per se* does not assist in solving the objective problem
  - Give arguments why starting from the closest prior art each other piece of prior art does not assist in solving the objective problem
- Check whether these inventive step arguments also apply for the dependent claims
- Deal with any other objection
- Sign the letter in an anonymous way

Step (10): Perform the final check
- Check the set of amended claims. Is this the set of claims intended to be uploaded or is it a draft set of claims? Are all claim numbers and dependencies correct?
- Check the letter to the EPO. Is it complete in that all objections have been addressed? Is it anonymous?
- Add the supplementary note, if there is any
- Upload your answer paper

These steps form the methodology for solving paper B. They are discussed in detail in Chapter 2.

1.6 How to use this book?

When Frederick Reif published his classical textbook on the theory of statistical physics in 1967, he gave the students the following advice:

> *"The only method of learning new ways of thinking is to practice thinking. Try to strive for insight, to find new relationships and simplicity where before you saw none. Above all, do not simply memorize formulas; learn modes of reasoning. ... Hence my last advice is that you try to understand simple basic ideas well and that you then proceed to work many problems, both those given in the book and those resulting from questions you may pose yourself."*

(F. Reif, Statistical Physics. Berkeley Physics Course, vol. 5, 1967, p. xiv–xv)

91 Having this in mind, there remains not much to add. Take your time to read the book, start early with trying to solve an old paper B and ask yourself at each instance, whether the advice from the book makes sense to you. If not, find out where you disagree. Think about ways and means to overcome the difficulties. Draw your conclusions and apply them, but don't forget to check at the end, whether you got the right result, or not. In this way you will test your understanding and gain the degree of independence, which you need when sitting the examination.

2 Methodology

2.1 Objective

Throughout this book, the term *"methodology"* refers to the practices and techniques used for tackling paper B, rather than to the theoretical analysis of the methods and principles in the field of patent law. Having an efficient methodology with clear outlines and procedures is essential in order to cope with the complexity of the paper and to accomplish the task. The two main objectives are to accelerate the processing time and to improve the quality by ensuring that the results are (i) comprehensive, (ii) consistent and (iii) in accordance with the requirements.

There exists no such thing as a unique method tailored to the needs of everybody who wants to sit paper B. When preparing for the EQE, you will have to acquire practical experience and learn what is effective for you yourself. Going quickly through the text of the paper, making some informal notes and drafting an answer on an *ad hoc* basis is hardly promising and generally leads to poor quality. On the other hand, thorough knowledge of best practices can help to avoid mistakes. But what does the concept of best practice mean in the context of paper B?

It means the following:
- The work is organised in a manner that the documents need not be read and evaluated several times, possibly a first time when the analysis of the paper is performed, a second time when the claims suggested by the client are to be amended, a third time when the letter to the Examiner is written and a fourth time when any corrections or additions become necessary.
- The information is processed as soon as it occurs. Thus, information retrieval does not absorb a lot of time.
- The risk of overlooking some important points of fact or law is minimised.
- All essential aspects of the paper are considered. There are no gaps and omissions.
- The results are clear and consistent.
- The answer has the right structure and is limited to those parts that are required. No time is spent on unnecessary issues.

Managing these aspects and bringing them under one roof is more an art than a set of technical skills. Nevertheless, there are good reasons to get acquainted with the technicalities of the case. This chapter is designed to help you familiarise yourself with the practical procedures for processing of paper B.

2.2 Preliminary steps

Before tackling any paper of the EQE, we strongly recommend you to check, whether you are really familiar with the relevant rules of the EQE.

Surprisingly, quite a number of candidates possess only superficial knowledge of the Regulation and Rules of the European qualifying examination, and some ignore them completely. This lack of knowledge may be dangerous and a major reason for failure at the examination. Ignorance of the rules means inevitably ignorance of the requirements that have to be fulfilled. Therefore, in order to avoid errors and misconceptions, it is indispensable to know and understand the rules laid down in the Regulation on the EQE, the Implementing provisions and the Instructions to candidates. Comprehensive knowledge of the legal framework is also required for developing a coherent strategy for solving paper B.

In the hierarchy of norms, the Regulation on the EQE (REE) comes first. The Implementing provisions to the Regulation on the European qualifying examination (IPREE) take the second place. Last, but not least, there are the Instructions to candidates concerning the conduct of the European qualifying examination (Instr.). From a practical standpoint, they are as important as the higher-ranking sources.

These three legal texts define the framework and the conditions of the EQE. The most important provisions are set out below, as far as they apply directly to paper B.

2.2.1 Regulation on the EQE

100 **Regulation on the European qualifying examination for professional representatives (REE)**

101 <center>**Art. 1(1) REE:**</center>

The European qualifying examination (hereinafter "the examination" or "the EQE") is designed to establish whether a candidate is qualified to practise as a professional representative before the European Patent Office (hereinafter "the EPO").

102 <center>**Art. 1(4) REE:**</center>

The examination shall cover, as a minimum: (…); the preparation of a reply to an official letter in which prior art has been cited; (…).

103 This provision determines the scope of paper B.

104 <center>**Art. 1(5) REE:**</center>

One or more of the examination papers may be set in more than one technical field.

105 Papers A and B used to be drawn up in two technical fields, namely Electricity/Mechanics and Chemistry, but are nowadays, starting from 2017, single papers.

106 <center>**Art. 6(2) REE:**</center>

Subject to the IPREE, the Examination Board shall give the members of the Examination Committees instructions for:
(a) preparing the examination papers
(b) preparing the marking sheets
(c) marking candidates' answers consistently.

107 The marking of the answer papers is performed on the basis of the marking sheet.

108 <center>**Art. 6(4) REE:**</center>

The Examination Board shall decide on the list of books and documents, including case law, which may be used by candidates during the examination.

109 As to the admitted books and documents, see below.

110 <center>**Art. 6(6) REE:**</center>

After the examination, the Examination Board shall transmit to the Examination Secretariat a report on each examination paper (examiners' report) and a model solution prepared by the relevant Examination Committee. The report and the model solution will be published in an examination Compendium to enable candidates to prepare for future examinations as specified in the IPREE.

111 These materials can all be downloaded from the website of the EPO. (https://www.epo.org/mobile/eqe/compendium/b.html ; http://documents.epo.org/projects/babylon/eponot.nsf/0/e1558f38ad0987cbc1257f780055e08d/$FILE/MockPaperB.pdf ; http://documents.epo.org/projects/babylon/eponot.nsf/0/603E34C657386DECC1257FA200300DBF/$-File/ExReport_MockB.pdf; https://www.epo.org/mobile/eqe/compendium/b/BEM.html; and https://www.epo.org/mobile/eqe/compendium/b/BCH.html)

112 <center>**Art. 8(1) REE:**</center>

Subject to Art. 6(2) the Examination Committees shall:
(a) be entrusted with the preparation of the examination papers
(b) be entrusted with the preparation of the marking sheets
(c) provide the Examination Board with any relevant information relating to (a) and (b)
(d) mark the answer papers and make a proposal for the grades to be awarded for each paper
(e) Each answer paper shall be marked by two committee members separately.

Art. 8(2) REE:

The Examination Committees shall advise the Examination Board on the list of books and documents, including case law, which may be used by candidates during the examination.

As to the admitted books and documents, see below.

Art. 9(1) REE:

The Examination Secretariat shall: (...)
(b) prepare and organise the examination (...)
(d) publish the Compendium and any other information relating to the examination or its conduct.

The Compendium can be downloaded from the website of the EPO; see herein-above on Art. 6(6) REE.

Art. 12(1) REE:

The examination papers shall be drawn up in the three official languages of the EPO and all candidates shall receive them in all three languages.

Art. 12(2) REE:

The candidates' answers shall be given in one of the three official languages of the EPO unless otherwise prescribed in accordance with paragraph 3.

Candidates may request to draft their answer in certain other languages than English, French or German, see Rule 5(1) and Rule 22(2) IPREE. However, the text of the papers is provided in these three languages only.

Art. 13 REE: Examination syllabus

The examination shall establish whether a candidate has:

(1) a thorough knowledge of:
   (a) European patent law as laid down in the EPC and any legislation relating to Community patents
   (b) the Paris Convention (Articles 1 to 5*quater* and Article 11)
   (c) the Patent Cooperation Treaty
   (d) all decisions of the Enlarged Board of Appeal and EPO case law as specified in the IPREE, and

(2) a general knowledge of the national laws of:
   (a) the contracting states to the extent that they apply to European patent applications and European patents
   (b) the United States of America and Japan to the extent that they are of importance in connection with proceedings before the EPO.

For paper B the legal sources listed under (1)(a) and (1)(d) are particularly important.

Art. 15 REE: Choice of papers

When enrolling, candidates shall indicate which paper or papers they intend to sit.

Candidates are free to choose the paper(s) they wish to sit. The former modular system ceased to exist when the new Regulation on the European qualifying examination came into force in 2009.

Art. 19(1) REE: Communications

Any communication concerning the examination shall be addressed to the Secretariat.

The Examination Secretariat is the only authority that can provide binding information on the EQE.

126 **Art. 21(1) REE: Anonymity**

Candidates' anonymity shall be respected when their answers are marked.

127 Candidates have to take care that their answer paper is anonymous, *i.e.* that neither their natural name, nor their initials appear in the text of the answer (see also Point 6 of the Instructions).

2.2.2 Implementing provisions to the Regulation on the EQE (IPREE)

128 **Rule 2 IPREE: Examination syllabus (as amended 29 September 2017)**

The examination syllabus referred to in Art. 13 REE shall cover only those legal texts referred to in Art. 13(1)(a) to (c) REE which are in force on 31 October of the year prior to the examination. The EPO case law referred to in Art. 13(1)(d) REE shall be that covered in the latest edition of *"Case Law of the Boards of Appeal of the European Patent Office"* (herein after *"the Case Law Book"*), the case law referred to in any case law special edition of the Official Journal published after the latest edition of the Case Law Book, and any case law published in the Official Journal on or before 31 October of the year prior to the examination.

129 For paper B, candidates need to be particularly conversant with the EPC, the PCT and the case law of the Boards of Appeal in so far as these texts apply to European patent applications. The content of the examination only relates to legal texts which were in force on 31 October of the year preceding the examination.

130 **Rule 3 IPREE: Marking**

When marking answer papers, the members of the Examination Committees shall bear in mind that candidates may have written their answers in a language other than their mother tongue. Errors of grammar or style shall therefore not be penalised.

131 Errors of grammar or style have no impact on the marking, as long as the answer paper is clear and can be understood by the members of the Examination Committees. When drafting the answer, candidates should bear in mind that the examiners may also have another mother tongue than the language of the answer paper. Therefore, it is appropriate to use clear and simple language.

132 **Rule 4(1) IPREE: Marking sheets**

Pursuant to Art. 8(1)(d) REE, details regarding the marking shall be entered on the marking sheets.

133 The marking sheets of the old papers are published in the Compendium and may be downloaded from the website of the EPO.

134 **Rule 6 IPREE: Grades/passing the pre-examination and the examination**

(1) Each answer paper shall be marked on a scale from zero to 100 by the relevant Examination Committee. (…)

(3) With regard to the examination as defined in Rule 21:
  (a) where, on the merits of an answer paper, 50 marks or more are awarded, a PASS grade shall be awarded for that paper, or
  (b) where, on the merits of an answer paper, fewer than 45 marks are awarded, a FAIL grade shall be awarded for that paper, or
  (c) where, on the merits of an answer paper, at least 45 but fewer than 50 marks are awarded, the grade awarded for that paper shall be COMPENSABLE FAIL.

135 In order to pass a minimum of 50 marks is required. If more than 50 marks are achieved, up to 5 marks can be used for compensating a compensable fail of another paper. An excess over 55 marks has no impact on the issue of passing the EQE.

Rule 19 IPREE: Conduct of the pre-examination or the examination 136

(1) If a candidate fails to comply with the instructions to candidates concerning the conduct of the pre-examination or the examination or with instructions given on the basis thereof by the invigilators, the following measures may be taken by the Examination Board in respect of that candidate:
(a) deduction of marks
(b) instructions (…) to mark the answer paper concerned only in part
(c) Instructions (…) not to mark the answer paper concerned and not to award any marks, and/or
(d) disqualification from the pre-examination or the examination for a given year.

(2) If a candidate disturbs other candidates during the pre-examination or the examination, the chief invigilator shall be empowered to suspend him at once from the paper during which this occurs. (…)

Candidates should make every effort to comply with the instructions concerning the conduct of the examination. Failure to comply may give rise to dramatic sanctions. 137

The 2021 EQE was conducted online, making that some provisions of the IPREE do not really apply. However, in the Instructions to candidates concerning the conduct of the European qualifying examination 2021 (Official Journal February 2021; https://www.epo.org/law-practice/legal-texts/official-journal/2021/02/a13.html) there are specific sections on Exam Invigilation and Misconduct that need to be taken into account. 138

(3) Complaints concerning the conduct of the pre-examination or the examination shall not be entertained by the Examination Board unless a written statement of the facts is submitted to the chief invigilator at the latest 30 minutes after the closing signal has been given on the final day of the examination. 139

Rule 21 IPREE: Examination papers 140

The [main] examination shall consist of four papers: Paper A, Paper B, Paper C and Paper D as defined in Rules 23 to 26 respectively.

Rule 22 IPREE: General instructions for answering the papers 141
(as amended 29 September 2017)

(1) Candidates are expected to be familiar with at least the following documents in the versions valid as at 31 October of the year prior to the pre-examination or the examination:
(a) the EPC
(b) the Implementing Regulations to the EPC
(c) the (…) Protocol on Centralisation
(d) the (…) Protocol on Recognition
(e) the Rules relating to Fees
(f) the notice of the President of the EPO concerning the arrangements for deposit accounts
(g) the PCT
(h) the Regulations under the PCT
(i) the Paris Convention for the Protection of Industrial Property
(j) the list of contracting states to the EPC and of contracting states to the PCT
(k) the Ancillary Regulations to the EPC
(l) the brochure entitled "National law relating to the EPC"
(m) the Guidelines for Examination in the EPO
(n) the content of the Official Journal of the EPO
(o) the Guidelines for Search and Examination at the EPO as PCT Authority.

For paper B the sources mentioned under (a), (b), (e), (g), (h), (m) and (n) are of particular importance. 142

It will be assumed that candidates have read the examination paper in the language in which they give their answer. Candidates who give their answer in a language 143 other than one of the EPO official languages, and have filed a corresponding request when enrolling for the examination, shall indicate on the front page of their answer papers which language they used in answering the examination papers.

144 Whenever the second or third language version of the paper is used, for example in case of a suspected error in the primary version of the text, it is advisable to indicate this either on the front page of the answer or in a supplementary note.

145 **Candidates shall accept the facts given in the examination paper and limit themselves to those facts. Whether and to what extent those facts are used shall be the responsibility of each candidate. Candidates shall not use any special knowledge they may have of the technical field of the invention.**

146 This paragraph is of utmost importance for candidates sitting paper B. Typically, the basis of paper B is often a real case which is simplified and adapted in order to meet the requirements of the examination. Occasionally, such modifications may lead to minor distortions regarding the technical content of in the paper. Experts in the concerned technical field will or may recognise such distortions, but they should refrain from casting doubt on the information given in in the paper. Paper B is not about technical intricacies, but about the ability to amend claims and drafting a response to a communication issued by an Examiner of the European Patent Office (Art. 1(4) REE; Rule 24 IPREE).

147   Rule 24 IPREE: Content of the examination – Reply paper
                                (Paper B)
(1) The purpose of this paper shall be to assess candidates' ability to reply to an official communication in which prior art has been cited as defined in Article 1(4) REE. The duration of this paper shall be three hours.

148 By Decision of the Supervisory Board of 17 November 2016, all candidates are granted an additional thirty minutes, so that effectively the duration of paper B shall be three and a half hours.

149 **(2) In this paper, candidates shall assume that a European patent application has been filed designating all the contracting states, and that the EPO has issued an official communication. The paper shall include a client's letter containing instructions about the way the client wishes to proceed with the European patent application and a draft set of claims to be filed with the candidates' response to the official communication.**

150 The client's letter and the draft set of claims are a mandatory part of paper B. This letter and the draft set of claims reflect the wish of the client and indicate <u>how he wishes you to proceed</u> with the European patent application.

151 **(3) Candidates are expected to respond to all points raised in the official communication. The response shall be in the form of a letter to the EPO accompanied by the claims supplied by the client, amended as appropriate to meet the requirements of the EPC. The description shall not, however, be amended. In their reply, candidates shall identify clearly all amendments made in the claims and their basis in the application as filed, and provide additional explanations where necessary. Candidates shall also set out their arguments in support of the patentability of the independent claim(s).**

152 The main tasks of paper B are
- to amend the client's draft set of claims which meet the following requirements:
  (i) the claims have to be in conformity with the EPC, in particular regarding support in the application as originally filed in the sense of Art. 123(2) EPC, novelty, inventive step, clarity, unity of invention and Rule 43(2) EPC;
  (ii) the claims are in accordance with the client's wish; and
  (iii) the claims have to be in line with the Guidelines, unless there is a clear reason to depart from them; and
- to draft a letter to the Examiner wherein all points raised in the official communication are responded to, wherein all amendments made in the claims are clearly identified and their basis in the application as filed is clearly elaborated, and wherein it is

explained why the claimed subject-matter is novel, involves an inventive step (showing all steps of the problem-solution approach), and, when appropriate, why the claimed subject-matter relates to an invention and would be industrially applicable, and why the set of claims meet the requirements of unity-of-invention and Rule 43(2) EPC.

In paper B, it is not necessary to file an amended description to bring it in line with the set of claims as amended. It may however be needed to indicate that to solve a particular point raised in the official communication that and how the description is to be amended to overcome that point raised.

> **(4) Candidates may give the reasons for their choice of answer in a supplementary note. If they consider that any part of the application ought to be made the subject of one or more divisional applications, they shall, in the note, clearly set out the independent claim(s) for such divisional application(s). The note shall also present the arguments in support of the patentability of the independent claim(s) in such divisional application(s). Supplementary notes to examiners cannot, however, replace essential parts of candidates' replies to the EPO.**

Supplementary notes should be written with caution. There are only a few exceptional situations, where supplementary notes serve a useful purpose. Examples of such situations are lack of unity of invention or a suspected error in the paper.

> **Rule 27 IPREE: Composition and number of Examination Committees**
>
> (…)
>
> (2) (…) Examination Committee I shall be in charge of Papers A and B, (…).

2.2.3 Instructions to candidates concerning the conduct of the European qualifying examination and Instructions to candidates concerning the conduct of the European qualifying examination 2021

In Supplementary Publication 2, Official Journal 2019, the Regulation on the European qualifying examination for professional representatives as in force is published (https://www.epo.org/law-practice/legal-texts/official-journal/2019/etc/se2.html). Part thereof is the Instructions to candidates concerning the conduct of the European qualifying examination. Because the 2021 EQE was conducted online, the general Instructions to candidates was replaced by the Examination Secretariat by the Instructions to candidates concerning the conduct of the European qualifying examination 2021 (https://www.epo.org/law-practice/legal-texts/official-journal/2021/02/a13/2021-a13.pdf). It may well be expected that also the coming years the EQE will be conducted on line. For this reason, the 2021 version of the Instructions to candidates will also be quoted.

> **I.   General**
>
> **I.1 (2021)   These instructions shall apply to (…) the main examination, which consists of the four papers A, B, C and D, and to each part of these papers.**

Explicit reference is made in this provision to "each part of these papers". This is because papers D and C were split up in separate parts (paper D in three and paper C in two parts), wherein each part must be completed before a break. Papers A and B had the same syllabus and character as the 2017–2019 papers.

> **I.2   (2021) The European qualifying examination (EQE) 2021 will be conducted online using the WISEflow platform in conjunction with a LockDown browser. The examination will be invigilated using online proctoring based on video and audio recordings, with the help of artificial intelligence combined with human invigilation.**
>
> **IV.32 (2021) In the event of any problems, invigilators can be contacted via the chat function. However, candidates must not ask any questions on the content of the paper or how it should be interpreted.**

There is an opportunity to ask questions, but there is no opportunity to obtain explanations regarding the wording of the papers.

163   I.5   Candidates are advised to bring to the (...) main examination any books and documents they consider useful for answering the examination papers.

164   In this respect, see the decision of the Examination Board of 24 October 2011, Art. 1 (OJ EPO 2011, 584; part of Supplementary publication 2 – OJ EPO 2017): "Candidates may bring to the examination any books and documents they consider useful for answering the examination papers."

165   III.18 (2021)   Candidates alone are responsible for their workstations. They must ensure that their workstation is well lit and that there is no prohibited equipment (see point 20) within reach. In addition, candidates are personally responsible for ensuring that any permitted equipment they use is used only in the permitted manner.

166   III.19 (2021)   Candidates must have the monitoring equipment (camera and microphone) and the chat function (Zendesk) activated throughout the examination, as set out in the User Guide.

167   III.20 (2021)   Other than the computer system required for the examination (PC or laptop, monitor, keyboard, mouse, etc.) and routers and printers, no other electronic equipment (calculators, digital watches, tablets, smartphones, smart watches, etc.) are permitted unless expressly authorised in advance by the Examination Secretariat. Candidates may not use headphones, headsets or any other non-electronic noise-cancelling items such as earplugs.

168   I.4 (2021)   Instructions given by the system or invigilators must be followed in full and at all times. (...)

169   I.5 (2021)   The examination papers will be provided to candidates as PDF files in the EPO's three official languages.

170   However, for Paper B 2021, candidates were allowed to print the prior-art documents and the drawing(s), but none of the following: the description and claims of the application, the EPO communication, the client's letter and the amended claims. The documents allowed for printing were said to be made available at least ten minutes before the start of the examination.

171   I.7 (2021)   Candidates for the main examination must write their answers in the dedicated text editor in WISEflow.

172   I.8 (2021)   Candidates must not use their name or initials in their answers.

2.3 Detailed methodology for solving paper B

Summary

173   The basic steps of the methodology for solving paper B can be summarised as follows:
    (1) Getting an overview of the components of your paper B
    (2) Performing a preliminary analysis of the subject-matter of paper B
    (3) Finding the objections
    (4) Performing a preliminary analysis of the prior art
    (5) Performing an in-depth analysis of the patent application
    (6) Drafting the set of amended claims
    (7) Determining for the draft set of amended claims whether the material requirements (Art. 52-57 EPC) have been met, and optionally adapting the draft set of amended claims
    (8) Drafting the supplementary note, if any
    (9) Drafting the letter in response to the communication
    (10) Performing the final check

174   These steps are explained in detail in the following sections.

2.3.1 Step 1: Getting an overview of the components of your paper B

According to R 24 IPREE, paper B comprises always a European patent application as filed designating all the contracting states, an official communication issued by the EPO, a client's letter containing instructions about the way the client wishes to proceed with the European patent application and a draft set of amended claims. The European patent application consists of a description of the application and a set of claims as filed; optionally with (an) accompanying drawing(s); all the 2017–2019, the 2021 and the Mock 2016 papers B had accompanying drawings. According to Art. 1(4) REE, in the official letter/communication prior art is cited. In the 2017–2019 papers B, three prior art documents were cited; and in the Mock 2016 paper B, two prior art documents were cited.

In the 2021 paper B, also 3 prior art documents were cited. In addition, anonymous third party observations were made, referring to a public prior use.

A quick look at the front page of paper B gives a first impression of the components comprised in the paper.

Examples:

The front page of single paper B 2017 illustrates the standard configuration of a letter from the client accompanied by three documents representing the state of the art:

"This paper comprises:
- Description of the Application   2017/B/EN/1-3
- Claims   2017/B/EN/4
- Drawings of the Application   2017/B/EN/5
- Communication   2017/B/EN/6-7
- Document D1   2017/B/EN/8
- Drawings Document D1   2017/B/EN/9
- Document D2   2017/B/EN/10
- Drawing Document D2   2017/B/EN/11
- Document D3   2017/B/EN/12
- Drawing Document D3   2017/B/EN/13
- Client's Letter   2017/B/EN/14
- Draft set of claims   2017/B/EN/15"

The front page of single paper B 2021 notes that:

"This paper comprises:
- Description of the application   2021/B/EN/1-5
- Claims   2021/B/EN/6-7
- Drawings of the application   2021/B/EN/8-9
- Document D1   2021/B/EN/10-12
- Document D2   2021/B/EN/13-14
- Document D3   2021/B/EN/15-16
- Communication pursuant to Article 94(3) EPC   2021/B/EN/17-18
- Anonymous third party observations   2021/B/EN/19
- Client's letter   2021/B/EN/20-21
- Amended claims   2021/B/EN/22-23"

Realising that, at the moment of writing this book, only four single papers B and one Mock Paper B provided as an example by the EQE Committee in 2016 are available, yet wishing to provide some additional examples, herein-below reference will be made to some earlier Electricity/Mechanics and Chemistry papers B. As from 2013, these Electricity/Mechanics and Chemistry papers B also had a client's letter and a draft set of claims. These older papers B either had 2 or 3 documents pertaining to the state of the art.

2.3.2 Step 2: Performing a preliminary analysis of the subject-matter of paper B

This step serves the purpose of providing a rough idea what the paper is about. It consists of reading the introductory paragraphs of the patent application, identifying the problem underlying the invention described and claimed in the patent application (the subjective problem) and reading the claims of the patent application. The result is a first impression of the technical content of the paper. Try to understand the outlines of the paper, but do not spend time on details. The comprehensive in-depth analysis will be made later.

182   No conclusions need be drawn in step 2. Yet, it is good to form already an idea of what the invention is, based on the content of the claims, and to determine what the technical field of the invention is and what the subjective problem, the problem identified in the patent application as underlying the invention, is. Since the set of claims suggested by the client will highly likely be close to the original set of claims, and the technical field and subjective problem will highly likely play a role in the problem-and-solution approach that will attract many marks in the answer paper, this step 2 is not just provisional in nature. This step will provide guidance in the subsequent steps.

183   Single Papers B 2017–2021 had 5–6 claims. The 2017 and 2018 papers both had 1 independent product/system claim with 5 and 4 dependent claims, respectively. In the 2019 paper, there was an independent process claim, and 2 independent product claims. Additionally, there were 3 dependent product claims.

184   The 2021 paper had 1 independent product claim with 2 dependent product claims; and 2 independent process claims with 1 dependent process claim.

185   If there is a product claim and a process claim, then attention needs to be paid to the fact that the product claim be amended with more limitations than the process claim. This occurred in paper B 2021.

186   The 2016 Mock Paper had three claims, 1 independent product claim and 2 dependent claims.

187   The papers B Electricity/Mechanics and Chemistry 2013–2016, all had 4–6 claims and in most cases 2 independent claims.

188   Quite often, if not always, this preliminary analysis already gives you a good impression of what the subject-matter of the patent application encompasses. It generally is sufficient not to seek further depth at this stage. However, if you feel totally insecure at this stage, there should be nothing to stop you from gathering additional information – but mind the clock!

189   For illustrating the methodology, paper B 2017 is used as example. It is recommended to download the text of this paper from the "*Compendium*" website of the EPO, but it is also attached as Appendix 1 to this Book.

190   First, one reads the introductory paragraphs – paragraph by paragraph – until it is clear that the patent application has started with the description of its invention:

191   **Description of the Application**

[01] The present application relates to monitoring at least one vital sign of the human body by optical means. The four vital signs, pulse, body temperature, blood pressure and blood oxygen saturation, have to be monitored regularly for controlling the medical status of a patient in hospital. Monitoring vital signs at home will play a more and more important role in remote medicine. D1 discloses monitoring vital signs by attaching sensors to the human body with a clip. This has the drawback that the clip is uncomfortable and that for long-term measurements the attachment is not reliable, because the clip can move. Therefore, the aim of this invention is to provide a reliable and comfortable system for long-term remote monitoring of the vital signs of patients, such as small children and babies.

192   In the first sentence of this paragraph, the technical field of the invention is sketched: the monitoring of at least one vital sign of human body by optical means. The second and third sentences give a basic explanation on what a vital sign is, why it is monitored and that apparently the future is to monitor at home.

193   Since the technical field of an invention may play an important role in the first step(s) of the problem-solution approach, it is important to mark in a manner that suits you, what the technical field of the invention is, whether this is by marking in a particular colour, using some way of underlying, writing down on a separate sheet (on paper or electronically) or in any other way.

194   I prefer a sheet of paper, on which I can write down – herein-below, I will use *italics* to show what I would write down on a sheet of paper:

Field of Invention: monitoring at least one vital sign of the human body by optical means

Subsequently, it is indicated that prior art document D1 discloses the monitoring of vital signs by attaching sensors to the human body with a clip. From Step 1 we know that Document D1 forms part of the paper. From this short discussion of D1, it seems that D1 is in the same or at least in a similar technical field as the invention.

Then, paragraph [01] refers to a drawback of D1, being that a clip is uncomfortable for attaching sensors to a human body and that for long-term measurements the attachment is not reliable, because the clip can move. This observation is followed by the aim of the invention, and that is to provide a reliable and comfortable system for long-term remote monitoring of the vital signs of patients, such as small children and babies.

This seems the subjective problem underlying the invention, and, also this, is marked in a suitable way:

Problem: provide a reliable and comfortable system for long-term remote monitoring of vital signs of patients (such as small children or babies)

This problem is relative to D1

I have used brackets, because of the "such as" wording.

Subsequently, we read the next paragraph:

> [02] The invention concerns a system comprising means for attaching an optical sensor and a motion sensor to the human body. The attaching means comprises means for transmitting output signals from the sensors to an evaluation means for calculating at least one vital sign from the output signals. The inventive idea is that the attaching means is a garment, such as a sock or a wristband, and that the evaluation means is configured to correct the output signal from the optical sensor based on the output signal of the motion sensor, and vice-versa. It is not important for the invention how the signals are transmitted to the evaluation means.

As from the start of this paragraph, it is clear that this paragraph relates to the invention described in the patent application. We are not yet reading in all detail, but it is clear that two sensors, an optical and a motion sensor, are used according to the invention, that the attaching means is a garment; and that evaluation means are used for correcting the output signal of the optical sensor using the output of the motion sensor or *vice versa*.

At this stage, this is more than sufficient and we switch to the claims. [In these claims, you may wish to apply Part F, Chapter IV, 4.13.1 of the Guidelines by adding to a claim directed to an entity (a product claim) with a "for clause" the term "suitable" and bring the "suitable for" part between rectangular brackets]:

Claims

1. System for monitoring at least one vital sign of a human body, the system comprising:
   - holding means (1, 11, 21) for holding an optical sensor (2, 12, 22) and a motion sensor (3, 13, 23) close to the human body (10, 27), the holding means (1, 11, 21) comprising in addition to the sensors (2, 12, 22, 3, 13, 23) transmitting means (4, 14, 24) for transmitting output signals from the sensors (2, 12, 22, 3, 13, 23),
   - evaluation means (5, 25) for receiving the output signals and calculating from the output signals the at least one vital sign,

   characterised in that the evaluation means (5, 25) is configured to correct the output signal from the optical sensor (2, 12, 22) based on the output signal of the motion sensor (3, 13, 23) or to correct the output signal from the motion sensor (3, 13, 23) based on the output signal of the optical sensor and in that the transmitting means (4, 14, 24) is a wireless transmitting means.

   This independent claim is directed to a system, that has holding means, an optical sensor, a motion sensor, transmitting means being wireless, and evaluation means.

2. System according to claim 1, wherein the at least one vital sign is pulse, body temperature, blood pressure and/or blood oxygen saturation.

3. System according to claim 1 or 2, wherein the wireless transmitting means (4, 14, 24) is a wireless local network emitter.

4. System according to any of claims 1 to 3, further comprising a screen (6) and configured to display the at least one vital sign on the screen.

205 5. System according to any of claims 1 to 4, wherein the holding means is an attaching means (1, 11, 21) such as a sock (1), a wristband (11) or a glove.
206 6. System according to any of claims 1 to 5, wherein the attaching means (1, 11, 21) is at least partly made of Optitex™.
207 These other claims are all dependent on claim 1 and seem not that complicated.
208 [Should you feel that the claimed invention is not yet sufficiently clear for you, it goes without saying that you may then read some additional (or even all) paragraphs of the description.]
209 Once you have formed a preliminary idea of the technical field of the invention, the subjective problem underlying it and a general idea on the claimed subject-matter, you may turn to finding the actual task of paper B. That is, it is now time to give substance to what points are raised in the official communication and how your client suggests to proceed with the European patent application.

2.3.3 Step 3: Finding the objections

211 For paper B, it is expected to draft an amended set of claims and to draft a response to an official communication, wherein all objections are addressed.
212 As far as the set of claims is concerned, it is necessary that the subject-matter thereof meets the requirements of the EPC, and hence
– is clear in the sense of Art. 84 EPC;
– is in conformity with the requirements of Art. 123(2) EPC;
– meets the requirements of Art. 52 EPC; that is
  – relates to an invention, that
  – is novel,
  – involves an inventive step, and
  – is industrially applicable;
– meets the requirements of unity-of-invention under Art. 82 EPC; and
– meets the requirements of R. 43(2) EPC.

213 Above this, it is required that the set of claims is according to the <u>way the client wishes to proceed</u>. Where in paper A the claims must meet the requirements of the EPC, and must provide the broadest possible scope of protection, ideally covering as many embodiments of the described invention, paper B is not focussing primarily on the broadest scope of protection. The wish of the client is to be used as guidance, and only in that light an optimal scope of protection is expected. Or put in other words, the amended set of claims must be in accordance with the client's instructions, while the claims are in conformity with the EPC. Only after these main considerations, there is room for trying to get the broadest scope of protection. However, normally no marks are available for drafting claims – whether independent or dependent - where the client did not ask for.
214 As said, all objections are to be addressed. In this step 3, I will refer not only to the objections raised in the Communication, but also to issues linked with the wishes of the client as expressed in the client's letter and coming from the draft set of claims. In this book, these other issues will also be referred to as "objections".
215 This step 3 needs to be carried out with concentration and perhaps even suspicion. If you miss one or more objections, you miss possibilities to score marks.

Reading the Communication

216 For finding objections, I consider it suitable to first turn to the Examiner's Communication. Although the position of the Examiner should always be checked, normally the position taken is correct. In addition, you may assume that everything written in the exam paper is there with an intention or purpose.
217 **Communication:**
  1. The examination is based on the application as originally filed. Documents D1-D3 are prior art according to **Art. 54(2) EPC**.
218 Apparently, there are three pieces of prior art: D1-D3. From the reading of the first two paragraphs of the patent application as originally filed, we already know that one of these

prior art publications, D1, was discussed and formed the basis for defining the subjective problem, *viz.* the problem underlying the invention as originally filed.

> **Communication:**
> 2. **Art. 54(1) and (2) EPC (Novelty)**
>   The subject-matter of **claims 1–4** is **not novel** within the meaning of **Art. 54(1) and (2) EPC**, because it is known from D2:
>   2.1 <u>Claim 1</u>: D2 discloses in paragraph [01] a system for monitoring at least one vital sign of a human body, the system comprising holding means (support for the camera (2), cf. par. [01]) for holding an optical sensor (camera sensor) and a motion sensor (motion sensor in the camera) "close" to the human body (cf. point 3.1 below), the holding means comprising a transmitting means for transmitting output signals from the sensors to evaluation means (smart phone), the evaluation means being configured to correct the output signal from the optical sensor based on the output signal of the motion sensor (SMOOTHY App, cf. par. [02]). The evaluation means calculates a vital sign (pulse, cf. par. [01]). The transmitting means is a wireless transmitting means (cf. par. [02]).
>   2.2 <u>Claim 2</u>: D2 further discloses in par. [01] measuring the pulse.
>   2.3 <u>Claim 3</u>: D2 further discloses in par. [02] a wireless local network emitter.
>   2.4 <u>Claim 4</u>: D2 further discloses in par. [01] as display means a screen.

The Examiner takes the position that claims 1–4 are not novel over D2. *A contrario*, one may (at least preliminary – one has to check!) take from this, that claims 5 and 6 are novel.

While defining the novelty objection against claim 1, the Examiner points to the terms ""close" to the human body", while referring to point 3.1 of the Communication.

Claims 1-4 as originally filed are not novel. Claims 5 and 6 apparently are novel.

> **Communication:**
> 3. **Art. 84 EPC (Clarity)**
>   3.1 <u>Claim 1</u>: The expression "[holding] ... **close** to the human body" is a relative term and thus unclear. An unclear term cannot be used by the applicant to distinguish the invention from the prior art (Guidelines F-IV, 4.6).

This clarity objection in respect of the relative term "close to", at least at first sight, seems justified. Recall that the Examiner in making his novelty objection put emphasis on the terms ""close" to the human body".

Claim 1 is not clear, because it uses the terms "holding close to".

> 3.2 <u>Claim 5</u>: The technical feature **"glove" is only mentioned in the claims and not in the description**. According to **Art. 84 EPC** it is required that **the claims are supported by the description**.

Apparently, there is no reference to a glove in the description. This objection requires that either the claim has to be brought into conformity with the description, or *vice versa*, the description has to be brought into conformity with the claim(s).

Claim 5 is not clear, because it uses the term "glove" that is not supported by the description, or the description must be brought in conformity with claim 5.

> 3.3 <u>Claim 6</u>: Optitex™ is a **Trademark**. The definition of a composition by a trademark may change and therefore is unclear under **Art. 84 EPC** (cf. Guidelines F-IV, 4.8).

The Guidelines are quite clear on this point: "*The use of trade marks and similar expressions in claims is not allowed as it does not guarantee that the product or feature referred to is not modified while maintaining its name during the term of the patent. They may be allowed exceptionally if their use is unavoidable and they are generally recognised as having a precise meaning.*" It needs to be checked, whether we can find arguments for the position that Optitex™ is generally recognised as having a precise meaning and its use is unavoidable. Otherwise, the term needs to be replaced by a clear term or be removed.

Claim 6 is not clear, because it uses the trademark "Optitex™".

226 **Communication:**
    4. If the applicant wishes to maintain the application, **new claims** should be filed which take the above objections into account.

227 Your task is to file new claims that overcome the Examiner's objections.

228 Apparently, only novelty and clarity objections were raised by the Examiner. Only prior art objections are raised against claims 1–4 based on D2.

229 Provisionally, it seems that inventive step for (preliminary) novel claims 5 and 6 is not contested.

230 The clarity objections seem *prima facie* justified.

Claims 5 and 6 do not only appear to be novel; they also appear to involve an inventive step.

231 **Communication**
    5. Care should further be taken that the **dependency** of the amended **dependent claims** is correct.

232 Your task is further to check and, if needed, adapt the dependencies of the claims. It is striking in this light, that no objections were made by the Examiner on the dependency of the claims. Bear this in mind when drafting amended claims!

Check the dependencies of all dependent claims. This is a matter of clarity and/or of support in the application as originally filed.

233 **Communication**
    6. In order to facilitate the examination as to whether the new claims contain subject-matter which extends beyond the content of the application as originally filed, the applicant is requested to indicate precisely where in the application documents any **amendments** proposed find a **basis (Art. 123(2) EPC and Rule 137(4) EPC). This also applies to the deletion of features.**

234 As you already know, paper B requires – like in real life – that amended claims do not violate Art. 123(2) EPC. It is emphasized that you indicate <u>precisely</u> were the support for claim amendments comes from. In addition, with no apparent reason found in the Communication, the Examiner all of a sudden refers to specific attention under Art. 123(2) EPC when features would be deleted from a claim.

Are all amendments in line with Art. 123(2) EPC?

235 **Communication**
    7. Care should be taken to ensure that the new claims comply with the requirements of the EPC in respect of **clarity, novelty, inventive step** and, if relevant, **unity (Art. 84, 54, 56 and 82 EPC)**.

236 The new claims must be clear and concise, must relate to subject-matter that is novel and involves an inventive step, and the set of claims must meet the requirements of unity-of-invention.

Are the amended claims clear? Do the amended claims meet the requirement of novelty? Do the amended claims involve an inventive step? Is the requirement of unity-of-invention met?

237 **Communication**
    8. In the letter of reply, the **problem and solution approach** should be followed. In particular, the **difference between the independent claim** and the **prior art (D1-D3)** should be indicated. The **technical problem** underlying the invention in view of the **closest prior art** and the **solution** to this problem should be readily derivable from the reply of the applicant.

238 When discussing the issue of inventive step, it is not only necessary to apply the problem-solution approach; it is necessary to take (and motivate) every step in the problem-solution approach. In addition, the Examiner asks for the difference between the independent claim and each document of the prior art. Apparently, only one independent

claim is expected! This question of the Examiner requires you to discuss the novelty of said independent claim relative to all three cited documents of the prior art.

Apply the problem and solution approach in all its steps!

The Communication is quite helpful. Not only are some objections clearly sketched, but also your task is clearly defined. In addition, the Communication hinted to potential problems with the dependency of dependent claims and hinted to the deletion of a feature from the claim(s).

Reading the client's letter

In the next step, it is time to read the client's letter. As already mentioned herein-above, one of your main tasks in paper B is to proceed in accordance with your client's wishes.

At this stage, we know what the field of the invention is and we know the subjective problem that underlies the invention, when starting from D1. Further, we have an idea of the claimed subject-matter and found out that the original claims 1-4 are held to be not novel over D2. Claims 5 and 6 appear to relate to novel subject-matter that may involve an inventive step. Finally, there are clarity objections raised with regard to the relative term "close to" in claim 1, to the use of the Trademark Optitex in claim 6, and to the fact that claim 5 uses the term "glove" that is not supported by the description.

Let us go to the client's letter.

Client's letter

Dear Ms. Evita Lee-Tea,

[01] Our invention has the advantage that the vital signs can be remotely monitored with a reliable, secure and comfortable attachment of the sensors in combination with a high signal quality, which is achieved by noise reduction through correcting the sensor output signals.

Your client starts with mentioning the advantage of the invention. This comes close to the subjective problem relative to D1, given in paragraph [01] of the patent application as filed:

Problem: provide a reliable and comfortable system for long-term remote monitoring of vital signs of patients (such as small children or babies).

It is not exactly the same, though. Your client refers to "secure" attachment and points to "high signal quality, achieved by noise reduction through correcting the sensor output signals".

Client's letter

[02] We propose filing the enclosed draft set of claims together with your reply to the official communication. We are convinced that the subject-matter of amended claim 1 is novel and inventive. Please make any amendments to the proposed set of claims you consider to be necessary for the claims to fulfil the requirements of the EPC, whilst giving us the broadest possible scope of protection for our invention.

A draft set of claims is introduced. Your client is convinced that the subject-matter of amended claim 1 is novel and involves an inventive step.

In addition, you are invited to make any amendments to the proposed set of claims needed to bring these claims in accordance with the requirements of the EPC. Your client knows in which way he wants to go, but is not a specialist in patent law. That part should be your contribution.

Since the single paper B 2017, you can score 30 marks for the amendment of the claims. Using the words of the Examiners' Report of paper B 2017, these 30 "(m)arks were awarded for making appropriate amendments to the draft set of claims for bringing it [said draft set of claims] into accordance with the EPC. **No marks** are awarded for merely filing the claim set proposed by the client or for the formulation of additional dependent claims."

Hence, although the client wishes that the set of claims gives him "the broadest possible scope of protection" for his invention, neither are points available for other inventions than the one(s) identified in the draft provided by your client, nor for any new dependent claims. The suggested set of claims in itself should be optimised to give the broadest possible scope of protection.

250 Knowing this, do not waste time on finding different and other inventions or different preferred embodiments, if there is no hint to those in either the draft set of claims or the client's letter!

251 **Client's letter**

[03] Claim 1 has been restricted by including the features of dependent claim 5. Claim 1 is drafted in the two-part form with respect to D1, because D2 and D3 are from remote technical fields. We have moved the wireless transmission from claim 1 to amended dependent claim 2, because for some applications this kind of transmission is not suitable. We do not want to have a dependent claim related to the subject matter of original claim 2. We only want to protect a system, where the attaching means is (any kind of) a garment. Please amend the claims accordingly, if possible.

252 Your client suggests to restrict claim 1 by including the features of claim 5.

253 From our preliminary analysis, we know that there were no novelty objections raised by the Examiner in respect of original claim 5, nor was there an explicit inventive step objection. We do know that there was a clarity issue with regard to claim 1 and a clarity issue with regard to claim 5, but not knowing yet how the amended claim 1 looks like, we cannot say anything in respect of these clarity issues.

254 In the second sentence of paragraph [03] of the client's letter, the client observed that amended claim 1 is drafted in the two-part form with respect to D1, because D2 and D3 are from remote technical fields.

255 This is already a second time that apparently the client considers that D1 is the closest prior art. First, D1 was discussed as prior art document in the description of the patent application and the subjective problem was based thereon. Second, its features are brought in the preamble of a two-part form claim. In addition, the client considers that D2 and D3 are from remote technical fields.

256 Since the client is not an expert in patent law, of course you have to check if D1 indeed can be the closest prior art in view of the problem-solution approach. Furthermore, if so, you also have to check whether the two-part form is correctly used.

Is D1 the closest prior art? Are D2 and D3 from remote technical fields?
Is the independent claim correctly put in the two-part form?

257 Then, the client informs you that the wireless transmission is moved to amended claim 2, "because for some applications this kind of transmission is not suitable".

258 This reason for the move, is of course irrelevant from a patent law point-of-view. You need to check whether the requirements of Art. 123(2) EPC have been met when a feature is removed from a claim. See in this light Part H, Chapter V, 3.1 of the Guidelines (Replacement or removal of features from a claim). A clear pointer to this part of the answer is found in point 6 of the Communication, wherein, so we know, the Examiner apparently without reason referred to providing basis under Art. 123(2) EPC when features were deleted.

Is there support under Art. 123(2) EPC to remove from claim 1 that the transmission is wireless?

259 [Part H, Chapter V, 3.1 of the Guidelines teaches that if an amendment by replacing or removing a feature from a claim fails to pass the following test by at least one criterion, it necessarily contravenes the requirements of Art. 123(2) EPC:
(i) the replaced or removed feature was not explained as essential in the originally filed disclosure;
(ii) the skilled person would directly and unambiguously recognize that the feature is not, as such, indispensable for the function of the invention in the light of the technical problem the invention serves to solve (in this context special care needs to be taken in cases where the technical problem is reformulated during the proceedings); and

(iii) the skilled person would recognize that the replacement or removal requires no modification of one or more features to compensate for the change (it does not in itself alter the invention).

However, even if the above criteria are met, it must still be ensured that the amendment by replacing or removing a feature from a claim satisfies the requirements of Art. 123(2) EPC as they also have been set out in G 3/89 and G 11/91, referred to in G 2/10 as "the gold standard".]

Originally filed claim 2 may be deleted, because the client explicitly states that he does not want to have a dependent claim related to the subject-matter of original claim 2.

When a feature is removed from claim 1, not only the support under Art. 123(2) EPC needs to be checked, but there may also be issues with the support in the application for the dependent claims. In addition, the dependency of the dependent claims must be checked. The latter certainly, because – apparently without any reason – the Examiner points in item 5 of its Communication that the dependency of amended dependent claims should be correct.

The last explicit wish of the client in paragraph [03] is the request to amend the claims to protect a system, where the attaching means is (any kind of) a garment.

Is there support under Art. 123(2) EPC to "generalize" original claim 5 to "any kind of garment"?

Client's letter

[04] The third embodiment is enjoying unexpected success in the sports article market. To cover this embodiment, we replaced the erroneous word "glove" in amended claim 1 by "headband for goggles". It is very important for us to have protection for this embodiment. Inspired by the erroneous word "glove" and by the teaching of D3 we intend to produce a glove comprising optical and motion sensors according to our inventive idea. If possible, please protect the option that the garment is a glove. In view of the comment of the examiner in section 3.2 you may have to provide corresponding reasoning. Otherwise we do not want you to add further dependent claims.

We have not yet read what the third embodiment is, but apparently it is a headband for goggles. [If you wish, you can quickly have a look in the description to have this information confirmed.] The client replaced the term "glove" in original claim 5 (now introduced in claim 1) by this term that appears to be supported by the application as originally filed as "third embodiment". If allowable, this replacement would overcome the clarity objection with respect to the "glove".

However, the client invites you to claim gloves, as well. In that case, you have to deal with the clarity objection raised in section 3.2 of the Communication.

Is there support under Art. 123(2) EPC to claim a headband for goggles? Is there a possibility to maintain a glove in the claims and hence solve the clarity issue raised to that term?

No other dependent claims are to be drawn up.

Reading the draft set of claims

In the final step of finding the objections, it is time to read the draft set of claims.

Draft set of claims
1. System for monitoring at least one vital sign of a human body, the system comprising:
    – ~~holding~~ attaching means (1, 11, 21) for ~~holding~~ attaching an optical sensor (2, 12, 22) and a motion sensor (3, 13, 23) ~~close~~ to the human body (10, 27), the ~~holding~~ attaching means (1, 11, 21) comprising in addition to the sensors (2, 12, 22, 3, 13, 23) transmitting means (4, 14, 24) for transmitting output signals from the sensors (2, 12, 22, 3, 13, 23),
    – evaluation means (5, 25) for receiving the output signals and calculating from the output signals the at least one vital sign, characterised in that <u>the attaching means (1, 11, 21) is one of a sock (1), a wristband (11) or a headband (21) for</u>

goggles (20) and in that the evaluation means (5, 25) is configured to correct the output signal from the optical sensor (2, 12, 22) based on the output signal of the motion sensor (3, 13, 23) or to correct the output signal from the motion sensor (3, 13, 23) based on the output signal of the optical sensor ~~and wherein the transmitting means is a wireless transmitting means (4, 14, 24)~~.

269 The first thing that draws the attention is that the term "holding means" is replaced by "attaching means" and that "holding (...) close" is replaced by "attaching". This would overcome the clarity objection, because the relative term "close" is no longer used. But the question is, is this replacement supported by the application as originally filed?

270 In the client's letter, it was noted that amended claim 1 is a combination of original claims 1 and 5. Does this combination of claims 1 and 5 support this replacement? Does the description support this replacement?

Is there support under Art. 123(2) EPC to replace holding means with attaching means?

271 In addition, the attaching means is limited to a sock, a wristband or a headband for goggles.

272 Again, in the client's letter, it was noted that amended claim 1 is a combination of original claims 1 and 5, yet the originally used term "glove" was replaced by "headband for goggles". Moreover, the client wishes to generalize to "(any kind of) a garment" and would also like to maintain the term "glove" in the claims. In the latter case, the clarity objection raised in point 3.2 of the Communication should be addressed in another way than just deleting this term.

273 The objection to generalize to any garment and the objection to claim gloves were already identified while going through the client's letter.

274 The last amendment is the deletion of the transmitting means being wireless transmitting means.

275 Also this objection was already identified while going through the client's letter.

Draft set of claims
2. System according to claim 1, wherein the ~~at least one vital sign is pulse, body temperature, blood pressure and/or blood oxygen saturation~~ output signals are transmitted by wireless transmitting means (4, 14, 24).

276 In the client's letter, it was noted that the feature removed from claim 1 was introduced in claim 2. The subject-matter of original claim 2 needed not be maintained in a claim.

277 When looking at the wording of amended claim 2, you can see that it is not the same wording as the wording removed from claim 1. Instead of a product feature, *viz.* that the transmitting means is a wireless transmitting means, process wording is introduced in claim 2, *viz.* output signals are transmitted by wireless transmitting means. Normally, in a product claim product features rather than process features are desired; otherwise a clarity objection may be raised.

Adapt the wording of proposed claim 2?

278 **Draft set of claims**
3. System according to claim 1 or 2, wherein the wireless transmitting means (4, 14, 24) is a wireless local network emitter.

279 The wording of claim 3 did not change. However, the removal of wireless transmitting means from amended claim 1 makes that the back-reference to amended claim 1 misses antecedent basis so that a clarity issue may be raised.

280 In addition, it is needed to check whether there is support for the potential new combinations coming from the amendments made in claim 1 and the features of claim 3.

Adapt the wording of proposed claim 3 in the light of the amendments in claims 1 and 2?

281 **Draft set of claims**
4. System according to any of claims 1 to 3, further comprising a screen (6) and configured to display the at least one vital sign on the screen.

282 The wording of claim 4 did not change, either. However, it is needed to check whether there is support for the potential new combinations coming from the amendments made

in claim 1 and the features of claim 4. In addition, the dependency on claims 2 and 3 need to be checked under Art. 123(2) EPC and in accordance with Art. 84 EPC.

Adapt the wording of proposed claim 4 in the light of the amendments in claims 1, 2 and 3?

Draft set of claims

5. ~~System according to any of claims 1 to 4, wherein the holding means is an attaching means such as a sock (1), a wristband (11) or a glove.~~

Claim 5 as filed was deleted. As noted in the client's letter, its content was introduced in amended claim 1 and the term "glove" was replaced by "headband for goggles". There was however the wish of the client to have a claim directed to a glove, as well, should it be possible to overcome the clarity objection.

If amended claim 1 can be generalized to (any kind of) a garment, can we maintain the preferred embodiments in a claim? Watch the dependency of such a dependent claim.

Draft set of claims

5.~~6.~~ System according to any of claims 1 to ~~5~~ 4, wherein the attaching means (1, 11, 21) is at least partly made of *Optitex*™.

The client essentially maintains original claim 6 and has amended the back-references to the preceding claims. It is needed to check whether there is support for the potential new combinations coming from the amendments made in claim 1 and the features of original claim 6. In addition, the dependency on claims 2, 3 and 4 needs to be checked under Art. 123(2) EPC and in accordance with Art. 84 EPC. No suggestion is made to deal with the clarity objection in view of the use of the Tradename *Optitex*™.

How can we overcome the clarity objection based on the Tradename Optitex? Watch the dependency of such a claim.

Résumé of the objections

Before going in the details of the invention as elaborated in the description of the application as filed and before having read the prior cited by the Examiner in his communication, we know that our task is to deal with the following points or objections:

<u>*On the claims as originally filed:*</u>
Claims 1-4 as originally filed are not novel.
Claims 5 and 6 apparently are novel.
Claims 5 and 6 do not only appear to be novel; they also appear to involve an inventive step.
Claim 1 is not clear, because it uses the terms "holding close to".
Claim 5 is not clear, because it uses the term "glove" that is not supported by the description, or the description must be brought in conformity with claim 5.
Claim 6 is not clear, because it uses the trademark "Optitex™".

<u>*On the amended claims:*</u>
Do the amended claims meet the requirement of novelty?
Do the amended claims involve an inventive step?
Are the amended claims clear?
Are all amendments in line with Art. 123(2) EPC?
Is there support under Art. 123(2) EPC to replace holding means with attaching means?
Is there support under Art. 123(2) EPC to remove from claim 1 that the transmission is wireless?
Is there support under Art. 123(2) EPC to "generalize" original claim 5 to "any kind of garment"?
Is there support under Art. 123(2) EPC to claim a headband for goggles?
Is there a possibility to maintain a glove in the claims and hence solve the clarity issue raised to that term?
If amended claim 1 can be generalized to (any kind of) a garment, can we maintain the preferred embodiments in a claim? Watch the dependency of such a claim.

Check the dependencies of all dependent claims. This is a matter of clarity and/or of support in the application as originally filed.
Adapt the wording of proposed claim 2?
Adapt the wording of proposed claim 3 in the light of the amendments in claims 1 and 2?
Adapt the wording of proposed claim 4 in the light of the amendments in claims 1, 2 and 3?
How can we overcome the clarity objection based on the Tradename Optitex? Watch the dependency of such a claim.
Is the requirement of unity-of-invention met?

<u>Apply the problem and solution approach in all its steps:</u>
Field of Invention: monitoring at least one vital sign of the human body by optical means.
Problem: provide a reliable and comfortable system for long-term remote monitoring of vital signs of patients (such as small children or babies).
This problem is relative to D1
Is D1 the closest prior art? Are D2 and D3 from remote technical fields?
Is the independent claim correctly put in the two-part form?

2.3.4 Step 4: Performing a preliminary analysis of the prior art

288   In the last step of the preliminary analysis, we read the state of the art.

289   From steps 1–3, we know that there are 3 pieces of prior art, D1, D2 and D3. The Examiner has raised novelty objections against original claims 1–4, based on D2. The client states in his letter that D1 is the closest prior art, and that D2 and D3 are from remote technical fields. In addition, in the originally filed application, D1 is discussed and the problem underlying the invention is defined *vis-à-vis* D1. As is clear from point 8 of his communication, the Examiner explicitly wishes you to indicate the difference between the independent claim and the prior art (D1–D3), and wishes you to follow the problem and solution approach, wherein you have to indicate what the technical problem is that underlies the invention in view of the closest prior art.

So let us read D1:

290   **Document D1: From textbook "Medical Technology"**

[01] Described is an optical pulse oximeter for measuring the pulse and the oxygen saturation in the blood.

291   From this first paragraph and compared with the first paragraph of the application as filed, it is clear that D1 belongs to the same or at least a similar technical field as the invention described in the patent application. In addition, D1 is presented as a textbook and hence a document that reflects basic knowledge of an average skilled person in that technical field.

292   **Document D1: From textbook "Medical Technology"**

[02] As shown in the figures the optical pulse oximeter typically utilizes a first LED (light-emitting diode) 221 and a second LED 222 facing an optical sensor 207 on both sides of a part of a patient's body, usually a fingertip or an earlobe. The first LED 221 emits red light and the second LED 222 emits infrared light. Absorption of light at these wavelengths differs significantly between blood loaded with oxygen and blood lacking oxygen. Oxygenated haemoglobin absorbs more infrared light and allows more red light to pass through. Deoxygenated haemoglobin allows more infrared light to pass through and absorbs more red light. The LEDs flash about thirty times per second. [03] The optical sensor 207 measures the intensity of the light that passes through, i.e. is not absorbed. The measurement fluctuates in time because the amount of arterial blood pulses with the heartbeat frequency. An evaluation means 205 calculates the oxygen saturation in the blood as well as the pulse from the ratio of the red light measurement to the infrared light measurement. The intensity of the infrared signal measured by the optical sensor 207 is proportional to the body temperature. From the blood oxygen saturation, pulse and body temperature, the blood pressure can be calculated. The calculated values are displayed on screen 206.

These two paragraphs sketch the underlying principles of how the optical pulse oximeter works.

Document D1: From textbook "Medical Technology"

[04] The LEDs 221, 222 and the optical sensor 207 are integrated into a clip 201 which is attached to a finger 210. The clip 201 is connected to the evaluation means 205 by means of a cable 204. In order to achieve better accuracy and reliability of the pulse measurement, the pulse can be measured independently from the optical pulse oximeter by means of a sensor 203, such as a pressure sensor or a motion sensor, which could also be integrated into the clip. Preferably a pressure sensor is used, because a motion sensor, which is reliable enough to measure the pulse, is typically large and heavy and therefore uncomfortable for the patient. The evaluation means 205 comprises simple, but fast software. This allows quick signal processing, but no further software can be installed in the evaluation means 205.

In this paragraph, a preferred embodiment of the optical pulse oximeter is described, further using an evaluation means, a sensor and fast software.

The discussion of D1 in the patent application as originally filed appears to reflect D1's content correctly.

We now turn to D2:

Document D2: Advertisement from the magazine "Smart phone & Co"

[01] Now there is the latest gadget for your jPhone: a jPhone babyphone! With the Wittings Smart Baby Monitor WSBW 4.0 you don't just simply monitor your child (also at night, thanks to a built-in infra-red image sensor), but you can directly interact with your child, e.g. by sending soothing music. Even better, the WSBW 4.0 not only transmits sound and images, but also monitors the current room temperature and the relative humidity of the air. The camera 1 detects small changes in the colour of the skin to measure the pulse of your baby and to display the pulse on a screen. The camera is mounted on a support 2 holding the camera close to the baby, but out of reach of the baby such that the camera cannot be damaged. The camera is movable about two axes. The infra-red sensor is used to automatically adjust the position of the camera 1 when your baby moves.

D2 is an advertisement from a particular magazine. It is in the field of babyphones. Yet, when compared to the first paragraph of the patent application as filed, D2 also monitors at least one vital sign of the human body by optical means: the pulse by detecting small changes in the colour of the skin. In that light, the statement in the client's letter that D2 is from a remote technical field may be questioned.

Document D2: Advertisement from the magazine "Smart phone & Co"

[02] The Wittings Smart Baby Monitor exchanges all data with your smart phone via wireless local network or any other wireless connection. Many jPhone apps are available for the WSBW 4.0. The SMOOTHY App installed in your jPhone 3 determines the motion of the camera 1 using a motion sensor in the camera. The SMOOTHY App corrects the sound and image signals from the camera on the basis of the motion data from the motion sensor in the camera, thereby reducing undesired noise from the signals. This achieves even better sound and picture quality.

When comparing the contents of these two paragraphs of D2 with the discussion of the Examiner in his communication, the Examiner's conclusions do not seem unreasonable.

Document D2: Advertisement from the magazine "Smart phone & Co"

[03] The Wittings Smart Baby Monitor is available for 130 Euros from October 2014 at www.arctic.com. SMOOTHY App: 1 Euro.

This third paragraph of D2 does not seem to add much to the first and second paragraphs.

The last document cited is D3. This document was not discussed in the application as originally filed, not discussed in the client's letter, other than that it is from a remote technical field, and not discussed by the Examiner in his communication.

304 **Document D3: Technical Disclosure from "Brooker, Phils & Siems"**

[01] Disclosed is a sock, comprising an electrical sensor for electrocardiography. Electrocardiography is the recording of the electrical activity of the heart. The electrical activity of the heart is detected by electrical sensors in contact with the skin of a human body.

305 In its first paragraph, D3 does not refer to the monitoring of a vital sign; it describes a sock comprising an electrical sensor, recording the electrical activity of the heart. Based on this paragraph alone, its technical field is a little further away than that of D1 and D2. In addition, it teaches electrical monitoring and not optical monitoring.

306 **Document D3: Technical Disclosure from "Brooker, Phils & Siems"**

[02] The figure shows a sock 301 comprising an electrical sensor 309 and a cable 304 that can be connected to an evaluation means 305 for processing the data from the sensor. The sock 301 is pulled over a patient's foot 310 such that the electrical sensor is in contact with the foot. The electrical signal from the electrical sensor 309 is evaluated and displayed by the evaluation means 305.

307 The sock does contain quite a number of features that also are present in the claims of the patent application as filed.

308 **Document D3: Technical Disclosure from "Brooker, Phils & Siems"**

[03] The sock 301 is a reliable, secure and comfortable means for attaching the electrical sensor 309 to the human body. The sock 301 is at least partially made of a material comprising 50–60 % cotton, 30–40 % polyurethane and 10–20 % polyethylene – glycol in % by weight. This material unfortunately allows measurements only with electrical sensors, because for any other type of sensor, e.g. optical sensor, the signal to noise ratio would be too low for measuring vital signs of the human body. Therefore, this material is not suitable for recording vital signs.

309 This paragraph makes that D3 teaches away from using its sock for monitoring a vital sign.

310 **Document D3: Technical Disclosure from "Brooker, Phils & Siems"**

[04]] Instead of a sock another kind of garment may be used, such as a glove, a wristband or a headband. A glove in particular is a reliable and comfortable means for attaching sensors to the human body.

311 This paragraph teaches that a sock is a garment, and that also other garments can be used, such as a glove, a wristband or a headband, so all the garments also referred to in the client's letter and the suggested set of claims.

312 Where the client wishes to generalize the claims to any kind of garment, D3 is a document that states that a sock, a glove, a wristband and a headband are species of the genus garment.

2.3.5 Step 5: Performing an in-depth analysis of the patent application

313 After finishing the preliminary analysis, we now know the objections and have a feeling on what the prior art teaches. It is time to tackle the objections and find solutions.

314 For this, read the description of the application as field with literally an eye on the objections identified in step 3.

315 It is good to be reminded on some of the notes and explanations that are also set out in the A-Book.

Notes and explanations:

316 Especially when you sit the Exam in a language that is not your mother language, keep the other language versions of the paper ready. They may be useful for clarifying issues of terminology or suspected errors. What appears to be unclear in one language is perhaps perfectly clear in another.

How can you recognise pertinent words, expressions and phrases? In the context of the EQE papers, *"keywords"* are not simply words that occur in the text more prominently than others. A keyword refers rather to an index term characterising important pieces of information. You will need experience and common sense to recognise such index terms. The best way to acquire a degree of reliability and routine is to solve old papers. By doing this, you will learn the language habits of those who draft the papers. The table below gives some examples of keywords and their significance.

Table of keywords and their significance

Keyword:	Significance:
"the invention concerns ..."	statement of invention
"the problem is ...", *"no solution was found"*	problem
"the advantage is ...", *"improved"*, *"better"*	positive effect
"the drawback is ...", *"insufficient"*, *"worse"*	negative effect
"the term ... means ...", *"X is the same as Y"*	definition
"it is essential that ...", *"must"*, *"inevitably"*	mandatory feature
"usually", *"typically"*, *"preferably"*, *"desirable"*	optional feature
"is known", *"commercially available"*	statement of prior art
"it is obvious that ..."	lack of inventive step

When marking any portions of text – whether a single word, a phrase or several sentences – minimalism is justified. In general, candidates mark too much, sometimes up to more than two third of the whole text. Such a proliferation may later cause only confusion, particularly if the meaning of the marked passages is not indicated or remains unclear.

It is essential to indicate consistently why passages have been marked. This can be done by means of marginal notes, preferably in the form of suitable abbreviations. The number of abbreviations should be kept small in order to avoid confusion. Some useful abbreviations are listed in the following table.

List of abbreviations

D, def	definition
eb1, eb2, emb1 ...	embodiment 1, 2 ... of the invention
e1, e2, eff1 ...	technical effect 1, 2 ...
Inst.	instructions given by the client
mf	mandatory feature of the invention
of	optional feature of the invention
p1, p2 ...	problem 1, 2 ...
s1, s2 ...	solution 1, 2 ...
STA	state of the art
TF	technical field of interest to the client

Some candidates distinguish between *"effects"*, *"advantages"* and *"disadvantages"*, but for the sake of simplicity, it is normally better to use the same abbreviation for all these effects.

Technical problems, technical effects and advantages mentioned in the patent application are often essential for the determination of the subject-matter to be claimed. These concepts may likely play a role in a problem-solution approach to show inventive step. Advantages and statements of problems and their solution should always be marked. Whenever a problem is solved or an advantage is obtained by more than one technical feature, it is important to list all involved features in combination.

The in-depth analysis is an essential part of the method and a key to success or failure. Therefore, there is every reason to perform step 5 with greatest care. Spend sufficient time on the proper analysis of the paper and try to arrive at the proper conclusions in the first round. There is no room for quick shots and decisions taken in haste. As a consequence of haste you may need a second or third round, and you have to read the texts twice or thrice. When sitting the examination, you cannot afford such escapades.

325 **Read the description in detail**

Description of the Application

[01] The present application relates to monitoring at least one vital sign of the human body by optical means. The four vital signs, pulse, body temperature, blood pressure and blood oxygen saturation, have to be monitored regularly for controlling the medical status of a patient in hospital. Monitoring vital signs at home will play a more and more important role in remote medicine. D1 discloses monitoring vital signs by attaching sensors to the human body with a clip. This has the drawback that the clip is uncomfortable and that for long-term measurements the attachment is not reliable, because the clip can move. Therefore, the aim of this invention is to provide a reliable and comfortable system for long-term remote monitoring of the vital signs of patients, such as small children and babies.

326 As already noted in the preliminary analysis of step 2, in the first sentence of this paragraph, the technical field of the invention is sketched: the monitoring of at least one vital sign of human body by optical means. The second and third sentences give a basic explanation on what a vital sign is, why it is monitored and that apparently the future is to monitor at home.

327 Subsequently, it is indicated that prior art document D1 discloses the monitoring of vital signs by attaching sensors to the human body with a clip.

328 Then, paragraph [01] refers to a drawback of D1, being that a clip is uncomfortable and that for long-term measurements the attachment is not reliable, because the clip can move. This observation is followed by the aim of the invention, and that is to provide a reliable and comfortable system for long-term remote monitoring of the vital signs of patients, such as small children and babies.

329 Relative to D1, the subjective problem underlying the invention is noted to provide a reliable and comfortable system for long-term remote monitoring of vital signs or patients.

330 Meanwhile, we know that
 – D1 is a textbook, and is in the same or at least in a similar technical field as the invention;
 – D2 is in the field of babyphones, but also teaches optical monitoring of the pulse of a baby; and
 – D3 relates to electronically monitoring the heart, while teaching that its solution is not suitable for monitoring vital signs; at least not by optical means.

331 In the light of this knowledge, knowing that the client considers that D1 is the closest prior art and that D2 and D3 are from more remote technical fields and knowing that the technical field of an invention may play an important role in the first step(s) of the problem-solution approach, either the invention should drastically shift in the coming paragraphs, for example because the novelty objection based on D2 is to be overcome, or D1 is likely the closest prior art, indeed. Selecting on the knowledge we have at this stage, I do not see good arguments to place D2 or D3 above D1 to be the closest prior art.

Subsequently, we read the next paragraph:

332 **Description of the Application**

[02] The invention concerns a system comprising means for attaching an optical sensor and a motion sensor to the human body. The attaching means comprises means for transmitting output signals from the sensors to an evaluation means for calculating at least one vital sign from the output signals. The inventive idea is that the attaching means is a garment, such as a sock or a wristband, and that the evaluation means is configured to correct the output signal from the optical sensor based on the output signal of the motion sensor, and vice-versa. It is not important for the invention how the signals are transmitted to the evaluation means.

333 This paragraph is on the invention described in the patent application. It provides basis for an attaching means for attaching sensors to the human body, rather than a holding means for holding sensors close to the human body. In addition, the attaching means is a garment, such as a sock or a wristband.

334 Paragraph [02] seems suitable support to deal with the following two objections:

Is there support under Art. 123(2) EPC to replace holding means with attaching means?

Is there support under Art. 123(2) EPC to "generalize" original claim 5 to "any kind of garment"?

In addition, this paragraph points to the evaluation means configured to correct the output signal from the optical sensor based on the output signal of the motion sensor, and vice-versa as (part of) the inventive idea. Apparently, this statement should be coupled to the term "reliable" in the subjective problem definition.

Furthermore, this paragraph [02] makes clear that the transmission means feature at the end of original claim 1 need not necessarily be wireless: "it is not important for the invention how the signals are transmitted to the evaluation means" (Part H, Chapter V, 3.1 of the Guidelines, requirement (i)).

Is there support under Art. 123(2) EPC to remove from claim 1 that the transmission is wireless?

This brings us to the next paragraph:

Description of the Application

[03] Figs. 1-3 show systems according to first, second and third embodiments of the invention. The invention will be described below with reference to the drawings.

This paragraph refers to the drawings and to the first, second and third embodiments of the invention. Recall that the client in its letter pointed to the unexpected success of the third embodiment and used that to replace the glove in the claims by a headband for goggles.

Nothing else can be taken from this paragraph.

Description of the Application

[04] Fig. 1 shows a system for remotely monitoring vital signs. The system comprises a sock 1 for attaching an optical sensor 2 and a motion sensor 3 to a human body 10. The sock 1 comprises transmitting means 4 for transmitting the output signals of sensors 2 and 3 to evaluation means 5. The transmitting means 4 may be any kind of transmitting means, such as a serial port for a cable, or wireless transmitting means, such as a wireless local network emitter.

This paragraph describes a sock as an embodiment of the invention. The sock is used to attach two sensors to a human body, rather than holding these close to a human body. Regarding the suggested wording of new claim 1, this is a further argument that this suggested claim meets the requirements of Art. 123(2) EPC at least on this aspect.

In addition, this paragraph teaches that the transmitting means may be any kind of transmitting means and not only a wireless transmitting means. This is after paragraph [02] a second time that the transmitting means is presented as not necessarily needing to be a wireless transmitting means. The embodiment of a sock is additionally coupled to the wireless transmitting means being a wireless local network emitter (original claim 3).

Description of the Application

[05] The evaluation means 5 is configured to receive and process the transmitted signals and may be a computer, a software application called App, or a smart phone, such as a jPhone. The vital signs are calculated from the output signals of the sensors and may be outputted as an audio signal or displayed on a screen 6 of the evaluation means 5.

This paragraph couples different evaluation means to the sock and indicates that the vital signs may be displayed on, *e.g.*, a screen (original claim 4).

For the originally filed claims and for the set of claims suggested by the client, paragraph [06] does not bring anything:

Description of the Application

[06] The optical sensor 2 comprises a light source 2a and a light detector 2b. The light source 2a emits a light beam 7a towards the human body 10 and the light detector 2b measures the light 7b having passed through the human body, i.e. not absorbed by the human body. 2a and 2b are part of an optical pulse oximeter as described in D1.

345 It describes the optical sensor of claim 1 and how it works. It is a known sensor in the sense that it is also described in D1.

346 **Description of the Application**

[07] Accommodating an optical sensor into a garment adds electrical noise to the output signal of the optical sensor 2. A sock 1 worn by a baby moves frequently, which adds further noise to the output signal from the optical sensor 2. This further reduces the quality of the output signal. In order to overcome this drawback, in the first embodiment, the motion sensor 3 is placed next to, preferably between, the light source 2a and the light detector 2b. However, motion sensor 3, light source 2a and light detector 2b may be placed at any position in the garment 1. The relative position of these components to each other is not important. The output signal of the motion sensor 3 is also transmitted by the transmitting means 4 to the evaluation means 5.

347 Paragraph [07] is also providing information on how the invention works. It describes the optical sensor and the motion sensor, not only while referring to the sock, but also to a garment. The teaching of this paragraph may hence be generalized to any garment.

348 **Description of the Application**

[08] In the evaluation means 5 the output signal from the optical sensor 2 is corrected based on the output signal from the motion sensor 3 such that noise is reduced. This leads to better signal quality, thereby preventing false measurements.

Example for correcting the signal: A quick movement of the foot causes an erroneous peak to occur in the output signal of the optical sensor 2 and simultaneously, a peak in the output signal of the motion sensor 3. The evaluation means 5 uses the output signal from the motion sensor 3 to remove the erroneous peak in the output signal of the optical sensor 2. Vice versa the output signal from the motion sensor 3, which may be used for directly measuring a patient's pulse, may be corrected by the output signal of sensor 2. The relative position of the motion sensor 3 with respect to the optical sensor 2 is not important for correcting the signals.

349 Where the previous paragraphs essentially focus on a garment, such as a sock, with sensors, paragraph [08] focuses on the "reliable" aspect of the subjective problem identified in paragraph [01] of the patent application: the correction in the evaluation means. Paragraph [08] describes the correction of the output signal from the optical sensor based on the output signal from the motion sensor (or *vice versa*) in the evaluation means, resulting in a better signal quality and the prevention of false measurements. In addition, in an example this correction is elaborated. This paragraph hence describes that this part of the subjective problem has been solved.

350 With an eye on the problem-solution approach, the correction in the evaluation means part of the characterizing portion of suggested amended claim 1 is associated with the technical effect of providing better signal quality and the prevention of false measurements.

351 **Description of the Application**

[09] The evaluation means 5 is configured to calculate from the corrected signals the vital signs as is described in more detail in D1. The sock 1 may be replaced by a wristband 11 as shown in Fig. 2. However, any garment may be used. The garment may be at least partially made of *Optitex*™, which is a material comprising 50–60 % cotton, 30–40 % polyurethane and 10–20 % polyethylene glycol in % by weight. The remaining technical features, such as the transmitting means 14, light source 12a, light detector 12b and motion sensor 13, are identical to the first embodiment.

352 The evaluation means do not seem to be special in that reference is made to D1.

353 More interesting is that the sock may be replaced by a wristband (second embodiment), with the remaining technical features, such as the transmitting means, light source, light detector and motion sensor being identical to the first embodiment. More importantly the sock can even be replaced by "any garment". This sentence is very relevant for the possibilities to generalize socks and wristbands to any garment. This sentence hence is relevant for the objections:

Is there support under Art. 123(2) EPC to replace holding means with attaching means?
Is there support under Art. 123(2) EPC to "generalize" original claim 5 to "any kind of garment"?
Is there support under Art. 123(2) EPC to remove from claim 1 that the transmission is wireless?

Furthermore, paragraph [09] teaches that the garment may be at least partially made of *Optitex*™. This material identified by a trademark is described to be a material comprising 50–60 % cotton, 30–40 % polyurethane and 10–20 % polyethylene glycol in % by weight.

We recall that the Examiner raised a clarity objection to claim 6 referring to *Optitex*™. This paragraph provides support for replacing the material *Optitex*™ by a material comprising 50–60 % cotton, 30–40 % polyurethane and 10–20 % polyethylene glycol in % by weight:

Claim 6 is not clear, because it uses the trademark "Optitex™".

The third embodiment, the one enjoying unexpected success in the sports article market according to the client's letter, yet was erroneously not claimed, is described in the paragraphs [10], [11] and [12]:

Description of the Application

[10] Fig. 3 shows a system for use while doing sport such as running or cycling. The system comprises a headband 21 for goggles 20. The goggles 20 protect the eyes from foreign objects and water. The optical sensor 22, i.e. light source 22a and light detector 22b, and the motion sensor 23 are attached to the ear 27 by means of the headband 21. The headband 21 is a garment and may be made of *Optitex*™ which provides reliable, secure and comfortable attachment of the sensors to the ear.

The headband for goggles is presented as a garment and may be made of *Optitex*™.

Description of the Application

[11] Accordingly, Fig. 3 shows a system for monitoring the vital signs of the human body, the system comprising the headband 21 for attaching the optical sensor 22 and the motion sensor 23 to the human body. The headband 21 comprises, in addition to the sensors 22 and 23, transmitting means 24 for transmitting the output signals from the sensors. The system further comprises an evaluation means 25 for receiving the output signals and calculating therefrom at least one of the vital signs. The evaluation means 25 is configured to correct the output signal from the sensor 22 based on the output signal of sensor 23, and vice-versa.

In paragraph [11], it is further described that also the headband is "for attaching" the sensors "to the human body".

Description of the Application

[12] In this embodiment it is essential that the vital signs are not displayed on the screen of the evaluation means 25, because the screen is used for other purposes, such as displaying a map. Instead the vital signs may be output as an audio signal, e.g. to an earphone 26 attached to the headband 21. The transmitting means 24 may be a wireless transmitting means or any other kind of transmitting means, such as described for the other embodiments.

The teachings in paragraphs [10] and [11] make that the headband can be linked to almost all originally filed claims and claims suggested by the client. However, in paragraph [12], it is described as essential that in the headband embodiment the vital signs are not displayed on a screen. That is, there is no support to link the headband embodiment with the screen claimed in original claim 4 and claim 4 as suggested by the client.

2.3.6 Step 6: Drafting the set of amended claims

In the previous steps, we have made a preliminary and detailed analysis of materials of paper B. It is now time to proceed according to the wish of the client.

364 Thereto, we either recall or read again the letter of the client, bearing in mind the Examiner's communication.

365 In the Examiner's communication, novelty objections were raised to claims 1–4. In addition, clarity objections were raised to "holding (...) close to" as used in claim 1, to the term "glove" as used in claim 5, because this term is not supported by the description, and to the Trade name Optitex™ used in claim 6. No other objections were raised by the Examiner; particularly the novelty of claims 5 and 6 was not contested and no inventive step objections were raised.

366 The client suggests a set of amended claims, wherein claim 1 is said to be restricted by including the features of claim 5 as filed therein; be it that the unclear term "glove" used in claim 5 is replaced by "headband for goggles". Further, the feature that the transmission is wireless has been removed from claim 1.

367 Your client is convinced that such a suggested new claim 1 is novel and inventive, and has "the advantage that the vital signs can be remotely monitored with a reliable, secure and comfortable attachment of the sensors in combination with a high signal quality, which is achieved by noise reduction through correcting the sensor output signals".

368 Claim 2 may be deleted and the feature removed from claim 1 is suggested to be in new claim 2.

369 The wording of claims 3, 4 and 6 remained the same.

370 Further, the client indicates the wish to protect a system, wherein the attaching means is (any kind of) a garment, and asks to protect, if possible, the option that the garment is a glove.

371 Let us have a close look at the suggested set of claims and check the wording of these claims for support in the application as originally filed, for meeting the requirement of clarity and for any other more formal objections. To avoid too much of duplication of work, it is advisable to keep track of the steps taken in this exercise. If the Exam is in electronic form, you may already start drafting a letter. If it works better for you to make notes on a sheet of paper, it is fine as well.

372 At this stage, I prefer postponing the material issues of novelty and inventive step, and optionally other patentability issues associated with Articles 52–57 EPC.

373 **Draft set of claims**
1. System for monitoring at least one vital sign of a human body, the system comprising:
   – ~~holding~~ attaching means (1, 11, 21) for ~~holding~~ attaching an optical sensor (2, 12, 22) and a motion sensor (3, 13, 23) ~~close~~ to the human body (10, 27), the ~~holding~~ attaching means (1, 11, 21) comprising in addition to the sensors (2, 12, 22, 3, 13, 23) transmitting means (4, 14, 24) for transmitting output signals from the sensors (2, 12, 22, 3, 13, 23),
   – evaluation means (5, 25) for receiving the output signals and calculating from the output signals the at least one vital sign,
   characterised in that the attaching means (1, 11, 21) is one of a sock (1), a wristband (11) or a headband (21) for goggles (20) and in that the evaluation means (5, 25) is configured to correct the output signal from the optical sensor (2, 12, 22) based on the output signal of the motion sensor (3, 13, 23) or to correct the output signal from the motion sensor (3, 13, 23) based on the output signal of the optical sensor ~~and wherein the transmitting means is a wireless transmitting means (4, 14, 24)~~.
2. System according to claim 1, wherein the ~~at least one vital sign is pulse, body temperature, blood pressure and/or blood oxygen saturation~~ output signals are transmitted by wireless transmitting means (4, 14, 24).
3. System according to claim 1 or 2, wherein the wireless transmitting means (4, 14, 24) is a wireless local network emitter.
4. System according to any of claims 1 to 3, further comprising a screen (6) and configured to display the at least one vital sign on the screen.
5. ~~System according to any of claims 1 to 4, wherein the holding means is an attaching means such as a sock (1), a wristband (11) or a glove.~~
5. ~~6.~~ System according to any of claims 1 to ~~5~~ 4, wherein the attaching means (1, 11, 21) is at least partly made of Optitex™.

Claim 1 374

Suggested claim 1, indeed, includes all features of original claim 5, except that the glove was replaced by a headband for goggles. For the drafting of the letter to the Examiner, bear in mind that suggested claim 1 is based on original claim 1, and make this explicit!

Because of the inclusion of the wording of claim 5, the terms "holding means" and "holding (...) close to" are replaced by "attaching means" and "attaching (...) to". This would overcome the clarity objection, wherein I note that the Examiner did not object to the wording of original claim 5 on the term "attaching". 375

Original claim 5 was dependent on any of claims 1 to 4, so for the embodiments "sock" and "wristband", the only issue with suggested claim 1 may be the removal of the feature that the transmitting means is a wireless transmitting means. 376

On the removal of this feature *per se*, I will revert herein-below. 377

The sock and the wristband are described as the first and second embodiment and are illustrated by FIG. 1 and FIG. 2, respectively. From [04], it is clear that the sock can be combined with any kind of transmitting means. Paragraph [09] states that the transmitting means for the wristband embodiment is identical to the first embodiment. 378

It can hence be concluded that for the support under Art. 123(2) EPC for the sock and the wristband there are no issues in claim 1 (nor in claims 2-4). 379

For the headband for goggles embodiment, it needs to be checked whether there is support in the description, because there is no reference to the headband in the original claims. As is also noted in the client's letter, the headband is based on the third embodiment, the one of FIG. 3. 380

In paragraph [11], it is stated that the system comprises the headband for attaching the optical sensor and the motion sensor to the human body. The "attaching" wording of suggested claim 1 does not introduce issues under Art. 123(2) EPC. 381

Neither does the removal of the feature that the transmitting means is a wireless transmitting means from claim 1 form a problem under Art. 123(2) EPC. According to paragraph [12] of the description, the transmitting means may be a wireless transmitting means or any other kind of transmitting means, such as described for the other embodiments. 382

The same paragraph [12], however, also teaches that the third embodiment cannot be combined with the feature that the vital signs are displayed on the screen of the evaluation means. This makes that suggested claim 4, with the present wording, cannot be combined with suggested claim 1. 383

Can the feature "that the transmitting means is a wireless transmitting means" be removed from claim 1? 384

For the acceptability under Art. 123(2) EPC of the removal of a feature from a claim, an aid in assessing the allowability is the essentiality test or three-point test as described in Part H, Chapter V, 3.1 of the Guidelines. This section of the Guidelines teaches that if an amendment by (replacing or) removing a feature from a claim fails to pass the following test by at least one criterion, it necessarily contravenes the requirements of Art. 123(2) EPC: 385

(i) the replaced or removed feature was not explained as essential in the originally filed disclosure;
(ii) the skilled person would directly and unambiguously recognize that the feature is not, as such, indispensable for the function of the invention in the light of the technical problem the invention serves to solve (in this context special care needs to be taken in cases where the technical problem is reformulated during the proceedings); and
(iii) the skilled person would recognize that the replacement or removal requires no modification of one or more features to compensate for the change (it does not in itself alter the invention).

However, even if the above criteria are met, it must still be ensured that the amendment by replacing or removing a feature from a claim satisfies the requirements of Art. 123(2) EPC as they also have been set out in G 3/89 and G 11/91, referred to in G 2/10 as "the gold standard" (directly and unambiguously derivable from the application as originally filed). 386

From the last sentence of paragraph [02] of the description, it follows that "it is not important for the invention how the signals are transmitted to the evaluation means". This is confirmed in [04], wherein the first embodiment/FIG. 1 is discussed, stating that 387 "the transmitting means may be any kind of transmitting means, such as a serial port for a cable, or wireless transmitting means, such as a wireless local network emitter". Moreover, in paragraph [09], it is noted that the sock may be replaced by a wristband, but that in fact any garment may be used, and that the remaining features, including the transmitting means are identical to the sock embodiment. Finally, in [12], last sentence, is it noted that also for the headband embodiment, the transmitting means "may be a wireless transmitting means or any other kind of transmitting means, such as described for the other embodiments".

388   The transmitting means, hence, is not presented as essential; it is not indispensable for the function of the invention in the light of the technical problem that is to be solved; and no modification of one or more features of the claim is required to compensate for the change.

389   In this light, the suggested claim 1 seems allowable under Art. 123(2) EPC.

390   But the wish of the client additionally is to use (any kind of) a garment as attaching means and, if possible, also maintain a claim on the "glove" embodiment.

391   Let us start with the generalization to "garment".

We read in paragraph [02] of the description that "(t)he inventive idea is that the attaching means is a garment, such as a sock or a wristband". This is already a strong argument to consider the generalization allowable. In addition, also paragraph [07] generally refers to a garment, and paragraph [09] is even more explicit: "(t)he sock 1 may be replaced by a wristband 11 as shown in Fig. 2. However, any garment may be used. The garment may be at least partially made of *Optitex*™". Further reference is made to paragraph [10], making clear that also a headband is a garment: "(t)he headband 21 is a garment and may be made of *Optitex*™ which provides reliable, secure and comfortable attachment of the sensors to the ear".

392   This makes that the application as originally filed has clear, direct and unambiguous support for any garment as attaching means.

393   And, based on this conclusion, the three garments which the client suggested to be incorporated in claim 1, *viz.* the sock, the wristwatch and the headband can be brought in a dependent claim. The only point of attention is that the headband may not be combined with the screen of suggested claim 4 (see paragraph [12]). This latter point can be dealt with by, for example, bringing the sock and wristband in a claim 5, referring back to claims 1-4; and the headband in a new claim 6, referring back to claims 1-3.

394   This leaves the objection coupled to the glove. As any person knows, a glove is also a garment. This additionally is backed up by paragraph [04] of D3, teaching that "(i)nstead of a sock another kind of garment may be used, such as a glove, a wristband or a headband. A glove in particular is a reliable and comfortable means for attaching sensors to the human body".

395   With this in mind, the glove may be maintained as a preferred embodiment. It has support in claim 5 as originally filed together with the sock and wristband. It can be added to the dependent claim wherein also these two embodiments are maintained.

396   We recall that a clarity objection was raised by the Examiner in view of the glove embodiment of original claim 5. It is however clear that a glove is a garment and therefore is supported by the description. Moreover, the description can also be brought into conformity with the claims by adding a sentence to the description that a preferred embodiment of a garment is a glove. However, you are reminded that within the framework of paper B you are not expected to amend the description

397   Finally, I note that the client has indicated that claim 1 is drafted in the two-part form with respect to D1. D1 teaches a clip as attaching means and not a garment. If D1 is indeed the closest prior art (this will be checked when discussing inventive step), then I note that with the term "garment" instead of the terms "sock (1), a wristband (11) or a headband (21) for goggles", the two-part form is correctly applied.

398   **Claim 2**

In the client's letter, it was noted that the feature removed from claim 1 was introduced in claim 2. The subject-matter of original claim 2 needed not be maintained in a claim.

399   When looking at the wording of amended claim 2, you can see that it is not the same wording as the wording removed from claim 1. Instead of a product feature, *viz.* that the transmitting means is a wireless transmitting means, process wording is introduced in

claim 2, *viz.* output signals are transmitted by wireless transmitting means. Normally, in a product claim product features rather than process features are desired; otherwise a clarity objection may be raised.

Claim 2 hence should be amended to introduce the exact wording of the feature deleted from claim 1.

Claim 3
In this claim dependent on claims 1 and 2, it is claimed that the wireless transmitting means is a wireless local network emitter. Note however, that the feature that the transmitting means is wireless is removed from claim 1 to new claim 2. To avoid a clarity objection because of a missing antecedent, suggested claim 3 should only depend on new claim 2.

Claim 4
The wording of claim 4 can be maintained as is. The changes in claims 1-3, and especially in claim 1, may all be combined with the original wording of claim 4.

Original Claim 5
The client suggested to bring the limitations of original claim 5 in claim 1. However, from the discussion of claim 1, herein-above, it can be taken that I propose maintenance of the original wording of claim 5. This is with the remark that the clarity objection to claim 5 made by the Examiner has to be dealt with in the letter to the Examiner.

In addition, I proposed a new **Claim 6**, directed to the garment being a headband for goggles. This embodiment cannot be combined with the screen limitation of new claim 4, so it should refer back to claims 1-3.

Suggested Claim 5
The client did only renumber original claim 6 to suggested claim 5 while adapting the dependency. The Examiner objected to original claim 6, because of a lack of clarity associated with the use of the Tradename *Optitex*™.

Based on paragraph [09], this product with the Tradename *Optitex* can be replaced by "a material comprising 50–60 % cotton, 30–40 % polyurethane and 10–20 % polyethylene glycol in % by weight".

For the dependency of this dependent claim, **Claim 7**, it needs to be checked whether it can also be linked with the introduced general term "garment" and the preferred embodiment "headband for goggles".

In paragraph [09], there is the teaching that "any garment may be used. The garment may be at least partially made of Optitex™, which is a material comprising 50–60 % cotton, 30–40 % polyurethane and 10–20 % polyethylene glycol in % by weight", so new claim 7 can depend on claim 1. Further, paragraph [10] states that "(t)he headband 21 is a garment and may be made of Optitex™", so this preferred embodiment can also be combined with new claim 7.

Based on this analysis, I come to the following set of claims (where the amendments are shown *vis-à-vis* the client's draft set of claims):

1. System for monitoring at least one vital sign of a human body, the system comprising:
   - attaching means (1, 11, 21) for attaching an optical sensor (2, 12, 22) and a motion sensor (3, 13, 23) to the human body (10, 27), the attaching means (1, 11, 21) comprising in addition to the sensors (2, 12, 22, 3, 13, 23) transmitting means (4, 14, 24) for transmitting output signals from the sensors (2, 12, 22, 3, 13, 23),
   - evaluation means (5, 25) for receiving the output signals and calculating from the output signals the at least one vital sign, characterised in that the attaching means (1, 11, 21) is ~~one of a sock (1), a wristband (11) or a headband (21) for goggles (20)~~ a garment and in that the evaluation means (5, 25) is configured to correct the output signal from the optical sensor (2, 12, 22) based on the output signal of the motion sensor (3, 13, 23) or to correct the output signal from the motion sensor (3, 13, 23) based on the output signal of the optical sensor.
2. System according to claim 1 wherein ~~the output signals are transmitted by~~ the transmitting means (4, 14, 24) is a wireless transmitting means (4, 14, 24).
3. System according to claim ~~1 or~~ 2 wherein the wireless transmitting means (4, 14, 24) is a wireless local network emitter.
4. System according to any of claims 1 to 3, further comprising a screen (6) and configured to display the at least one vital sign on the screen.

> 5. <u>System according to any of claims 1 to 4, wherein the garment is a sock (1), a wristband (11) or a glove.</u>
> 6. <u>System according to any of claims 1 to 3, wherein the garment is a headband (21) for goggles (20).</u>
> 7. System according to any of claims 1 to 4 6, wherein the attaching means (1, 11, 21) at least partly made of ~~Optitex~~™ <u>a material comprising 50-60% cotton, 30-40% polyurethane and 10-20% polyethylene glycol in % by weight.</u>

410   We need to remember with this set of claims that we have to check whether D1 is indeed the closest prior art in view of the two-part form of claim 1.

411   We further have to remember that we provide support in the description for the glove embodiment.

412   When looking at this set of claims in its entirety, there is one independent claim with six dependent claims.

413   Further, there appears to be no issue with lack of unity, nor with any problem under R 43(2) EPC.

2.3.7 Step 7: Determining for the draft set of amended claims whether the material requirements (Art. 52-57 EPC) have been met, and optionally adapting the draft set of amended claims

414   In the client's letter, the client indicated to be convinced that the subject-matter of amended claim 1 is novel and inventive. In addition, the client drafted claim 1 "in the two-part form with respect to D1, because D2 and D3 are from remote technical fields". Further, the client stays close to the problem identified in the description, which is associated with the present of a clip as attaching means used in D1. The client did put emphasis on a higher signal quality.

415   It is time to check whether you can agree to these positions with the draft set of amended claims. This is also the moment to read the prior art, in this case D1-D3, in detail.
     Let us start with the novelty requirement.

416   Thereto, one has to compare the wording of the only independent claim, claim 1, with each of the documents of the prior art, separately.

417   A document takes away the novelty of any claimed subject-matter derivable directly and unambiguously from a particular document including any features implicit to a person skilled in the art in what is expressly mentioned in that document. Hence, if there is at least one claim feature in independent claim 1 that is not directly, unambiguously and implicitly derivable from each document of the prior art, the requirement of novelty is met.

418   It is helpful in the analysis if each document separately is described using the wording of independent claim 1. The relevant references to the prior art disclosure may be written in brackets after each feature found. Points of interpretation that arise as a result of the analysis, for example how a feature in a claim or disclosure is interpreted, or why a feature is implicitly known from a disclosure, can be written immediately into the text within brackets.

419   At the same time, it is good to collect information on the technical field and the technical effects mentioned in each prior art document.

420   D1 is not just a book; it is a textbook. It teaches a system (an optical pulse oximeter; [01]) for monitoring at least one vital sign of a human body (the pulse and the oxygen saturation in the blood; [01]), the system comprising: attaching means (clip 21; [04], first and second sentence) for attaching an optical sensor (207; [02]) and a motion sensor (sensor 203, optionally being a motion sensor, which could be integrated into the clip: [04], third sentence) to the human body (part of a patient's body, usually a fingertip or an earlobe; [02]), the attaching means (207) comprising in addition to the sensors transmitting means (cable 204; [04], second sentence) for transmitting output signals from the sensors, evaluation means (205; [03], [04]) for receiving the output signals and calculating from the output signals the at least one vital sign ([03], third sentence).

421   D1 does not teach that the attaching means is a garment. Further, it does not teach that the evaluation means is configured to correct the output signal from the optical sensor based on the output signal of the motion sensor or to correct the output signal from the motion sensor based on the output signal of the optical sensor.

If D1 is indeed identified as the closest prior art, it is correctly brought in a two-part form.

In that light, it is noted that D1 is a textbook and is directed to measuring the pulse and oxygen saturation in blood. Further, D1 contains quite some information on the sensors and other technical equipment and on the measuring techniques applied. In [04] of D1, it is observed that when the optical pulse oximeter is used together with a second pulse measurement sensor, such as a pressure sensor or a motion sensor, "better accuracy and reliability of the pulse measurement" is achieved.

D1 is thus a textbook that relates to the same technical field as the invention in the patent application and also refers to at least part of the subjective problem definition. In addition, it has a high number of features in common with independent claim 1. In this light, D1 is a good candidate to become the closest prior art.

For the evaluation of D2, we may already make some use of the position taken by the Examiner in his novelty objection.

Advertisement D2 discloses a system (babyphone, baby monitor; [01], first sentence) for monitoring at least one vital sign of a human body (the pulse of your baby; [01], third sentence), the system comprising an optical sensor (built-in infra-red image sensor; [01], first and last sentence) and a motion sensor (motion sensor in the camera; [02], second sentence), the system further comprising a transmitting means (WSBW 4.0; [01], first and second sentence) for transmitting output signals from the sensors to evaluation means (smart phone; [02], first sentence), the evaluation means being configured to correct the output signal from the optical sensor based on the output signal of the motion sensor (SMOOTHY App, cf. par. [02]).

The system of D2 does not teach attaching means for attaching an optical sensor and a motion sensor to the human body. Neither does D2 teach that the attaching means may be a garment.

According to the client, D2 is from a remote technical field. Likely, this means that very convincing arguments are needed to come to D2 as closest prior art.

When D1 and D2 are compared, such convincing arguments do not come up easily. D1 is a textbook really focussing on measurement of vital signs and wishing to obtain detailed information thereof. D2 is an advertisement for a babyphone with, as one of the options, an optical measurement of the baby's pulse, one of the four vital signs. D1 points to a reliable measurement, and D2 contains a feature wherein sound and image signals from the camera are corrected on the basis of motion data. Both D1 and D2 share a good number of claim features with independent claim 1 of the application

To me, in principle, D2 could also have been a suitable starting point. However, the clear hint of the client to D1 being the closest prior art, and D1 being a textbook in the same technical field as the invention, where D2 is primarily in the field of babyphones of D2, makes that I consider D1 closer than D2.

D3 teaches a system for monitoring a human body, the system comprising: attaching means for attaching a sensor to the human body (electrical sensors in contact with the skin of a human body; [01], third sentence), the attaching means comprising in addition to the sensors transmitting means for transmitting output signals from the sensors (cable 304; [02], first sentence), and evaluation means for receiving the output signals and processing these signals, wherein the attaching means is a garment (a sock, a glove, a wristband, a headband; [04]).

D3 does not teach the monitoring of one of the four vital signs of a human body. In addition, D3 does not teach to use an optical sensor and a motion sensor. D3 further does not teach that the evaluation means is configured to correct the output signal from the optical sensor based on the output signal of the motion sensor or to correct the output signal from the motion sensor based on the output signal of the optical sensor.

According to the client, D3 is from a remote technical field. Likely, this means that very convincing arguments are needed to come to D3 as closest prior art.

D3 does not measure a vital sign, and even points away from measuring vital signs ([03]), so is not in the same technical field as the invention and D1. D3 does teach that a sock or other garment is a reliable, secure and comfortable means for attaching a sensor to the human body, so it addresses at least a part of the subjective problem.

To me, D3 was further away from the invention than D2, and certainly than D1.

436 [The above analysis for finding the closest prior art is my own. When you look in the Examiners' Report for paper B 2017 (attached as Appendix 2 to this Book), the Examination Committee stated as follows:

> "D1 is considered to represent the closest prior art according to GL-VII, 5.3, since it addresses the same field as that of the invention and is the best starting point for the most convincing problem-solution-approach in favour of inventive step (…).
> D2 is not a suitable starting point for assessing inventive step, because it is not in the same technical field. This is true even if D2 has many technical features in common.
> D3 could *prima facie* also be a suitable starting point. However, it has fewer features in common than D1."

And

437 "Closest prior art is D1, because D1 is the only available document in the field of the invention. D1 mentions indirectly in the last paragraph the underlying purpose of the invention, i.e. attaching the optical and motion sensor to the human body in a comfortable and reliable manner. Therefore, D1 is the closest of the available prior art
D2 has as many features in common as D1, but is in a remote technical field with respect to the invention, i.e. in the field of baby phones and remotely monitoring the behaviour of babies. The system in D2 is not adapted for monitoring the vital signs of a human body in a reliable manner as required in the medical sector. This however is a key feature of the invention.
D3 could also be a suitable starting point. However, it has fewer features in common than D1 and is silent about a motion sensor, which is of fundamental importance for the invention."]

438 The draft set of amended claims hence is novel over each of the prior art references and with D1 being the closest prior art, I conclude that the draft set of amended claims may become final.

439 The final issue to be discussed in this step is, whether the independent claim involves an inventive step.

440 As the Examiner also indicated in his Communication, for inventive step the problem-solution approach is to be used showing all the steps.

441 This means that first it has to be determined and motivated which piece of prior art forms the closest prior art.

442 Then, the technical feature(s) forming the difference between the claimed subject-matter and the closest prior art has (have) to be identified.

443 In a next step the technical effect associated with the technical feature(s) forming difference should be determined.

444 This step is followed by the definition of the objective problem underlying the invention; *viz.* the technical problem relative to the closest prior art.

445 It should be checked that this objective problem is indeed solved by the technical feature(s) forming the difference with the closest prior art. If this is not the case, or not the case over the full scope of the claim, the objective problem needs to be redefined.

446 Finally, it needs to be determined whether or not the solution to the problem is obvious. For a correct set of claims for paper B, the answer should be that the objective problem is not solved in an obvious manner.

447 For paper B, the route to go is that first it is checked whether the closest prior art itself gives a pointer to the solution present in the discussed claim.

448 If that is not the case, you have to check the combination of the closest prior art with each of the other pieces of prior art available. Thereto, arguments can first be made at the level that the combination of the closest prior art with one or more of the other pieces of prior art cannot be made. Secondly, when the combination of the closest prior art and a further piece of prior art would be made, it should be argued why that combination would still not bring the skilled person to the claimed subject-matter.

449 We already decided that D1 is the closest prior art, and while checking novelty we also noted two differences between independent claim 1 and D1.
D1 does not teach that the attaching means is a garment.

D1 does not teach that the evaluation means is configured to correct the output signal from the optical sensor based on the output signal of the motion sensor or to correct the output signal from the motion sensor based on the output signal of the optical sensor.

What are the technical effects of these differences? I myself always turn back to the patent application to check the technical effects.

For the technical effect of the garment, we know from paragraph [01] of the application that discusses D1 using a clip that "the clip is uncomfortable and that for long-term measurements the attachment is not reliable, because the clip can move" and that the invention wishes to provide a "reliable and comfortable system for long-term remote monitoring of the vital signs of patients". In paragraph [10], this is confirmed by the statement "The headband 21 is a garment and may be made of *Optitex*™ which provides reliable, secure and comfortable attachment of the sensors to the ear".

For the technical effect of the feature "that the evaluation means is configured to correct the output signal from the optical sensor based on the output signal of the motion sensor or to correct the output signal from the motion sensor based on the output signal of the optical sensor", the wording of [01] may give basis for the technical effect that the correction would lead to a more reliable system, but this is not very clear. An argument supporting this position is that the invention as presented in [02] with both the garment and the correction feature apparently solves the subjective problem presented in [01]. An argument against this position is that the wording could also be seen as supporting that a garment would not move in the way a clip would (see also the last sentence of [10]).

Paragraphs [07] and [08], however, are clear on the technical effect of the correction feature: the correction "leads to better signal quality, thereby preventing false measurements".

From [07] it becomes clear that "(a)ccommodating an optical sensor into a garment adds electrical noise to the output signal of the optical sensor 2. A sock 1 worn by a baby moves frequently, which adds further noise to the output signal from the optical sensor 2. This further reduces the quality of the output signal". Thereto, also a motion sensor is present. Paragraph [08] sets out that "(i)n the evaluation means 5 the output signal from the optical sensor 2 is corrected based on the output signal from the motion sensor 3 such that noise is reduced. This leads to better signal quality, thereby preventing false measurements".

Hence, the following technical effects are associated with the distinguishing features:
- the attaching means in the form of a garment provides reliable and comfortable attachment of the sensors to the human body; and
- at the same time the configuration of the evaluation means overcomes the drawback of using a garment as attaching means, namely that accommodating an optical sensor or a motion sensor into the garment adds electrical noise to the output signal of the sensor.

These technical effects are helpful in defining the objective technical problem: to provide a reliable and comfortable system for long-term remote monitoring of the vital signs of patients with sensors attached to the patient's body, in combination with a high quality signal. This problem definition comes close to the advantage that the client sketches in paragraph [01] of the client's letter.

Paragraphs [02], [07] and [08] of the patent application provide support for the position that this problem has been solved by the features of claim 1.

Does D1 bring you to this solution?

Reading D1 in detail again, and now only focussing on inventive step, says no.

D1 only teaches the use of a clip as an attaching means. D1 does describe the use of an optical sensor and mentions that, in order to achieve better accuracy and reliability of the pulse measurement, the pulse can be measured independently from the optical pulse oximeter by means of a sensor 203, such as a pressure sensor or a motion sensor, which could also be integrated into the clip. However, preferably a pressure sensor is used, because a motion sensor, which is reliable enough to measure the pulse, is typically large and heavy and therefore uncomfortable for the patient. D1 does not describe anything on an evaluation means combining signals coming from different sensors. Hence, D1 does not bring a skilled person closer to the invention.

D2 is not concerned with attaching sensors to a body, let alone doing so in a comfortable and reliable way. As such there is not a motivation to combine D1 with D2. Should however a combination of both D1 and D2 be made, the garment is still absent. D2 does teach a correction method, but that is not for reducing electrical noise; it is to improve the sound and image signals from the camera used in D2.

460   D3 is directed to the use of electrical sensors for electrocardiography. This is not exactly the same technical field as the claimed invention, but likely the skilled person would take it into account.

461   D3 teaches to use a sock (or another kind of garment, such as a glove, a wristband or a headband) as a reliable, secure and comfortable means for attaching the electrical sensor 309 to the human body. The sock 301 is at least partially made of a material comprising 50–60 % cotton, 30–40 % polyurethane and 10–20 % polyethylene-glycol in % by weight. However, D3 also states for the material used for its garment, that it "unfortunately allows measurements only with electrical sensors, because for any other type of sensor, e.g. optical sensor, the signal to noise ratio would be too low for measuring vital signs of the human body. Therefore, this material is not suitable for recording vital signs". D3 hence does not contain any pointer to solving the objective problem other than by teaching to use a garment for another type of sensor.

462   And when the three documents would be combined, the combined teaching would still not bring the skilled person to the claimed invention.

463   The only conclusion to be drawn hence is that independent amended claim 1 involves an inventive step.

Step 7 is completed.

2.3.8 Step 8: Drafting the supplementary note, if any

464   If you feel that your solution of paper B needs a comment, you may write a supplementary note and attach it to your answer. Rule 24(4) IPREE notes that you may give the reasons for your choice of answer in a supplementary note.

465   As a general rule, however, supplementary notes are not required, except in the situations of lack of unity of invention and possible violation of Rule 43(2) EPC (see below). Incidentally, there exists no obligation to set out the reasons for the choice of answer, and often it is only wise to exercise restraint. The Examiners´ report of paper A 2006 Chemistry brings it up to the point: "*Good candidates generally did not submit notes to the examiner. Time preparing notes was often time not well spent*". But also in Examiners' reports for paper B this message was given. For example in the Examiners' report B 2007 Chemistry, it was observed that "The examiners were pleased to see a reduction in the number of notes to examiners. They had no objection to such notes being submitted and gave any submitted due consideration. In most cases it was found that they were not an effective use of the candidates' time and rarely enhanced the candidates' answer", while the Examiners' report of paper B 2010 posed that "The committee was pleased to note that very few candidates chose to submit notes to the examiner". There is no reason why you should lose time writing extensive comments about what you have done and what you have left out. Marks are awarded for your answer, not for your comments. Put in the words of the final sentence of Rule 24(4) IPREE "Supplementary notes to examiners cannot (…) replace essential parts of candidates' replies to the EPO".

466   If you nevertheless wish to explain your answer, bear in mind the following principles.
467   Any supplementary note should:
- address a relevant issue; and
- be brief and concise.

468   As mentioned above, an exceptional situation, where a supplementary note may be required, is lack of unity of invention. What has to be done in this case is set out in Rule 24(4) IPREE.

Supplementary notes addressing the issue of unity of invention

469   Rule 24(4) IPREE reads:

> "**If (candidates) consider that any part of the application ought to be made the subject of one or more divisional applications, they shall, in the note, clearly set out the independent claim(s) for such divisional application(s). The note shall also present the arguments in support of the patentability of the independent claim(s) in such divisional application(s)**".

Lack of unity of invention does not arise often in paper B, the last couple of years. Actually, since the introduction of the single paper B, there has not yet been a unity-of-invention problem.

In addition, it is noted that, in case a divisional application is to be expected as part of the answer, there will be hints, for example in the Examiner's communication and/or in the client's letter to attract attention to this issue.

If such hints are missing, you are pointed to the Examiners' Report of paper B 2015 Chemistry, saying "Candidates who decide to include a new independent claim are expected to provide complete arguments for such a claim. (…) As Paper B is an amendment paper, the drafting of new independent and/or dependent claims is usually not considered as time well spent if not specifically requested by the client in his letter".

But, having Rule 24(4) IPREE, this is not a guarantee for future papers. From before 2017, if there was an issue with unity-of-invention, there was normally only one further application and a single independent claim. There was neither a need to draft any dependent claims, nor to explain in much detail why there was lack of unity. A short remark outlining the additional protection provided by the further application was sufficient.

Regarding unity of invention, it is essential that clear decisions be taken. The supplementary note must be conclusive. Vague statements such as a reference to a further application that could possibly be envisaged *"when required"* are inadequate and lead to a loss of marks.

Mind inconsistencies in supplementary notes:

Supplementary notes containing inconsistent statements are at best useless. The Examiners' report of paper A 2004 Chemistry describes a typical example as follows:

> *"A number of candidates filed a single set of claims, which was stated in the accompanying notes to lack unity of invention. Such candidates were not able to obtain full marks, since the claims in the answer are required to fulfil the requirements of unity of invention. A candidate who has identified more than one invention should indicate the claims of the supplementary invention(s) in a note.*
>
> *Other candidates lost marks for proposing to file separate applications for sets of claims which did not lack unity of invention with the claims of their first invention."*

Drawn to paper B: use the set of suggested claims of the client. If these contain independent claims not meeting the requirement of unity-of-invention, then either amend this situation by adapting the claim wording, or by deleting one or more independent claims to solve the unity problem.

In paper B 2017, there is no reason to have a supplementary note on lack of unity.

Reasoning relating to Rule 43(2) EPC

Where the set of claim contains more than one independent claim in the same category, you are either expected to deal with that issue in the letter to the Examiner, if this would be allowable. There are only three possibilities, namely the three exceptions a), b) or c) set out in Rule 43(2) EPC: a European patent application may contain more than one independent claim in the same category (product, process, apparatus or use) only if the subject-matter of the application involves one of the following:
(a) a plurality of interrelated products,
(b) different uses of a product or apparatus,
(c) alternative solutions to a particular problem, where it is inappropriate to cover these alternatives by a single claim.

Other options do not exist under the EPC.

Should it not be allowable to have more than one independent claim in the set of claims, it will be appropriate to indicate in a supplementary note why these claims are not in accordance with Rule 43(2) EPC, and what you suggest to do with the non-selected independent claim(s).

Other situations where a supplementary note is useful

There are a few further situations, where a supplementary note was useful in the past. The most prominent are outlined below.

Specific interpretations of terms

481 The Examiners' report of paper A 1997 Electricity/Mechanics contains the following statement:

> *"If a candidate makes a note to the effect that he has understood a particular term to have a particular meaning, the examiners considered it to be appropriate to construe that term when used in claims as having that meaning."*

Such situations should occur only very exceptionally, however.

Suspected errors in the text of paper B

482 Although the texts of the Exam papers are drafted with greatest care, it cannot be ruled out that there may be an error, for example an error of translation.

483 If you come across a suspected error of any significance, it is appropriate to draft a short supplementary note to the effect that presumably there is an error. Of course, you should explain in a few words what the error could be and how you have coped with it.

484 The Examiners' reports, however, have reported various situations, where supplementary notes are not useful or even detrimental. The following examples speak for themselves.

485 Most of these examples come from Examiners' reports for paper A.

Situations where a supplementary note is not useful or detrimental
Addressing unimportant issues

486 Supplementary notes dealing with unimportant issues, for example the title of the application, are a waste of time (see Examiners' report of paper A 1993 Chemistry).

Suggestions of alternative independent claims

487 It happens that candidates draft supplementary notes because they hesitate to take clear decisions. The Examiners' report of paper A1997 Electricity/Mechanics describes such a situation:

> *"A number of candidates also appear to be unable to decide on the exact scope of their main claim and attempt to overcome this by writing notes to the examiner which it is hoped will broaden or otherwise affect the scope of the claims drafted. This is not accepted by the examiners as it would give such candidates an unfair advantage of having in effect more than one try at writing a good claim."*

Suggestions of claims extending beyond the disclosure of the invention

488 There is no point in drafting supplementary notes to the effect to suggest the filing of further applications extending beyond the disclosure of the invention provided in the letter from the client. Such speculative proposals are meaningless and cause only a loss of time.

Explaining why something is not claimed

489 In paper B it occurs regularly that certain embodiments of the invention described by the client cannot or can no longer be claimed, for example because they lack novelty or inventive step. In such cases, it is not appropriate to draft a supplementary note in order to explain, possibly in every detail, why the embodiments concerned are not included in the claims.

Presenting unfounded statements

490 Occasionally, candidates are aware of well-established principles of law, but for one reason or another, they prefer not to apply them. In such situations even the most elaborate supplementary note will not save them from losing marks.

491 An example are product-by-process claims. According to the case law of the Boards of Appeal and the Guidelines (F-IV, 4.12), a claim defining a product in terms of a process is to be construed as a claim to the product as such, irrespective of whether the term *"obtainable"*, *"obtained"*, *"directly obtained"* or an equivalent wording is used in the product-by-process claim. It is a hopeless exercise to draft a supplementary note to the contrary, arguing that a different construction would be more appropriate.

While supplementary notes are useful in certain situations, they have a considerable potential of becoming counter-productive. To write unnecessary or erroneous supplementary notes does not only mean a loss of time, but it shows also that the candidate has gaps in the understanding of important principles of the exam.

Therefore, the general recommendation is:

Write a supplementary note only when you have a strong reason to do so.

2.3.9 Step 9: Drafting the letter in response to the communication

In addition to the set of amended claims, a response to the official communication is to be prepared.

In the words of Rule 24(3) IPREE, the response shall be in the form of a letter to the EPO, wherein the candidates are expected to respond to all points raised in the official communication. In their reply, candidates shall identify clearly all amendments made in the claims and their basis in the application as filed, and provide additional explanations where necessary. Candidates shall also set out their arguments in support of the patentability of the independent claim(s).

The description shall not, however, be amended.

From the response, it must be clear that it is directed to the EPO Examiner. It is not necessary to provide all address details, and to be overly polite. Just a plain formal letter suffices. Neither is it necessary to request Oral Proceedings. What you upload as your answer paper should either result in a communication, wherein the Examiner only invites you to file a description that is brought into conformity with the amended claims, or in a communication under Rule 71(3) EPC. A suitable response can just start with "It is requested to grant a European patent on the basis of the attached set of claims".

Or said in the words of an Examiners' report (B 2007 Chemistry) "As in previous years some candidates apparently spent considerable time in including things such as the date, the address of the EPO or requests for oral proceedings. Candidates may find it a better use of their time to concentrate on substantive issues first. Few, if any, marks are available for including matters such as the address of the EPO".

To maximize the possibilities to collect marks, it is of the utmost importance to work in a structured way. That is, deal with each type of objection in a separate section and work claim-by-claim.

At least the following types of objections are generally expected to be answered: support in the application as originally filed under Art. 123(2) EPC; clarity of the claims; novelty, wherein each independent claim is discussed in view of all references cited and this is advisably done by using one paragraph per piece of prior art; inventive step, wherein each independent claim is discussed using the problem-solution approach in all its steps; often unity-of-invention and/or Rule 43(2) EPC; and optionally any other objection based on any of the Articles 52-57 EPC or any other issue that was raised in the communication.

Let me start with giving the set of amended claims wherein the underscored portions have been added and crossed-out portions have been deleted:

1. System for monitoring at least one vital sign of a human body, the system comprising:
   - <u>attaching</u> ~~holding~~ means (1, 11, 21) for <u>attaching</u> ~~holding~~ an optical sensor (2, 12, 22) and a motion sensor (3, 13, 23) ~~close~~ to the human body (10, 27), the <u>attaching</u> means (1, 11, 21) comprising in addition to the sensors (2, 12, 22, 3, 13, 23) transmitting means (4, 14, 24) for transmitting output signals from the sensors (2, 12, 22, 3, 13, 23),
   - evaluation means (5, 25) for receiving the output signals and calculating from the output signals the at least one vital sign, characterised in that <u>the attaching means (1, 11, 21) is a garment</u> and in that the evaluation means (5, 25) is configured to correct the output signal from the optical sensor (2, 12, 22) based on the output signal of the motion sensor (3, 13, 23) or to correct the output signal from the motion sensor (3,13,23) based on the output signal of the optical sensor ~~and in that the transmitting means (4, 14, 24) is a wireless transmitting means~~.
2. System according to claim 1 wherein ~~the at least one vital sign is pulse, body temperature, blood pressure and/or blood oxygen saturation~~ <u>the transmitting means (4, 14, 24) is a</u> wireless transmitting means <u>(4, 14, 24)</u>.

3. System according to claim 1 or 2 wherein the wireless transmitting means (4, 14, 24) is a wireless local network emitter.
4. System according to any of claims 1 to 3, further comprising a screen (6) and configured to display the at least one vital sign on the screen.
5. System according to any of claims 1 to 4, wherein ~~the holding means is an attaching means (1, 11, 21) such as~~ <u>the garment is</u> a sock (1), a wristband (11) or a glove.
6. <u>System according to any of claims 1 to 3, wherein the garment is a .headband (21) for goggles (20).</u>
7. ~~6.~~ System according to any of claims 1 to ~~5~~ <u>6</u>, wherein the attaching means (1, 11, 21) at least partly made of ~~Optitex™~~ <u>a material comprising 50-60% cotton, 30-40% polyurethane and 10-20% polyethylene glycol in % by weight.</u>

502 Most candidates start with the section dealing with support in the application as originally filed under Art. 123(2) EPC. According to Art. 123(2) EPC, the European patent application or European patent may not be amended in such a way that it contains subject-matter which extends beyond the content of the application as filed. In paper B, the arguments showing that the amendments meet the requirements of Art. 123(2) EPC attract a high number of marks, generally 20 marks and even more. This means that you should elaborate quite a bit on this requirement.

503 In the Guidelines Part H, Ch. IV, 2.1, the underlying idea and basic principle of Art. 123(2) EPC are sketched.

504 The underlying idea of Art. 123(2) is that an applicant is not allowed to improve its position by adding subject-matter not disclosed in the application as filed, which would give him an unwarranted advantage and could be damaging to the legal security of third parties relying on the content of the original application (see G 1/93).

505 An amendment is regarded as introducing subject-matter which extends beyond the content of the application as filed, and therefore unallowable, if the overall change in the content of the application (whether by way of addition, alteration or excision) results in the skilled person being presented with information which is not directly and unambiguously derivable from that previously presented by the application, even when account is taken of matter which is implicit to a person skilled in the art (see G 2/10).

506 The so-called "gold standard" according to G 2/10 (also called "relevant disclosure test" in G 1/16) hence is that a document discloses subject-matter (implicitly or explicitly) if the skilled person directly and unambiguously derives that subject-matter from the document, using common general knowledge and seen objectively and relative to the relevant date. In other words, the disclosure content of a document is the information that the skilled person derives – explicitly or implicitly – directly and unambiguously from the document as a whole.

507 For discussing claim 1, three issues have to be dealt with: the replacement of "holding means" by "attaching means" and of "holding (...) close to" by "attaching to"; the generalization of particular species to the genus "garment", and the removal of the transmitting means being wireless transmitting means.

508 In step 6, we have carried out the exercise to find the support, and the arguments should now be written in the letter. In this light, and to collect all marks, it is important to give all the support for an amendment that you can find. This encompasses to refer explicitly to, for example, original claim 1, if that claim is amended ("Amended claim 1 is based on original claim 1, with the following amendments ...").

509 Particular attention is to be paid to the deletion of a feature from the claim. Like it is indicated in step 6, if a feature is removed from a claim, it necessarily contravenes the requirements of Art. 123(2) EPC, if that removal fails to pass at least one criterion of the essentiallity test or three-point test described in Part H, Ch. V, 3.1 of the Guidelines. But, even if the removal meets these three criteria, it must still be ensured that the amendment satisfies the gold standard. From your letter, it must be clear that this double requirement (meeting the essentiality test and meeting the gold standard) has been met.

510 And when the removal is allowable, it is essential that you check whether this removal affects the dependency of the other claims. Not only may this be an issue under Art. 123(2) EPC, but in addition or alternatively it may also be an issue under the section clarity of the claims. As already indicated, it is advised not to make arguments in respect of different

objections in one and the same paragraph or section, but to raise issues on support in the section on Art. 123(2) EPC and to raise issues on clarity in the section on Art. 84 EPC.

With the set of claims suggested by the client, there is no issue under Art. 123(2) EPC with claim 3 being dependent on claims 1 and 2, but only under Art. 84 EPC.

The newly introduced preferred embodiment of the headband for goggles could only be supported by the description, and in the description, it is described that this embodiment cannot be combined with the screen of dependent claim 4. This makes that this newly introduced preferred embodiment may not refer back to claim 4.

The last issue under Art. 123(2) EPC is the replacement of the trade name *Optitex* by a material describing it. This is not a 1:1 replacement, but pointing out support will not be a major problem in the claim itself. However, the indication of support in the application as filed also encompasses checking the dependency of that claim.

It is good custom to end a section, in this case the section on Art. 123(2) EPC with the statement: "It is concluded that the requirements of Art. 123(2) EPC have been met".

After discussing support in the application as originally filed, it generally makes sense to discuss any potential clarity issues.

One of these issues is associated with the dependency of the claims. The removal of the feature that the transmitting means needs to be a wireless transmitting means from claim 1 makes that there is no antecedent basis in claim 1 anymore for "the wireless transmitting means" and for that reason amended claim 3 should only refer to dependent claim 2.

The clarity objection raised by the Examiner on the term "(holding (...)) close to" is overcome by replacing the term "holding" in claim 1 as filed by "attaching". Not only should this amendment be made, but also the response to the communication should explain this.

A similar issue is the replacement of the trade name *Optitex* by a material describing it. Also here a clear statement that the unclear trade name is exchanged by terms describing a particular material in "chemical" terms.

The last clarity issue is the objection raised in respect of the term "glove" appearing in the original set of claims, because it is not supported by the description.

There are two clear ways to deal with this objection. The first is that the description is brought into conformity with the originally filed claims. This can be done by, for example, adding the terms "or by a glove" at the end of the second sentence of paragraph [09] following "Fig. 2". Another possibility is explaining that the invention is supported for any garment, and hence also for a glove, since a glove is a garment. This is known to any person skilled in the art, and this position is supported by the last paragraph of D3.

Hence, the set of claims as amended meets the requirements of Art. 84 EPC.

In a next session, the novelty may be discussed.

A claim is novel relative to a particular piece of prior art, if it contains at least one feature that is not directly and unambiguously derivable from that particular piece of prior art.

So, when discussing novelty, it is advisable to discuss the novelty of an independent claim relative to each piece of prior art in a separate paragraph.

Independent claim 1 is drafted in the two-part form differentiating it from D1, which, so we determined, is the closest prior art. The differences between D1 and independent claim 1 are hence the features in the characterizing part. Claim 1 hence is novel over D1.

There are two differences between D1 and independent claim 1, and in principle it would have been sufficient to just refer to one of these differences. However, because the differences need to be given in the problem-solution approach anyway, it makes sense to refer to both.

In step 7, herein-above, also the differences between D2 and independent claim 1 and between D3 and independent claim 1 are given. For the discussion on novelty, it now suffices to refer just to one difference. However, I myself prefer to give all differences, if there is no discussion on the terms used.

When an independent claim is novel over a particular piece of prior art, normally it is not required to discuss the claims dependent on that independent claim. However, always check the specific claim wording of the dependent claims.

Since the set of amended claims is comprised of one independent claim and a number of real dependent claims, one can conclude that the requirement of novelty has been met.

529 The next issue to be discussed is the matter of inventive step. For this issue, the number of marks is generally even higher than for the discussion of Art. 123(2) EPC.

530 In principle, this discussion is to be carried out for each independent claim. And just like I indicated for the discussion on novelty, if an independent claim meets the requirement of inventive step, normally also the claims depending on that independent claim involve an inventive step.

531 In paper B, this discussion always uses the problem-solution approach as set out in the Guidelines Part G, Ch. VII, 5. The problem-solution approach has three main stages: (i) determining the "closest prior art"; (ii) establishing the "objective technical problem" to be solved; and (iii) considering whether or not the claimed invention, starting from the closest prior art and the objective technical problem, would have been obvious to the skilled person.

532 For the response to be uploaded as part of the answer to paper B, each step of problem-solution approach must be taken, indicated and motivated.

533 This starts with the determination of the closest prior art.

534 The closest prior art is that which in one single reference discloses the combination of features which constitutes the most promising starting point for a development leading to the invention. In selecting the closest prior art, the first consideration is that it must be directed to a similar purpose or effect as the invention or at least belong to the same or a closely related technical field as the claimed invention.

535 This first consideration makes clear why in the methodology of paper B, the technical field and the technical effect, purpose or (dis)advantages are collected; not only for the patent application, but also for the documents forming the prior art.

536 In practice, the closest prior art is generally that which corresponds to a similar use and requires the minimum of structural and functional modifications to arrive at the claimed invention. This, however, is a secondary consideration. Such a secondary consideration may play a role in the determination of the closest prior art, if the first consideration is not sufficient. That is, if on the basis of the first consideration there is more than one candidate, then it may be needed to argue why the other candidates should not be the closest prior art.

537 This is reflected in the marking. Normally, one gets at least one mark for an explicit statement that a particular piece of prior art forms the closest prior art; and one gets additional marks for providing arguments why that particular piece of prior art is the closest prior art, and one gets marks for providing arguments why each of the other pieces of prior art do not form the closest prior art.

538 In step 7, the relevant arguments as to why D1 was the closest prior art, and D2 and D3 are not, are given.

539 Once you have selected the closest prior art for a particular independent claim, you have to determine what the difference is. The difference between the independent claim and the closest prior art is expressed in features of the independent claim that are not directly and unambiguously derivable from the closest prior art.

540 Independent claim 1 of our set of amended claims is in a correct two-part form, making that the difference are the features following "characterised in that".

541 Subsequently, the technical effect(s) associated with the difference(s) is (are) sought. This was done in detail in step 7:

542 The following technical effects are associated with the distinguishing features:
  – the attaching means in the form of a garment provides reliable and comfortable attachment of the sensors to the human body; and
  – at the same time the configuration of the evaluation means overcomes the drawback of using a garment as attaching means, namely that accommodating an optical sensor or a motion sensor into the garment adds electrical noise to the output signal of the sensor.

543 Then, one has to establish in an objective way the technical problem to be solved relative to the closest prior art. In the context of the problem-solution approach, the technical problem means the aim and task of modifying or adapting the closest prior art to provide the technical effects that the invention provides over the closest prior art. The technical problem thus defined is often referred to as the "objective technical problem".

544 Based on the technical effects associated with the differences between D1 and independent claim 1, we may define the objective technical problem as follows: to provide a reliable

and comfortable system for long-term remote monitoring of the vital signs of patients with sensors attached to the patient's body, in combination with a high quality signal.

Subsequently, it is always good to check whether this problem is indeed solved by the features that distinguish independent claim 1 from the closest prior art, here D1.

Now that we have the closest prior art and the objective technical problem, the question is whether there is any teaching in the prior art as a whole that **would** (not simply could, but actually would) have prompted the skilled person, faced with the objective technical problem, to modify or adapt the closest prior art while taking account of that teaching, thereby arriving at something falling within the terms of the claims, and thus achieving what the invention achieves.

In paper B, one starts with providing arguments, why the closest prior art taken *per se* would not bring the skilled person to the claimed subject-matter.

If this hurdle is taken, arguments are provided why the closest prior art in combination with another prior art document would not bring the skilled person to the claimed subject-matter.

At this stage, there can be two types of arguments. The first type of argument is to find and give arguments why a skilled person starting from the closest prior art would never have turned to the second piece of prior art.

The second type of argument is to find arguments as to why, when the skilled person starting from the closest prior art would turn to the second piece of prior art, he still would not come to the claimed invention.

These first and second types of arguments are checked for all other pieces of prior art, separately.

Normally (partial problems excluded; see thereto chapter 7 of this book on Inventive Step), it is not convincing when a combination of the closest prior art with two or more other documents are needed to contest inventive step. However, if you have time, you may wish to provide an argument as to why a combination of three documents would still not bring you to the claimed invention.

This section ends again with the statement that hence the claimed subject-matter involves an inventive step.

The above-discussed concepts essentially always are present in paper B. But also other objections could have been raised, such as unity-of-invention problems, issues under Rule 43(2) EPC and/or issues under other grounds of Articles 52-57 EPC. For paper B 2017, these issues did not play a role.

What needs further to be borne in mind is that you do not sign the letter in your own name. The answer paper must be anonymous.

In Appendix 3 to this book, an example of the response and a set of claims is given in the form of the CEIPI model solution.

2.3.10 Step 10: Final check

The answer papers are corrected in the form in which they are uploaded on the day of the examination. Before finalizing your answer paper, you may wish to make a final check. The following essential points should still be checked:

Checklist for the final check of the answer paper

> The answer paper is complete and contains the following components:
> - The set of amended claims
> - The response to the communication
> - An optional supplementary note
>
> The answer paper should be anonymous, i.e. it does not contain your real name or any other element that identifies you.
> Each component of the answer paper is complete and placed in the correct order.
> Particularly, the claims in the set of amended claims are correctly numbered and the back references are correct as well.
> In the response, the different sections on support in the application as originally filed, on clarity, on novelty, on inventive step, and possibly on unity, Rule 43(2) EPC and any other ground on which the Examiner raised objection, are clearly identified.

2.4 Strategy for solving paper B

559 There is no such thing as a general strategy for solving paper B. You have to develop your own strategy, which should be adapted to your experience and skills. The most important requirements are to have a strategy at all, and to follow it as closely as possible.

560 You can get good advice from several sources, particularly from the following publications:

561 Regulation on the European qualifying examination for professional representatives (EQE) published as supplementary publication to the Official Journal EPO 2, 2019.

562 The most important parts are:
- Regulation on the European qualifying examination for professional representatives (REE)
- Implementing provisions to the Regulation on the European qualifying examination for professional representatives (IPREE)
- Instructions to candidates concerning the conduct of the European qualifying examination

563 The Regulation on the European qualifying examination is available online on the website of the EPO in English, French and German.
www.epo.org/law-practice/legal-texts/official-journal/2019/etc/se2.html

564 Most points of the strategy for tackling paper B are in explanation and amplification of matters which are explicitly mentioned in the REE, IPREE and the Instructions to candidates. Therefore, comprehensive knowledge of the Regulation on the EQE is a must.

565 Another source of primary importance are the examiners' reports of single papers B 2017, 2018, 2019 and 2021 and those of papers B Chemistry and B Electricity/Mechanics, in particular those issued in the years 2013-2016 (the older papers B Chemistry and Electricity/Mechanics differ in style, especially because these do not come with a suggested set of claims in combination with a rather explicit instruction letter of the client). They contain essential information about the content of the papers and the expected solutions, as well as detailed comments about the marking scheme. The Examiners' reports are available online on the *"Compendium"* website of the EPO in English, French and German.
www.epo.org/learning-events/eqe/compendium.html

566 The European Patent Academy of the EPO has published and edited a guide for preparation containing valuable information about the EQE, the order in which to tackle the subject-matter, hints on the examination technique and insight into how the Examination Committees mark the papers.

European qualifying examination. Guide for preparation.
9th edition, Munich: EPO, 2019.

567 A revised version is in preparation. The publication is available in English and can be downloaded from the EQE website of the EPO.
www.epo.org/learning-events/materials/study-guide.html

Things to consider when developing a strategy for tackling paper B

568 The following suggestions are a synthesis of the advice given in the sources referred to above and information provided by experienced tutors and candidates, who have passed the examination.

569 **First steps of the preparation**
(1) Provide sufficient time for your preparation. Presumably you need at least six months, preferably longer.
(2) Study carefully the examination syllabus as defined in Art. 13 REE, Rule 2 IPREE and Rule 22 IPREE. In-depth knowledge of the documents, particularly the EPC and the Guidelines for Examination in the EPO is crucial for passing paper B.
(3) Study the decisions of the Enlarged Board of Appeal *("G-decisions")* and the Case law of the EPO boards of appeal, 9th edition, July 2019. This publication is available online in English, French and German in HTML format at:
www.epo.org/law-practice/case-law-appeals/case-law.html
It can also be downloaded in PDF format.

(4) Study the Regulation on the EQE in-depth to learn what is expected from you at the examination, and – equally important – what is not expected.
(5) Actually, paper B comes quite close to real-life situations. The most important difference is that you have to file a set of claims and a thoroughly elaborated response to get an immediate grant. Understand the consequences of this difference.
(6) Update your knowledge by regularly consulting the EPO website.

During the in-depth preparation phase ...
(7) Attend high-quality courses for paper B, wherein you have to practice yourself.
(8) Prepare and train on templates, standard clauses, samples of independent claims in various categories, a model structure of the response to the communication, checklists and any further tools, which you wish to use at the examination.
Do not include any such materials in your answer paper, though.
(9) Study the allocation of marks awarded in the past to the various parts of the answer paper. Typically, marks were awarded as follows:

Paper B	2017	2018	2019	2021
amendments to the draft set of claims	30	30	30	30 marks
amendments (Art. 123(2) EPC)	24	22	18	17 marks
clarity	8	6	2	3 marks
novelty	6	6	10	12 marks
inventive step	32	36	40	26 marks
prior use arguments				8 marks
Art. 52 arguments				4 marks

Investigate how the marks are distributed, especially for the Art. 123(2) EPC amendments and for the inventive step discussion.
(10) Gain practice by solving old papers B, preferably the single papers and the more recent papers of 2016-2013 Chemistry and Electricity/Mechanics. Use a systematic methodology. Solve one or two examination papers without time constraints. Subsequently, solve a few papers within the time available at the examination, i.e. 3½ hours (+ ½ an hour). Check how much time you need for each type of activities. Do not read the Examiners´ report until you have worked out the entire answer paper yourself. Once you have completed drafting your answer, compare your result with the Examiners´ report. Analyse your strengths and your weaknesses. Mark any points about which you are not sure. Study any issues that you find difficult.
(11) Seek feedback from your superiors, colleagues and tutors.
(12) Set up a working group together with fellow candidates. Discuss any points, which are unclear. Share your experience and your knowledge with others.
(13) Draw up in writing your personal strategy in terms of work priorities and allocation of time.
Take the marking scheme as a basis and determine the sequence of the tasks to perform. Evaluate the experience that you have acquired in solving old examination papers.
Fix the amount time to be provided for each task.
Whatever you are doing, strive for a good ratio of marks to time spent.
(14) Make a list of books, documents and additional materials you consider useful for answering the examination paper. Make sure that your documentation is up to date. In addition to your books, documents, templates, standard clauses, checklists, etc., bring at least the following materials with you to the examination:
– several pens and markers
– scrap paper
– convenient food and beverages
(15) Get used to your materials before the examination
(16) Prepare a checklist to ensure that you do not forget anything when sitting the examination.

3 Interpretation and analysis of disclosures

3.1 Legal basis

EPC Articles and Rules
Art. 69 EPC
Protocol on the Interpretation of Art. 69 EPC of 5 October 1973 as revised by the Act revising the EPC of 29 November 2000

Guidelines
B-III, 3.2: Interpretation of claims
F-IV, 4.2: Interpretation

Case Law Book
I.C.4: Determining the content of the relevant prior art
I.C.4.1: General rules of interpretation
I.C.4.2: Combinations within a prior art document
I.C.4.3: Taking implicit features into account

Further reference
C-Book, Chapter 4, p. 87–107: Interpretation and analysis

3.2 Relevance to paper B

First of all, the description and claims of the application as filed by the client have to be interpreted and understood. Also the technical content of the documents representing the state of the art has to be determined. This may also need interpretation. Further, the suggested set of amended claims provided by the client and the amendments thereto to bring these in line with the client's wishes and in conformity with the EPC need to satisfy the rules of interpretation applicable to the procedures before the EPO set out in the Guidelines. It is obvious that the documents comprised in the state of the art should be interpreted according to the same standards as those applied to the claims. Finally, the content of the communication may provide specific interpretations that have to be addressed or may itself need interpretation.

The EPC does not contain any provisions on the interpretation of terms and expressions used in the items making up a European patent application or a patent, but there is extensive case law issued by the Boards of Appeal of the EPO on this. Accordingly, a number of principles of interpretation have been established, including those outlined below.

3.3 Interpreting features

Any document contained in the state of the art has to be considered as a whole. It is not permissible to consider individual paragraphs of a document, let alone individual phrases or words in isolation. Each part of a document has to be construed taking the content as a whole into account.

For the interpretation of the content of a document, it is decisive how a skilled person would have understood the document at the publication date. The content of a document is what the skilled person derives directly and unambiguously from the text, taking common general knowledge into account.

It is not permissible to combine two or more separate documents, or to combine separate parts belonging to different embodiments described in a single document, unless such a combination is suggested explicitly. The content of a document cannot be construed to be a reservoir, from which features pertaining to separate embodiments may be drawn in order to artificially create a further embodiment.

Any document has to be read with an attempt to make technical sense out of it. Such a reading may involve a departure from the strict literal wording. The interpretation must not be made on the basis of a narrow, literal or academic approach.

581   It is tradition not to assess the scope of protection of claims and use this to interpret the claims. This makes that claims are, for instance, not interpreted as embracing equivalent embodiments. Accordingly, when assessing novelty, it is also not relevant whether a prior art document would disclose something which would fall under the scope of protection of a claim by way of equivalency.

3.3.1 Interpreting technical terms and expressions

582   The terms and expressions in a document have to be read giving the words the meaning and scope which these normally have in the relevant technical field, unless a special meaning is expressly stated in the document. If such a special meaning is indicated, it takes precedence over the usual meaning. A document may be its own dictionary.

583   Any non-specific definitions of terms and expressions should be given the broadest technically reasonable meanings.

584   **Example:**

In D3 of paper B 2021, it is observed that earthworms belong to the class of worms, which comprises many different distantly related animals which develop in a plethora of substrates. However, in the patent application forming the core of paper B 2021, there is a paragraph [006] stating that "in the context of the present invention, the terms worms and earthworms are used interchangeably to refer to earthworms", and the Examiner raised a clarity objection to a claim, wherein the term worm was used.

3.3.2 Non-limiting features

585   Expressions such as *"preferably"*, *"for example"*, *"such as"*, *"particularly"*, *"especially"*, *"typically"*, *"normally"*, *"usually"* or *"may"* have no limiting effect; that is to say, the feature following any such expression is to be regarded as optional (Guidelines F-IV, 4.9)

586   **Example:**

In the suggested set of amended claims for paper B 2016 Electricity/Mechanics, the client proposes to solve an objection under R. 43(2) EPC by making claim 5 dependent on claim 1. Claim 1 is directed to a warning system; claim 5 to a warning pole comprising a warning system. The proposal of the client reads as follows:
    "5. Warning pole (20) comprising a warning system preferably according to claim 1".
    The preferably-clause is not limiting.

3.3.3 Identical features

587   A specific feature may have different names. It is possible that a feature described by the client as pertaining to the invention is disclosed in a document representing the state of the art, but not with the same wording. Whether such a situation of synonyms exists has to be investigated on a case to case basis, using the information provided by the examination paper as a guide.

588   **Examples:**

In paper B 2021, the invention relates to a compost container for producing organic fertilizer from organic refuse using worms, in particular earthworms. In paragraph [006] the description notes that "In the context of the present invention, the terms worms and earthworms are used interchangeably to refer to earthworms".

589   The Examiner noted in his communication that "Method claim 4 refers to worms in general for which no support in the description in the sense of Article 84 EPC can be found. It is clear from the application (see paragraph [6] of the description) that only earthworms can be used in the claimed invention (see also document D3, first two paragraphs)".

3.3.4 Generic versus specific features

A generic disclosure does not usually take away the novelty of any specific example falling within the terms of that disclosure, but a specific disclosure does take away the novelty of a generic claim embracing that disclosure (Guidelines G-VI, 5).

Examples:

A disclosure of copper takes away the novelty of metal as a generic concept, but not the novelty of any metal other than copper.

A disclosure of rivets takes away the novelty of fastening means as a generic concept, but not the novelty of any fastening means other than rivets, such as nails or adhesives.

The generic term "alkane" is not novelty-destroying for the compound "methane" (i.e. the alkane having one atom of carbon and four atoms of hydrogen), but "methane" destroys the novelty of "alkane".

In paper B Chemistry 2015, claim 3 of the application as filed contained as a feature "hydrotalcite". The Examiner raised a novelty objection to this claim based on D1, of which paragraph [005] shows that clays can be used. The Examiner then argued that "it would appear that hydrotalcite falls within this definition". He hence raised a novelty objection based on a prior art teaching a genus against a claim that referred to a species. The candidates were expected to argue that the Examiner's position was incorrect.

3.3.5 Features incorporated by reference

If a document representing the state of the art explicitly refers to another document as providing more detailed information on certain specific features, the teaching of the latter document is to be regarded as incorporated (Guidelines G-IV, 8).

Examples:

In Document D1 of paper B 2018, it is taught that the average surface roughness Ra is a well-known parameter defined in accordance with the International Standards Organization (ISO).

Document D1 of paper B Chemistry 2016 teaches that the preparation of polymers with a methacrylic acid ester such as butyl methacrylate and another monomer such as, for example styrene or methacrylic acid is described in the patent specification EP8975654 for the controlled release of fertilisers.

3.3.6 Implicit features

The disclosure of a document is not limited to what is explicitly described, but includes everything that is *"directly and unambiguously derivable"* from the document. In particular, the state of the art comprises implicit features. The limitation to features *"derivable directly and unambiguously"* from the document is essential. According to the case law of the Boards of Appeal and the Guidelines, the teaching of a document must not be interpreted as embracing equivalents not disclosed explicitly in the document (Guidelines G-VI, 2).

Example:

In the paper B 2021, claim 1 refers to "drain holes (5) permitting moisture to drain from the upper to the lower compartment". The Examiner raises novelty objections using the following argument "Note that the mesh used in D2 and D3 is considered a support with drain holes, since the mesh of D2 or D3 is also suitable for draining excess moisture from the organic substrate".

4 State of the Art

4.1 Legal basis

EPC Articles and Rules 600
Art. 54 EPC: Novelty
Art. 55 EPC: Non-prejudicial disclosures
Art. 56 EPC: Inventive step

Guidelines 601
B-VI, 6: Contents of prior-art disclosures
G-IV: State of the art
G-IV, 1: General remarks and definition
G-IV, 7: State of the art made available to the public "by means of a written or oral description, by use or in any other way"

Case Law Book 602
I.C.2: State of the art
I.C.2.8: Common general knowledge
I.C.2.5: Non-prejudicial disclosures under Art. 55 EPC
I.C.4: Determining the content of the relevant prior art

Further reference 603
C-Book, Chapter 5, p. 109–126: State of the Art

Important decisions 604

Disclosure of commercially available products — G1/92 — 605

The chemical composition of a product forms part of the state of the art when the product as such is commercially or otherwise available to the public and can be analysed and reproduced by the skilled person, irrespective of whether or not particular reasons can be identified for analysing the composition. The same principle applies *mutatis mutandis* to any other product.

Prior use by sale — T 482/89 — 606

The sale of a product without an obligation of confidentiality makes the product available to the public.

Written account published after a use or an oral disclosure — T 154/88 — 607

If a use or an oral disclosure was made available to the public before the relevant date, but published in writing only afterwards, the written account may be deemed to give a true account of the use or oral disclosure, unless there is a good reason why this should not be the case (Guidelines G-IV, 1 and 7.4). However, if there is a considerable gap between the date of the use or oral disclosure and the date of publication of the written account, such an assumption cannot be made without further proof.

Non-written state of the art — T 939/92 — 608

Art. 54(2) EPC does not limit the state of the art to written disclosures in specific documents. Rather, it defines it as including all other ways (*"in any other way"*) by which technical subject-matter can be made available to the public. Therefore, the absence of a reference to a particular document does not mean that there is no state of the art, as this could reside solely in the relevant common general knowledge, which, again, may or may not be in writing, i.e. in textbooks or the like, or be simply a part of the unwritten *"mental furniture"* of the person skilled in the art. In the case of a dispute as to the extent of the relevant common general knowledge this, like any other fact under contention, has to be proven, for example by documentary or oral evidence (see also T 766/91, reasons Point 8.2).

4.2 Relevance to paper B

609 The basis of paper B is a patent application (that is: a description of and a set of claims for an invention for which the client wishes to obtain a European patent), references forming pertinent prior art, a communication wherein an Examiner raises objections, and an instructions letter of the client together with a set of his suggested amended claims. The main tasks consist of adapting the suggested amended claims and of drafting a response to the communication dealing with all objections raised.

610 It is evident that the proper assessment of the state of the art is critical for the solution of paper B. Determining the content of the state of the art is relatively easy, because the relevant documents are included in the paper. It is far more difficult to understand the invention and to delimitate it properly against the prior art.

4.3 State of the art

611 Art. 54(2), (3) EPC defines the state of the art as follows:

> **(2) The state of the art shall be held to comprise everything made available to the public by means of a written or oral description, by use, or in any other way, before the date of filing of the European patent application.**
>
> **(3) Additionally, the content of European patent applications as filed, the dates of filing of which are prior to the date referred to in paragraph 2 and which were published on or after that date, shall be considered as comprised in the state of the art.**

612 The three types of prior art specifically mentioned in Art. 54(2) EPC, namely written description, oral description and use, are the most common forms of disclosure, but the state of the art is by no means limited to these. It should be noted, however, that in paper B any disclosure is presented in writing, either in the form of the text of a publication, or of an acknowledgment of prior art in the letter from the client. If oral disclosure or public prior use is involved, a summary of the oral disclosure or use is given.

613 The state of the art comprises the whole disclosure of the prior documents. In the case of a patent application, the description, claims and any drawings are comprised. Any matter explicitly disclosed, but also any implicit disclosure form part of the prior art. Disclaimed matter is also regarded as being disclosed, with the exception of disclaimers for non-working embodiments (Guidelines G-IV, 5.1). Another part of the state of the art are references to other documents, as far as they are allowable (Guidelines G-IV, 5.1 and F-III, 8). Publications on the internet and online databases form also part of the state of the art from the date the information is publicly posted (Guidelines G-IV, 7.5).

614 Furthermore, conflicting European patent applications falling under Art. 54(3) EPC are comprised in the prior art. As of the 2013 papers B, no such documents occurred in paper B. The same applies to non-prejudicial disclosures under Art. 55 EPC. This is, however, not a guarantee for future papers!

Written disclosure

615 Nearly always the letter from the client contains one or more statements relating to the state of the art; similarly one or more statements relating to the state of the art are occasionally made in the description of the patent application. Such statements may be hidden and have to be retrieved when analysing the text of the letter and/or of the description. They may refer to documents published before the relevant date, but they may also relate to facts acknowledged by the client as comprised in the state of the art. In the absence of evidence to the contrary, any acknowledgment of prior art by the client should be accepted, see for example T 654/92, T 691/94, T 87/01, T 730/05, T 1449/05, T 211/06. Usually, paper B is accompanied by two or three separate documents representing the state of the art. These documents may have different forms, including articles in magazines, patent applications, advertisements, textbooks, research papers, etc.

616 It can be assumed that any technical subject-matter present in the prior art documents belongs, in fact, to the state of the art and is technically correct (Rule 22(3) IPREE).

Oral disclosure

Oral disclosure takes place when facts are unconditionally brought to the knowledge of members of the public in the course of a conversation or a lecture or by means of radio, television or sound reproduction equipment (Guidelines G-IV, 7.3.1).

Any statement in paper B referring to oral disclosure may be taken at face value, unless there is evidence that further investigations regarding the circumstances of the oral disclosure are required (Guidelines G-IV, 1 and 7.4).

Prior public use

Public prior use may be constituted by producing, offering, marketing or otherwise exploiting a product, by offering or marketing a process or its application, or by applying the process. Marketing may be effected, for example, by sale or exchange (Guidelines G-IV, 7.1). The condition is, as in the case of oral disclosure, that there is no obligation of confidentiality.

Usually, public prior use is revealed in paper B in the form of a statement in the patent application or in the letter from the client, that a particular product or process is *"conventional"*, *"known to the skilled person"*, *"commercially available"*, etc. Occasionally, there may be other forms for presenting public prior use, for example, the third party observation dealing with a public prior use in the 2021 paper B (*vide infra*). It may be assumed that such statements relating to the availability of products and processes give a true account of the facts, unless there is evidence to the contrary (Rule 22(3) IPREE).

4.4 Examples from past papers

In the communication of the Examiner in paper B 2021, he pointed to the fact that an observation by a third party pursuant to Art. 115 EPC has been filed with respect to an alleged prior use. The applicant is invited to provide arguments to suitably address the prior use or to amend the claims accordingly.

The anonymous third party observation states the following:

[001] We file observations in accordance with Article 115 EPC with respect to published patent application EP 19 222 222.7 with a filing date of 10 September 2018.

[002] The subject-matter of claim 1 is not novel, because the container of claim 1 was presented to the public before the filing date as evidenced by the following internet announcement. In our opinion during the guided tour on 02 August 2018 at 11:45 the public had access to the facilities where the apparatus of claim 1 was located.

[003] The following announcement was published on the internet under www.opendayincotsford.com on 6 June 2018:

[004] "Farm Open Day at The Cycle Farm in Cotsford Come and find out what we do at our Farm Open Day 2018. Learn about biodynamic farming, our farm and how we plan to expand our amazing work. You'll also meet our animals, get a chance to feed the chicks and learn how our earthworms and house flies produce fertilizer and feed. A great day for kids and adults!

Programme:
Sunday August 2nd 2018 from 10 to 14 h
10:00 Welcome
10:15 What we do and what we plan
10:30 Snacks and drinks from our farm
11:00 Guided tour to visit our chicks
11:45 Guided tour to meet with our earthworms and house flies
12:00 Lunch at our farmhouse kitchen"

[005] According to the local newspaper "Cotsford Herald" (www.cotald.com) on Monday 3rd August 2018 the open day attracted approximately 100 visitors who were impressed by the guided tours.

The when, where and how questions to be answered for a public prior use do not seem to provide a problem. However, the "what has been disclosed to the public" is not elaborated at all. It is only noted that: "the container" of claim 1 was presented, without providing any details or claim features. Knowing that a public prior use must be evidenced to quite an extend, this is insufficient to base an objection thereon.

5 Patentable and non-patentable inventions

5.1 Legal basis

EPC Articles and Rules

Art. 52(1), (2), (3) EPC
Art. 53 EPC
Art. 54 EPC
Art. 56 EPC
Art. 57 EPC
Rule 28 EPC
Rule 42 EPC
Rule 43 EPC

Guidelines

G-II, 1: Inventions – general remarks
G-I, 2: Patentability – further requirements of an invention
G-III: Industrial application
G-VI: Novelty
G-VII: Inventive step
G-II, 4: Exceptions to patentability
G-II, 4.1: Matter contrary to *"ordre public"* or morality
G-II, 4.2: Surgery, therapy and diagnostic methods
G-II, 4.2.1: Limitations of exception under Art. 53(c)
F-II, 4.9: Industrial application
G-III, 3: Industrial application vs. exclusion under Art. 52(2)
G-VI, 7.1: First or further medical use of known products
F-IV, 2.1: Technical features
G-VII, 5.4: Claims comprising technical and non-technical features
B-VIII, 2.2: Subject-matter excluded from patentability under Art. 52(2) and (3)
B-VIII, 2.2.1 Computer-implemented business methods
G-II, 3.6: Programs for computers

Case Law Book

I.A: Patentable inventions
I.A.1: Patent protection for technical inventions
I.A.2: Non-inventions under Art. 52(2) and (3) EPC
I.B: Exceptions to patentability
I.B.2: Breaches of *"ordre public"* or morality
I.B.3: Patentability of biological inventions
I.B.4: Medical methods

Further reference

C-Book, Chapter 9.1, p. 199–201: Patentability

Important decisions

Second and further medical indications   G 5/83

A European patent may be granted with claims directed to the use of a substance or composition for the manufacture of a medicament for a specified new and inventive therapeutic application (Headnote II).
    Such a use claim is called a "Swiss-type" claim.

Dosage regime   G 2/08

Where it is already known to use a medicament to treat an illness, Art. 54(5) EPC does not exclude that this medicament be patented for use in a different treatment by therapy of the same illness. Such patenting is also not excluded where a dosage regime is the only feature claimed which is not comprised in the state of the art.

630   The format of the so-called *"Swiss-type"* claims is abolished. The main reason therefor is that EPC 2000 contains Art. 54(5) EPC allowing to claim second and further medical indications in another way: product for specific use in a method described in Art. 53(c) EPC.

631   **Diagnostic methods**   G 1/04

In order that the subject-matter of a claim relating to a diagnostic method practised on the human or animal body falls under the prohibition of Art. 52(4) EPC [1973], now Art. 53(c) EPC, the claim is to include the features relating to:
(i) the diagnosis for curative purposes *stricto sensu* representing the deductive medical or veterinary decision phase as a purely intellectual exercise,
(ii) the preceding steps which are constitutive for making that diagnosis, and
(iii) the specific interactions with the human or animal body which occur when carrying those out among these preceding steps which are of a technical nature (Headnote I).

632   **Medical imaging method**   G 1/07

A claimed imaging method, in which, when carried out, maintaining the life and health of the subject is important, and which comprises or encompasses an invasive step representing a substantial physical intervention on the body, which requires professional medical expertise to be carried out, and which entails a substantial health risk, even when carried out with the required professional care and expertise, is excluded from patentability as a method for treatment of the human or animal body by surgery pursuant to Art. 53(c) EPC (Headnote 1).

633   The exclusion from patentability under Art. 53(c) EPC can be avoided by disclaiming the embodiment, it being understood that in order to be patentable the claim including the disclaimer must fulfil all the requirements of the EPC and, where applicable, the requirements for a disclaimer to be allowable as defined in decisions G 1/03 and G 2/03 of the Enlarged Board of Appeal (Headnote 2b).

634   **Purely cosmetic treatment of humans**   T 144/83

A purely cosmetic treatment of a human by administration of a chemical product does not fall under the exceptions to patentability defined in Art. 53(c) EPC and is, therefore, susceptible of being patented.

635   **Method of manufacturing an endoprosthesis**   T 1005/98

A method of manufacturing an endoprosthesis outside the body, but requiring a surgical step to be carried out for taking measurements, is excluded from patentability under Art. 53(c) EPC. In contrast, a method involving no surgical step is patentable under Art. 52(1) EPC.

636   **Inventions consisting of a mixture of technical and non-technical features**   T 641/00

When an invention consists of a mixture of technical and non-technical features and has a technical character as a whole, it has to be assessed with respect to the requirement of inventive step by taking account of all those features which contribute to said technical character, whereas features making no such contribution cannot support the presence of inventive step.

637   **Non-technical features conferring novelty to a claimed method**   T 2050/07

Two non-technical features relating to mathematical algorithms were found to confer novelty to a method for analysing DNA mixtures, because they interacted with the remaining steps of the claimed method in order to produce a common technical result, namely a genotype estimate with an improved confidence compared to the quantitative method analysis known from the prior art.

5.2 Relevance to paper B

638   In paper B one or more independent claims have to be amended according to the client's wishes, which should offer the client the broadest possible protection in accordance with

the EPC (Rule 24 IPREE). Accomplishing this task requires in-depth knowledge of the provisions laid down in the EPC regarding patentable and non-patentable inventions, as well as inventions excepted from patentability by virtue of Art. 52 and Art. 53 EPC.

In order to comply with the requirements of the EPC, the claims must not encompass any non-patentable inventions within the meaning of Art. 52(2), (3) EPC, and they have to be formulated in a manner to exclude any inventions falling under the exceptions set out in Art. 53 EPC. 639

Depending on the circumstances of a case, the proper delimitation of the subject-matter of the claims against "*non-inventions*" and inventions excepted from patentability may be quite difficult. Relevant knowledge of the law and practical skills in claim drafting are indispensable. 640

5.3 Patentable inventions

A technical item is patentable under Art. 52(1) EPC, if it satisfies simultaneously the following four requirements: 641

First requirement

The item must be an "*invention*" susceptible of being patented. The EPC does not define what the term "*invention*" precisely means, but it gives in Art. 52(2) EPC a non-exhaustive list of objects, which are not regarded as patentable inventions within the meaning of Art. 52(1) EPC. These "*non-inventions*" are all either abstract or non-technical items. Therefore it may be concluded *a contrario*, that patentable inventions must have a "*technical character*" and, in addition, a sufficient degree of "*tangibility*" or "*concreteness*", as opposed to purely abstract ideas (Guidelines G-II, 1). 642

The requirement of a "*technical character*" implies a number of subsequent conditions, namely: 643
- The invention must relate to a technical field. Otherwise it would not be possible to indicate the technical field as required by Rule 42(1)(a) EPC. It may be in any field of technology
- There has to be a technical problem underlying the invention, see Rule 42(1)(c) EPC
- The invention must have technical features, for which protection can be sought, see Rule 43(1) EPC

(Guidelines G-I, 2(ii))

Second requirement

(2) The invention has to be novel within the meaning of Art. 54 EPC 644

(Guidelines G-VI)

Third requirement

(3) The invention has to involve an inventive step within the meaning of Art. 56 EPC 645

(Guidelines G-VII)

Fourth requirement

(4) The invention has to be "*susceptible of industrial application*" as defined in Art. 57 EPC 646

(Guidelines G-III)

When all four requirements are met simultaneously, an invention is susceptible of being patentable. This applies to virtually all technical fields. In certain areas special rules apply, however. Thus, a non-exhaustive list of patentable biotechnological inventions is set out in Rule 27 EPC. The list comprises the following items: 647
- Biological material which is isolated from its natural environment or produced by means of a technical process even if it previously occurred in nature (Rule 27(a) EPC)
- Plants or animals if the technical feasibility of the invention is not confined to a particular plant or animal variety (Rule 27(b) EPC). A claim wherein specific plant varieties

are not individually claimed is not excluded from patentability under Art. 53(b) EPC, even though it may embrace plant varieties (G 1/98, and Guidelines G-II, 5.4)
- A microbiological or other technical process, or a product obtained by means of such a process other than a plant or animal variety (Rule 27(c) EPC)

648 Other special provisions apply to biotechnological inventions, in particular inventions relating to the human body and its elements, including gene sequences or partial sequences, or relating to nucleotide and amino acid sequences. The relevant legislation is laid down in Rules 28 to 30 EPC (Guidelines G-II, 5.2).

649 An important group of patentable inventions is formed by substances and compositions having a medical use. According to Art. 54(4) EPC a substance or composition known as such may be patented for use in a medical method as defined in Art. 53(c) EPC, provided that the use in surgery, therapy or diagnostic methods practised on the human or animal body does not belong to the state of the art (*"first medical use"*).

650 If a known substance or composition is previously disclosed for use in surgery, therapy or diagnostic methods practised on the human or animal body as defined in Art. 53(c) EPC, it may be patented for use in a <u>specific</u> therapeutical, surgical or diagnostic method by virtue of Art. 54(5) EPC (*"second or further medical use"*).

651 Where it is already known to use a medicament to treat a specific illness, Art. 54(5) EPC does not exclude that this medicament be patented for use in a different treatment by therapy of the same illness. Such patenting is also not excluded where a dosage regime is the only feature claimed, which is not comprised in the state of the art (G 2/08).

652 Claims according to Art. 54(4) EPC or Art. 54(5) EPC involving a first or further medical use are limited to the medical indication referred to. In this respect, they are different from other claims containing a statement of the purpose in the preamble (Guidelines F-IV, 4.13). That is, Art. 54(4) and Art. 54(5) EPC results in a product claim for any or a specific medical use, respectively; in these cases, the "for"-clauses are not to be read as "suitable for".

5.4 Non-inventions according to Art. 52(2), (3) EPC

653 There exists subject-matter which cannot be patented by virtue of Art. 52(2) EPC and Art. 53 EPC, respectively.

654 A non-exhaustive list of so-called *"non-inventions"* which are not regarded as inventions within the meaning of Art. 52(1) EPC is given in Art. 52(2) EPC:
- Discoveries, scientific theories and mathematical methods (Art. 52(2)(a) EPC)
- Aesthetic creations (Art. 52(2)(b) EPC)
- Schemes, rules and methods for performing mental acts, playing games or doing business, and programs for computers (Art. 52(2)(c) EPC)
- Presentations of information (Art. 52(2)(d) EPC)

655 *"Non-inventions"* are by definition non-technical and involve non-technical features. Art. 52(3) EPC makes plain that *"non-inventions"* are excluded from patentability only to the extent to which they are claimed "as such". Thus, a program for computers in the form of an abstract set of computer code is not patentable. In contrast, having regard to Art. 52(3) EPC, nothing prevents the patentability of computer-implemented inventions (G 1/19; Guidelines B-VIII, 2.2 and 2.2.1; and Guidelines G-II, 3.6). The same applies *mutatis mutandis* to *"non-inventions"* other than programs for computers.

656 It is important to note, that the requirement of *"susceptibility of industrial application"* does not override the restrictions laid down in Art. 52(2) EPC. For example, an administrative method of stock control is not patentable, having regard to Art. 52(2)(c) EPC, even though it can be applied to a factory store-room for spare parts. On the other hand, although an invention must be *"susceptible of industrial application"*, the claims need not necessarily be restricted to applications in industry (Guidelines G-III,3).

5.5 Exceptions to patentability under Art. 53 EPC

657 According to Art. 53 EPC there are several exceptions to patentability, namely:
- Inventions, the commercial exploitation of which would be contrary to *"ordre public"* or morality (Art. 53(a) EPC)

- Plant or animal varieties or essentially biological processes for the production of plants or animals; this provision shall not apply to microbiological processes or the products thereof (Art. 53(b) EPC)
- Methods for treatment of the human or animal body by surgery or therapy and diagnostic methods practiced on the human or animal body; this provision shall not apply to products, in particular substances or compositions, for use in any of these methods (Art. 53(c) EPC)

(Guidelines G-II, 4.1; G-II, 4.2; 4.2.1)

658 The exceptions to patentability defined in Art. 53(a) EPC have been specified in Rule 28 EPC for biotechnological inventions, particularly cloning and modifying the genome of human beings, and using human embryos for industrial or commercial purposes (G 2/06; Guidelines G-II, 5.3).

659 Non-patentability under Art. 53(a) EPC or Art. 53(b) EPC occur only rarely (G 2/07, G 1/08, G 2/12, G 2/13). In contrast, inventions involving surgery, therapy or diagnostic methods occur regularly. In each case a thorough analysis has to be made in order to ensure that the subject-matter of the claims complies with Art. 53(c) EPC. Details regarding the practice to be followed are explained in the Guidelines in sub-paragraphs G-II, 4.2.1.1 (surgery), 4.2.1.2 (therapy) and 4.2.1.3 (diagnostic methods).

660 The exceptions under Art. 53(c) EPC are confined to the methods mentioned in the Article. Other methods of treatment of human beings or animals, or other methods of measuring characteristics of the human or animal body are patentable, provided that they are of technical and not of essentially biological character. For example, the purely cosmetic treatment of a human by administration of a chemical product is patentable (T 144/83). In contrast, cosmetic treatment involving surgery or therapy is not patentable (Guidelines G-II, 4.2.1).

661 Treatment of body tissues or fluids, after these have been removed from the human or animal body, or diagnostic methods applied thereon, are not excluded from patentability insofar as these tissues or fluids are not returned to the same body (Guidelines G-II, 4.2.1). In general, extensive interpretations of Art. 53(c) EPC should be avoided. Whether a method falls under the exceptions from patentability under Art. 53(c) EPC, or not, does not depend on the person carrying it out (G 1/04 and G 1/07, Reasons 3.4.1).

5.6 Non-technical features

662 Rule 43(1) EPC requires that the claims define the matter for which protection is sought in terms of the *"technical features of the invention"*. Statements of purpose are permissible and current in claims, as long as they are useful for the definition of the claimed matter. As a rule, non-technical features such as references to commercial advantages are not permissible (Guidelines F-IV, 2.1).

663 There is an important exception, however. Claims consisting of a mixture of technical and non-technical features may be allowable, and the non-technical features may even form a major part of the claimed subject-matter (Guidelines G-VII, 5.4). Typical cases are claims containing features of technical items and, in addition, features of a *"non-invention"* such as a mathematical method or a program for computers.

664 How claims consisting of a mixture of technical and non-technical features should be assessed is set out in decision T 641/00. The headnote I of said decision reads as follows:

"I. An invention consisting of a mixture of technical and non-technical features and having technical character as a whole is to be assessed with respect to the requirement of inventive step by taking account of all those features which contribute to said technical character, whereas features making no such contribution cannot support the presence of [an] inventive step."

665 The latter situation arises, for example, if a feature contributes only to the solution of a non-technical problem, e.g. a problem in a field excluded from patentability (Guidelines G-VII, 5.4.1).

666 The question arises, whether the principle outlined above is restricted to the assessment of inventive step, or not. Regarding the assessment of novelty, T 642/00 provides no guidance. It may reasonably be assumed, however, that non-technical features making

a technical contribution have to be taken into consideration in respect of novelty. For example, in decision T 2050/07 the Board of Appeal arrived at the conclusion, that two non-technical features relating to mathematical algorithms conferred novelty to a method for analysing DNA mixtures, because they interacted with the remaining steps of the claimed method in order to provide a common technical result, namely a genotype estimate with an improved confidence compared to the quantitative method analysis known from the prior art (T 2050/07, reasons 6–13).

5.7 Industrial application

667 Whenever it is not evident from the description or from the nature of the invention, whether the requirement of industrial application is met, the description should indicate explicitly the way in which the invention can be exploited in industry (Guidelines F-II, 4.9). In the vast majority of cases, there can be no reasonable doubts as to the industrial application of an invention. Therefore, no explanations are needed in the description in this respect.

5.8 Examples from past papers

668 The Examiner raises an objection under Art. 52(2)(c) EPC in paper B 2021.
Claim 6 reads on a calculation method for optimizing processing organic refuse, comprising the steps of
  a. defining a target value TV at time point tp > 0 for the amount of the earthworms (8) present in the refuse (7) at said time point tp;
  b. receiving data relating to the moisture of refuse (7) and the amount of earthworms (8) at a plurality of time points tp;
  c. determining if the value for the amount of earthworms (8) present in the refuse (7) at tp > 0 is equal to the defined target value TV for the amount of earthworms (8); and
  d. recommending adjusting the amount of moisture added to the refuse (7) at said time point tp, if the value for the amount of earthworms (8) present in the refuse at tp > 0 is not equal to the defined target value TV for the amount of earthworms (8).

669 The Examiner considers the subject-matter of claim 6 to be a method for performing mental acts and not to recite a technical feature. The method of claim 6 is, hence, considered excluded from patentability under Article 52(2)(c) EPC.

670 There were two options to deal with this objection.
The client proposed to add the step of "providing a container according to any one of claims 1 to 4". This wording is to be adjusted to bring antecedent basis for the terms "refuse" and "earthworms". The introductory part of said claim 6 could then read:
"A calculation method for optimizing processing organic refuse, comprising the steps of <u>providing a container according to any one of claims 1 to 4</u>, **holding organic refuse (7) populated with earthworms (8),** and a. defining (…)"

671 The second option makes use of the fact that in the description of the patent application of paper B 2021, it is noted that "One, more or all steps of the method can be implemented by a computer". This is an invitation to go to a computer implemented invention. At the end of claim 6, it could be added that "at least one of these steps being implemented by a computer"; yet, the claim that got the highest number of marks in the Examiners' report just referred to "A <u>computer-implemented</u> method for optimizing (…)".

672 I note that the Examiner did not make any unity-of-invention objections to the set of claims as originally filed. According to the Examiners' report, it was "expected that the method of claim 6 be amended to refer to a computer-implemented method. This suitably addresses the Article 52(2)(c) EPC objection. (…) Adding a technical feature (such as a container according to claim 1 is more limiting".

6 Novelty

6.1 Legal basis

EPC Articles and Rules 673
Art. 52(1) EPC
Art. 54 EPC

Guidelines 674
G-VI: Novelty
G-VI, 7: Examination of novelty
G-VI, 7.1: First or further medical use of known products
G-VI, 7.2: Second non-medical use
G-VI, 8: Selection inventions
G-VI, 8.1: Error margins in numerical values
G-VI, 9: Novelty of *"reach-through"* claims

Case Law Book 675
I.C: Novelty
I.C.5: Ascertaining differences
I.C.6: Chemical inventions and selection inventions
I.C.7: First and second medical use
I.C.8: Second (or further) non-medical use

Further references 676
C-Book, Chapter 5, p. 109–126: State of the Art
C-Book, Chapter 8, p. 169–179: Ranges

Important decisions

Distinguishing feature G 2/88 677
The claims of a European patent should clearly define the technical features of the invention and, thus, its technical subject-matter, so that the protection conferred by the patent can be determined and a comparison can be made with the state of the art, to ensure that the claimed invention is *inter alia* novel. A claimed invention lacks novelty unless it includes at least one (essential technical) feature, which distinguishes it from the state of the art. When deciding upon the novelty of a claim, a basic initial consideration is therefore to construe the claim in order to determine its technical features (G 2/88, reasons Point 7).

Assessment of novelty T 153/85 678
When assessing novelty, the disclosure of a prior document must be considered in isolation. It is only the actual content of a document, as understood by the person skilled in the art, which destroys novelty (T 153/85, headnote 3 and reasons Point 4.2).

Difference in wording T 114/86 679
A mere difference in wording is insufficient to establish novelty (following T 12/81, T 198/84 and T 248/85).

Specific reference in a document T 153/85 680
A prior document may on its proper construction, i.e. when its meaning to the person skilled in the art is determined, incorporate part or all of a second prior document into its disclosure, by specific reference to the second document.

Intrinsic and inherent features G 1/92 681
A commercially available product discloses implicitly its composition and its internal structure.

682 Other features, which are only revealed when the product is exposed to interaction with specifically chosen outside conditions in order to provide a particular effect or result, or to discover potential results or capabilities, are dependent on deliberate choices and thus cannot be considered as disclosed to the public.

683 **Parameters** T 94/84

The requirement of clarity may be fulfilled in a definition of a product, when the characteristics of the product are specified by parameters related to the physical structure of the product, provided that those parameters can be clearly and reliably determined by objective procedures which are usual in the art.

684 **Unusual parameters** T 1764/06

The only difference between the definition of the claimed polycrystalline titania powder having photo-activity in catalytic processes on the one side, and the photo catalyst of the state of the art on the other side, consisted in a parameter called "X-Index". By the index the proportion of ultraviolet-visible light that was absorbed in the visible region was characterised. Since the parameter was not usual, let alone common, for the skilled person, there was a presumption of lack of novelty.

685 **Implicit features** T 701/09

Implicit features are features, which a person skilled in the art would unequivocally gather from the overall context of a cited document.

It is an established principle in the case law since decision T 12/81, that the product inevitably resulting from a process properly defined as to its starting substance and reaction conditions is considered to be disclosed, even if it is not cited *expressis verbis* in the prior document (T 270/97).

686 **Features shown solely in a drawing** T 272/92)

Features shown solely in a drawing form part of the state of the art when a person skilled in that art is able, in the absence of any other description, to derive a technical teaching from them (T 272/92).

687 **Dimensions obtained from a diagram** T 857/91

Dimensions obtained merely by measuring a diagrammatic representation in a document do not, however, form part of the disclosure (T 857/91).

688 **Prior documents are not reservoirs of features** T 305/87; T 656/92

In assessing novelty, the content of a document must not be considered as a reservoir from which features pertaining to separate embodiments could be combined in order to create artificially a particular embodiment (T 305/87, reasons Point 5.3; T 656/92, reasons Point 2.3).

689 **Disclosure of separate dependent claims** T 525/99; T 42/92

The argumentation that the dependent claims 4, 5, 7 and 8 of document D5 are to be considered together in the assessment of novelty, and that the combined teaching of these claims discloses the claimed invention, was not accepted by the Board of Appeal.

690 The Board of Appeal held that in accordance with the established case law, the disclosure of a patent document does not embrace the combination of individual features claimed in separate dependent claims, if such combination is not supported by the description.

691 The disclosure of a prior-art patent specification does not cover combinations of individual features arising from reference back to the claims, if these features are claimed separately. Combining them is not supported by the description (T 42/92, headnote and reasons Point 3.4).

Specification of chemical substances   T 12/81

It is permissible to make the definition of a chemical substance more precise by additional product parameters such as melting point, hydrophilic properties, NMR coupling constant or product-by-process claims, if it cannot be defined by a sufficiently accurate generic formula (reasons Point 6).

If two classes of starting substances are required to prepare the end products, and examples of individual entities in each class are given in two lists of some length, then a substance resulting from the reaction of a specific pair from the two lists can nevertheless be regarded for patent purposes as a selection and hence as new (reasons Point 13).

6.2 Relevance to Paper B

Among the tasks of paper B, drafting one or more independent claims which meet the requirement of novelty is an important one. Not only because up to some 10 marks are available for discussing novelty of the independent claim(s) over all separate prior art references, but also because in the problem-solution approach the feature(s) making an independent claim novel play(s) an important role in the argumentation for inventive step.

For paper B, normally the following pattern is followed:

The examiner raises at least one novelty objection in its communication. The client describes his perception of the invention and generally provides amended claims that are novel. At the same time, the client often indicates that he wishes to have an independent claim that has a broader scope of protection. Based on support in the application as filed, you must come up with a claim that is novel. The novelty is motivated by pointing in the letter to the examiner to at least one feature of the claim that is not described directly and unambiguously in each piece of prior art. It goes without saying that for different prior art documents, the difference with the claim discussed may be another feature.

A major task of paper B consists in drafting one or more independent claims and motivating why this claim or these claims are novel. For this purpose the invention has to be compared with each piece of the prior art, with an aim to finding at least one distinguishing feature. As is well known, the subject-matter of a claim is novel if there is at least one distinguishing feature.

In case of more than one invention, it is generally efficient to start with the main invention and to analyse the remaining invention subsequently. Quite often the main invention confers novelty and inventive step to further inventions, since there exists usually a close relationship between the main and the other inventions.

6.3 Analysis of novelty

When assessing the state of the art, the case law of the Boards of Appeal and the guidance given in the Guidelines should be taken into account, in particular paragraphs F-IV, 4.6 to 4.13 and 4.21. The general approach to novelty can be summarised as follows:

The claims of a European patent should clearly define the technical features of the invention and, thus, its technical subject-matter, in order that the protection conferred by the patent can be determined and a comparison can be made with the state of the art, to ensure that the claimed invention is *inter alia* novel. A claimed invention lacks novelty unless it includes at least one essential technical feature, which distinguishes it from the state of the art. When deciding upon the novelty of a claim, a basic initial consideration is therefore to construe the claim in order to determine its technical features (G 2/88, reasons Point 7).

In determining novelty, each prior document must be read as a person skilled in the art would read it on the relevant date of said document, using his common general knowledge, but no expert knowledge (Guidelines G-VI, 3).

When an invention is compared for novelty purposes with the state of the art, this must be done on the basis of each element of prior art taken as a whole (T 153/85, T 124/87, T 233/90, T 904/91).

When assessing novelty, the disclosure of a prior document must be considered in isolation. It is only the actual content of a document, as understood by the person skilled in the art, which destroys novelty (T 153/85, headnote 3 and reasons Point 4.2).

703 A mere difference in wording is insufficient to establish novelty (following T 12/81, T 198/84 and T 248/85).

704 A prior document may on its proper construction (*i.e.* when its meaning to the skilled man is determined) incorporate part or all of a second prior document into its disclosure, by specific reference to the second document (T 153/85, headnote 4 and reasons Point 4.2).

705 A document representing the state of the art is prejudicial to the novelty of the invention to the extent that the claimed subject-matter concerned is directly and unambiguously derivable from the document.

706 All features must be disclosed in a single embodiment described in a single document, either explicitly or implicitly. It is not permissible to combine separate features described in a single document and pertaining to different embodiments, unless such a combination is specifically suggested by the document (T 305/87).

707 A prior document anticipates the novelty of an invention, if the latter is directly and unambiguously derivable from that document, including any features implicit to a person skilled in the art. However, an alleged disclosure can only be considered *"implicit"* if it is immediately apparent to the skilled person that nothing other than the alleged implicit feature forms part of the subject-matter disclosed (T 95/97, reasons Point 3.3). Implicit features are features, which a person skilled in the art would unequivocally gather from the overall context of a cited document (T 709/09, reasons Point 1.2).

708 It is an established principle in the case law since T 12/81 (OJ 1982, 296), that the product inevitably resulting from a process properly defined as to its starting substance and reaction conditions is considered to be disclosed, even if it is not cited *expressis verbis* in the prior document (T 270/97, reasons Point 3.1).

709 A commercially available product discloses its composition and its internal structure. Other features, which are only revealed when the product is exposed to interaction with specifically chosen outside conditions, in order to provide a particular effect or result, or to discover potential results or capabilities, depend on deliberate choices being made and thus cannot be considered as disclosed to the public (G 1/92).

710 Features shown solely in a drawing form part of the state of the art when a person skilled in that art is able, in the absence of any other description, to derive a technical teaching from them (T 272/92). Dimensions obtained merely by measuring a diagrammatic representation in a document do not, however, form part of the disclosure (T 857/91).

711 The teaching of a document, independent of its nature, is not to be interpreted as embracing equivalents not disclosed in that document (Guidelines G-VI, 2). Equivalents can only be taken into account when considering inventive step (T 517/90).

712 On the other hand, individual features in a document can be combined, if the skilled person, taking the technical facts into account and using his common general knowledge, would seriously contemplate the combination of the features concerned (T 305/87; T 656/82; Guidelines G-VI, 1; G-VI, 8(iii)).

713 It is not permissible to combine two or more documents representing the state of the art, unless (one of) the document(s) itself suggests the combination.

714 The disclosure of a patent document does not embrace the combination of individual features claimed in separate dependent claims if such combination is not supported by the description (T 525/99; T 42/92).

715 A mere difference in wording is insufficient to establish novelty (T 114/86, headnote 2; following T 12/81, T 198/84, T 248/85).

716 Non-distinctive characteristics of a particular intended use of a product should be disregarded, unless the use referred to implies particular features of the product.

717 A known compound is not rendered novel merely because it is available with a different degree of purity if the purity can be achieved by conventional means (T 360/07).

718 For claims to a first or further medical use, see Guidelines G-VI, 7.1.

6.4 Parameters

719 A product may be defined by one or more parameters, possibly in combination with structural features. In general, any continuous variable of a physical property can be regarded as a parameter. Examples are mass, density, colour, boiling point, temperature, volume, but also more complex properties such as stiffness, compression strength, surface energy, hardness, electrical conductivity, *etc.* Certain parameters can be measured

directly, for example the length of a macroscopic object, others such as the BET surface area are determined indirectly, and still others result from mathematical calculations.

Whenever a parameter is used for specifying the physical structure of a product, an objective procedure for the determination of the parameter is required. Otherwise no meaningful comparison between the product and the state of the art is possible.

Parameters which are well recognised in a particular technical field are normally unproblematic, since the person skilled in the art knows their meaning and how these can be measured.

The same does not always apply to unusual parameters. There may be difficulties regarding the precise meaning of an uncommon parameter, and special equipment or unusual methods may be required for its measurement. It may happen that in the state of the art a different parameter, or no parameter at all, is disclosed. In such situations a thorough analysis is required, whether the different parameter implies a technical difference in terms of the subject-matter concerned, or not. It may well be that the use of a particular parameter disguises a lack of novelty.

If a product according to the invention is identical to a product of the state of the art, except in respect of a parameter, the presumption of lack of novelty should be made, unless it can be shown on the basis of the available information that there exists, in fact, a difference. A typical example of such situations are two products which are produced, using the same starting products and the same manufacturing process. Then, in the first place an objection of lack of novelty arises (Guidelines F-IV, 4.11).

6.5 Novelty of selection inventions

The sections below follow closely the Guidelines and the Case Law Book, I.C.6. These sources should be consulted for detailed information.

The state of the art often comprises documents disclosing subject-matter in general terms. Such disclosures encompass a number of more specific technical teachings. In assessing the novelty of subject-matter encompassed by the general teaching, the question arises whether the latter makes the more specific teachings fully or partially accessible to the public. In other words, it has to be established, whether the general term used in the citation discloses the more specific subject-matter. In such cases the disclosure of the state of the art needs to be identified with great care.

Since situations of this kind occur frequently in Chemistry, the relevant case law usually relates to this technical field.

There are two main types of situations:
- Assessment of the novelty of chemical substances and groups of substances in respect of generic formulae, for example Markush formulae (i.e. single claims or groups defining alternatives (an entity selected from the group consisting of A, B, C and D)).
- Assessment of the novelty of products or processes defined by a range of a parameter, compared with products or processes comprised in the state of the art and characterised by a broader or overlapping range of the same parameter.

These types differ mainly in technical terms, but the same principles of patent law apply to both.

6.5.1 Selection of chemical substances or groups of substances from generic formulae comprised in the state of the art

(Reference is made to the Guidelines G-VI, 8(i)(a), (b) and Case Law Book I.C.6.1 and 6.2.

In determining the novelty of a selection, it has to be decided, whether the selected elements are disclosed in an individualised, i.e. concrete form in the prior art (T 12/81).

Single list principle

A selection from a single list of specifically disclosed elements does not confer novelty.

Two lists principle

732 If a selection from two or more lists of a certain length has to be made in order to arrive at a specific combination of features, then the resulting combination of features, not specifically disclosed in the prior art, confers novelty.

Examples: Selections from two or more lists

733 Example 1: The selection of individual chemical compounds from a known generic formula, whereby the compound selected results from the selection of specific substituents from two or more "*lists*" of substituents given in the known generic formula. The same applies to specific mixtures resulting from the selection of individual components from lists of components making up the prior art mixture.

734 Example 2: The selection of starting materials for the manufacture of a final product.

6.5.2 Selection of sub-ranges from broader ranges comprised in the state of the art

735 Reference is made to the Guidelines G-VI, 8(ii) and Case Law Book I.C.6.3.

736 A sub-range selected from a broader numerical range of the prior art is considered novel, if both of the following two criteria are simultaneously fulfilled (T 261/15; T 279/89):
(1) The selected sub-range is narrow compared to the known range;
(2) The selected sub-range is sufficiently far removed from any specific examples disclosed in the prior art and from the end-points of the known range.

737 In addition, the selection should not be arbitrarily.

738 An effect occurring only in the claimed sub-range cannot in itself confer novelty on that sub-range. However, such a technical effect occurring in the selected sub-range, but not in the whole of the known range, can confirm that the selection is not arbitrary, i.e. that the invention is novel and not merely a specimen of the prior art.

739 The meaning of "*narrow*" and "*sufficiently far removed*" has to be decided on a case-by-case basis. It is important that not just an arbitrary choice is made. For the latter, it is helpful if there is a specific technical effect associated with the claimed sub-range. That technical effect occurring within the selected range may also be the same effect as that attained with the broader known range, but to a greater extent.

740 The "*two lists principle*" applies to the selection of sub-ranges of two or more parameters from corresponding known ranges (Guidelines G-VI, 8(i)(c)).

6.5.3 Overlapping ranges

741 Reference is made to the Guidelines G-VI, 8(iii) and Case Law Book I.C.5.2.2.

742 The assessment of novelty in the case of overlapping ranges, for example numerical ranges or chemical formulae, is made on the basis of the same principles as in other cases of selection inventions (T 666/89). The whole content of the document representing the state of the art has to be taken into consideration.

743 As to overlapping ranges or numerical ranges of physical parameters, novelty is destroyed by the following items:
- An explicitly disclosed end-point of the known range;
- Any explicitly disclosed intermediate values;
- Any specific examples of the state of the art in the area of overlap.

744 It is not sufficient to exclude specific novelty destroying values comprised in the state of the art. It must also be considered, whether the skilled person, having regard to the technical facts and taking the general technical knowledge into account, would seriously contemplate applying the technical teaching of the prior art document in the range of overlap. If it can be fairly assumed that he would do so, the conclusion is that novelty is lacking.

745 The criteria mentioned in the context of the selection of sub-ranges (see above) can be applied in an analogous manner for assessing the novelty of overlapping numerical ranges (T 17/85).

746 As far as overlapping chemical formulae are concerned, novelty is acknowledged if the claimed subject-matter is distinguished from the prior art in the range of overlap by a new technical element, i.e. a new technical teaching (T 12/90, reasons Point 2.6). If this is not the case, then it must be considered whether the skilled person would seriously

contemplate working in the range of overlap and/or would accept that the area of overlap is directly and unambiguously disclosed in an implicit manner in the prior art (T 536/95). If this is the case, then novelty is lacking.

6.5.4 Multiple selections

Reference is made to the Case Law Book I.C.6.3.3.

In decision T 653/93 the Board of Appeal held that the claimed process was novel since it involved a selection in the form of a combination of three process features with selected ranges, and product features with specific limits, a combination not disclosed in the prior document.

In such situations the novelty cannot be assessed by contemplating the ranges of the various parameters separately. This would amount to an artificial and unjustified approach.

6.6 Novelty test

According to the *"novelty test"*, an invention lacks novelty, if all features are disclosed in combination in a single document. There is no need that all features be expressly mentioned in the document, since the disclosure comprises also any implicit features. Equivalents are not prejudicial to the novelty, even if they are well known (Guidelines G-VI, 2).

Vice versa, an invention is novel if the combination of all its features cannot be derived directly and unambiguously from any single document contained in the state of the art.

The novelty test is also used as a tool for assessing, whether an amendment made by way of addition complies with Art. 123(2) EPC, or not (Guidelines H-IV, 2.2).

6.7 Examples from past papers

Genus – species

The Examiner raised a novelty objection based on [005] of D1 against claim 3 as filed in paper B Chemistry 2015.

Claim 3 of the application as filed claims an airbag composition (…) in which the composition comprises (…) hydrotalcite as a secondary slag forming agent.

The Examiner observes that "Document D1 discloses an airbag composition comprising a triazole or tetrazole-type compound as fuel, an oxidant and a carbide or nitride as a slag forming agent. Oxides or hydroxides of titanium or aluminium can be added to the slag forming agent in order to improve the slag formation. Paragraph [005] also shows that clays can be used. It would appear that hydrotalcite falls within this definition. The subject-matter of claims 1 to 6 lacks novelty over this disclosure".

It was expected from the candidates that the Examiner uses a genus to anticipate a species. This is not in line with normal practice.

Difference in wording

In paper B 2021, claim 1 refers to "drain holes (5) permitting moisture to drain from the upper to the lower compartment". The Examiner raises novelty objections using the following argument: "D1 to D3 disclose the container of claim 1. Note that the mesh used in D2 and D3 is considered a support with drain holes, since the mesh of D2 or D3 is also suitable for draining excess moisture from the organic substrate".

7 Inventive Step

7.1 Legal basis

EPC Articles and Rules

Art. 52(1) EPC
Art. 56 EPC

Guidelines

G-VII: Inventive step
G-VII, 2: State of the art; date of filing
G-VII, 3: Person skilled in the art
G-VII, 4: Obviousness
G-VII, 5: Problem-solution approach
G-VII, 6: Combining pieces of prior art
G-VII, 7: Combination *vs.* juxtaposition or aggregation
G-VII, 9: Origin of an invention
G-VII, 10: Secondary indicators
G-VII, 12: Selection inventions
G-VII, 14: Dependent claims; claims in different categories
G-VII, 15: Examples
G-VII, Annex: Examples relating to the requirement of inventive step – indicators

Case Law Book

I.D: Inventive step
I.D.1: Introduction
I.D.2: Problem and solution approach
I.D.3: Closest prior art
I.D.4: Technical problem
I.D.5: "Could-would approach"
I.D.7: Expectation of success, especially in the field of genetic engineering and biotechnology
I.D.8: Skilled person
I.D.9: Assessment of inventive step
I.D.10: Secondary indicia in the assessment of inventive step

Important decisions

See Case Law Book.

Problem inventions, *"one way street"*, *"bonus"*, *"could/would"* — T 2/83

The discovery of a yet unrecognised problem may, in certain circumstances, give rise to patentable subject-matter in spite of the fact that the claimed solution is retrospectively trivial and in itself obvious (*"problem inventions"*). For instance the so-called analogy processes in chemistry are only claimable as long as the problem, *i.e.* the need to provide certain patentable products as their effect, is not yet within the state of the art.

It appears, however, that whenever the modification of a known device does not involve a real choice in the direction of a clearly desired improvement, i.e. the skilled man is in an inevitable *"one-way-street"* situation, the additional provision of a yet unsuspected *"bonus"* or side effect, which may be interpreted as a solution of a yet unknown problem, should not necessarily be decisive for patentability.

The question regarding inventive step is not whether the skilled man could have made a particular modification, but whether he actually would have done so in expectation of some improvement or advantage.

Partial problems — T 389/86

The characterising portion of claim 1 contains two sets of features relating to two solutions of *"partial problems"*. There is no interaction between these two sets of features that brings about a technical solution in excess of the sum of their individual effects, the said features being merely juxtaposed. Although the two partial problems have a common basis in so far as they both derive from use of a plastic tube plate, the fact still remains, that the two claimed sets of features are not functionally interdependent for the purpose of solving the two partial problems. In these circumstances, the combined effect of the two sets of features cannot be said to involve an inventive step.

766 What has to be established instead is, whether each of them separately is obvious in the light of the prior art. The subject-matter of claim 1 can be regarded as involving an inventive step if at least one of the sets is found to be inventive.

767 **Analogy processes, advantages and disadvantages, prejudice** T 119/82

The effect of a process manifests itself in the result, i.e. in the product in chemical cases, together with all its internal characteristics and the consequences of its history of origin, *e.g.* quality, yield and economic value. It is well established that analogy processes are patentable insofar as they provide a novel and inventive product. This is because all the features of the analogy process can only be derived from an effect which is as yet unknown and unsuspected (problem invention). If, on the other hand, the effect is wholly or partially known, *e.g.* the product is old or is a novel modification of an old structural part, the invention, i.e. the process or the intermediate therefore, should not merely consist of features which are already necessarily and readily derivable from the known part of the effect in an obvious manner having regard to the state of the art.

768 Obviousness is not only at hand when the skilled man would have seen all the advantages of acting in a certain manner, but also when he could clearly see why he should not act in the suggested manner in view of its predictable disadvantages or absence of improvement, provided he was indeed correct in his assessment of all the consequences.

769 Appellants who wish to rely on a prejudice which might have diverted the skilled man away from the alleged invention have the onus of demonstrating the existence of such prejudice.

7.2 Relevance to Paper B

770 Although the Implementing provisions to the Regulation of the EQE for paper B are not as clear as these for paper A, which instruct candidates to bear in mind the requirements of the EPC, in particular regarding novelty and inventive step, when they draft the claims (Rule 23(3) IPREE), the issue of inventive step is much more important in paper B than it is in paper A. Rule 24(3) IPREE does require that for paper B a response is expected that shall be in the form of a letter to the EPO accompanied by the claims supplied by the client, amended as appropriate <u>to meet the requirements of the EPC</u>. In the response, a convincing, detailed and meaningful analysis of inventive step has to be developed. This importance for the concept of inventive step is expressed in marks. For paper A, one can obtain around 5 marks for a decent problem definition in the introductory part of the description of an application; for paper B, one can normally get around 25 marks, and sometimes even up to 40, for the inventive step argumentation.

771 The claimed invention has to meet the requirement of inventive step in order to be patentable in accordance with the EPC (Art. 52(1) and Art. 56 EPC). It is not feasible to draft claims which embrace obvious subject-matter. The argumentation in support of an inventive step must be presented in the letter to the EPO, necessary to show that the independent claims are in conformity with the EPC.

772 The inventive step argumentation in paper B should be following the problem-solution approach described in all details in the Guidelines, Part G, Ch. VII, 5. And for each step in the problem-solution approach marks are available.

7.3 Outlines of the problem and solution approach

773 The question, whether there is an inventive step or not, arises only if the invention is novel. Thus, before any conclusions on inventive step can be drawn, the novelty of the claimed subject-matter must be firmly established.

774 The relevant state of the art consists of the prior art acknowledged in the patent application filed by the client, the content of the separate documents representing the state of the art and mentioned in the communication, and the common general knowledge of the person skilled in the art, which is not necessarily available in writing, *i.e.* in textbooks or

the like. It may also form part of the unwritten *"mental furniture"* of person skilled in the art (Guidelines G-VII, 2; T 939/92, reasons Point 2.3). Any acknowledgement of the state of the art in the patent application as filed or in the letter from the client should be regarded as being correct (Rule 22(3) IPREE).

The relevant person skilled in the art is a practitioner in the technical field concerned, who has average knowledge and abilities and is aware of the common general knowledge (Guidelines G-VII, 3).

The question to consider is, whether it would have been obvious to the person skilled in the art to arrive at the claimed subject-matter (or better: something falling within the terms of a claim) at the time of the invention. If this is the case, the invention is lacking inventive step (Art. 56 EPC; Guidelines G-VII, 4).

According to the case law of the Boards of Appeal the assessment of inventive step has to be based on objective criteria. Taking the state of the art as the starting point, the technical problem and its solution have to be evaluated. For this purpose the Boards of Appeal apply consistently the *"problem-and-solution approach"*. According to the Guidelines the application of the problem-and-solution approach is quasi mandatory (Guidelines G-VII, 5). For paper B of the EQE, the problem-solution approach actually is mandatory!

The problem-and-solution approach involves three main tasks which have to be performed, namely:
(1) Determining the closest prior art
(2) Defining the technical problem underlying the invention
(3) Considering whether the invention would have been obvious to the person skilled in the art, or not.

These tasks are outlined below in turn.

(1) Determining the closest prior art

There exists extensive case law of the Boards of Appeal regarding the determination of the closest prior art. Usually, the following criteria are applied for selecting the closest prior art. They are not mutually exclusive. On the contrary two or three of them, or even all four may be fulfilled simultaneously.

Criteria for the selection of the closest prior art

- Same technical field
- Same purpose or effect (Case Law Book I.D.3.2)
- Similarity of the technical problem (Case Law Book I.D.3.3)
- Maximum number of relevant features in common, or minimum number of structural modifications (Case Law Book I.D.3.1; 2)

Another criterion used incidentally by the Boards of Appeal is the selection of the *"most promising springboard"*, which is defined as the prior art which, when taken as the starting point, renders the invention most obvious (Case Law Book I.D.3.4.1)

In selecting the closest prior art, the first consideration is that it should relate to the same technical field. If, for example, the invention resides in an industrial process for forming artificial patinas, it is likely that the closest prior art is another industrial process for producing patinas, rather than a research paper.

The next consideration is usually the purpose or effect, or the technical problem addressed by a particular prior art.

There is a broad consensus that the number of relevant features in common is the least important among the selection criteria.

Once the closest prior art has been selected, the features which distinguish the invention from the closest prior art are identified. There must be at least one distinguishing feature. If there is none, the invention lacks novelty. The distinguishing features may be structural, functional or, in exceptional cases, non-technical.

Mixtures of technical and non-technical features

Any non-technical features are taken into account only to the extent that they make a contribution to the technical effects of the invention, which normally requires an interaction with the technical subject-matter. Non-technical features as such, and technical features that give only rise to non-technical effects, for example effects relating to subject-matter excluded from patentability, are disregarded (Guidelines G-VII, 5.2; 5.4; 5.4.1).

(2) Defining the technical problem underlying the invention

786 Before the technical problem can be established, the effects produced by the distinguishing features, possibly in combination with some other features of the invention, have to be assessed. To do this, the content of the letter from the client, the closest prior art and the distinguishing features are studied. All technical effects resulting, or at least associated with the distinguishing features are identified and noted. Subsequently the technical problem is formulated.

787 Within the framework of the problem-and-solution approach, the technical problem, occasionally called *"objective technical problem"* to distinguish it from the technical problem as presented by the client – the subjective technical problem-, can be defined as follows:

788 The objective technical problem consists in modifying or adapting the closest prior art, to provide the technical effects that the invention provides over the closest prior art.

789 For the special case of mixtures of technical and non-technical features, the procedure is explained in the Guidelines G-VII, 5.4; 5.4.1.

790 The technical problem defined in this manner is not necessarily identical with the problem presented by the client, since the objective technical problem is based on the objective facts of the case, not on subjective perceptions (Guidelines G-VII, 5.2).

791 When defining the technical problem, care should be taken not to include any pointers to the solution. In the problem-and-solution approach, the technical problem is defined in terms of the technical effects to be achieved. In contrast, the solution of the problem is defined in terms of the technical features of the invention. These two issues must not be mixed up.

792 It may happen that two or more distinguishing features are unrelated and give rise to separate technical effects. Then each effect is treated separately, with the result that there is a plurality of distinguished technical effects and solutions. Such a scenario is called a situation of an aggregation of *"partial problems"* (Guidelines G-VII, 5.2; 6; 7; T 389/86).

(3) Considering whether the invention would have been obvious to the person skilled in the art

793 Here, the question is, whether the state of the art contained any pointer that would – not simply could, but actually would – have prompted the skilled person, faced with the technical problem, to modify or adapt the closest prior art in the manner suggested by the invention, thus arriving at the latter without exercising inventive skills (Guidelines G-VII, 4; 5.3; T 2/83). Each document comprised in the state of the art has to be assessed in respect of its structural and functional similarity with the invention.

Combining pieces of prior art

794 In the context of the problem-solution approach, it is permissible to combine the disclosure of one or more documents, parts of documents or other pieces of prior art, for example a public prior use or general technical knowledge, with the closest prior art.

795 When more than one disclosure has to be combined with the closest prior art in order to arrive at the combination of features of the invention, this may be taken as an indication of the presence of an inventive step (Guidelines G-VII, 6).

Combination of features versus juxtaposition or aggregation

796 When a claim consists of a combination of features, it is not correct to argue that the separate features of the combination taken by themselves are known or obvious and that, consequently, the whole subject-matter claimed is obvious. The situation is different, however, where a claim is merely an *"aggregation"* or *"juxtaposition"* of features (Guidelines G-VII, 5.2).

A set of technical features is regarded as a combination of features, whenever the features interact to produce a combined technical effect, which is different from the sum of the technical effects of the individual features (Guidelines G-VII, 7).

Indications of inventive step

There are various indications in support of the presence of an inventive step, in particular the following:
- The presence of an unexpected technical effect (Guidelines G-VII, 10.2)
- A long-felt need (Guidelines G-VII, 10.3)
- Selection inventions (Guidelines GL-VII, 12)

The following indication is neutral regarding the presence of an inventive step:

Commercial success alone is not to be regarded as an indicator in support of inventive step (Guidelines G-VII, 10.3).

A wide variety of indications and examples in favour or against the presence of an inventive step is set out in the Annex to Chapter VII of the Guidelines. These relate to the application of known measures, the combination of features, obvious and non-obvious selections and technical prejudice.

Dependent claims

If the subject-matter of an independent claim is novel and involves an inventive step, there is no need to investigate separately, whether any dependent claim referring directly or indirectly back to the independent claim is novel and inventive. These requirements are automatically met by virtue of the reference to the independent claim (Guidelines G-VII, 13). The condition is that the dependent claims are truly dependent within the meaning of Rule 43(4) EPC.

Independent claims in different categories

Similarly, if a claim to a product is new and non-obvious there is no need to investigate the novelty and non-obviousness of any claims for a process which inevitably results in the manufacture of that product or of any claims for a use of that product. In particular, analogy processes, *i.e.* processes which themselves would otherwise not involve an inventive step, are patentable insofar as they provide a novel and inventive product (Guidelines G-VII, 13).

7.4 The meaning of the requirement of inventive step in Paper B

Paper B is based on the assumption that a client wishes to obtain a patent based on an invention described in a European patent application (Rule 24(2) IPREE). Against this background, it may be assumed that all positive facts described in the patent application and reported by the client are true, unless there are indications to the contrary. Undoubtedly there is an invention involving an inventive step described in the patent application, and there are no reasons to look for arguments which could raise doubts as to the technical effects and advantages of the invention.

For paper B, it may well be that the client himself describes certain limitations in his instructions letter. For example, if the invention relates to a process for producing a chemical compound, the client may explain that the desired product is not obtained, when the process is carried out in the presence of an acid. The client may also admit that a particular feature is obvious to any skilled person, *etc.* Such evidence should be accepted and taken seriously (Rule 22(3) IPREE). Whenever a particular embodiment is not working properly, for example, or not working at all, it has to be excluded from the scope of the claim, even if it is novel, because it does not involve an inventive step. To draw up a claim that is clearly not in accordance with the provisions of the EPC would be a major mistake. Similarly, to draw up a claim that is clearly not in accordance with the wishes of the client, would not result in marks.

806 In paper B the following things should be done regarding inventive step:
- To establish the novelty of the invention described by the client
- To determine the closest prior art; to collect all marks, an explicit statement is expected on which piece of prior art forms the closest prior art. Further, arguments are expected as to why that piece of prior art forms the closest prior art AND why the other piece(s) of prior art is(are) less suitable.
- To identify the distinguishing features of the invention
- To identify the technical effects produced by, or at least associated with the distinguishing features
- To formulate the technical problem underlying the invention
- To check whether this technical problem is solved by the claimed features and either to rephrase the technical problem or to exclude any non-working embodiments from the scope of the independent claim
- To exclude any other subject-matter which manifestly does not involve an inventive step
- To argue why the closest prior art taken *per se* does not bring the skilled person to the claimed subject-matter
- To argue why, when starting from the closest prior art, the skilled person would not come to the claimed subject-matter taking into account the other pieces of prior art. This may involve providing arguments why the closest prior art document would not be combined with a particular other piece of prior art, and/or arguments why, when the closest prior art document would be combined with another piece of prior art, this combination would not result in the claimed subject-matter.

7.5 Examples from past papers

807 **Selecting the closest prior art**

Paper B 2018 contains three prior art documents, which all deal with fuses. The Examiner raises an inventive step objection in respect of claim 4: "D2 discloses in paragraphs [001], [002] a fuse (201) having a cover layer (205) covering the fuse track (203). The skilled person, seeking to improve the fuse of D1, would consider employing the cover layer of D2 in the fuse of D1. Furthermore, D1 clearly discloses in Figs. 1A and 2 a fuse track (103) having a neck portion.". So, apparently, the Examiner started from D1 as closed prior art; for, a problem is formulated relative to D1.

808 In the Examiners' report, this fact is used as an argument for selecting D1 to form the closest prior art: "The closest prior art is D1. It is noted that the examiner himself/herself starts from D1 in the inventive step assessment in point 4 of the communication. The fuse disclosed in D1 displays the fewest differences from the invention set out in independent claim 1 of the present application, (…). Furthermore, D1 addresses the same purpose of reducing reflow of the fuse track made of AlCu alloy after blowing because it refers in par. [002] to the problem that fuses made with some alloys may become conducting again after blowing and states that the fuses made with the above-mentioned alloy have improved values when assessed using the standard reflow index".

809 So, three arguments were made as to why D1 is the closest prior art. Normally, the third argument is the most important one to start with.

810 Also D2 and D3 were related to the same technical field of fuses.

'The Examiners' report states for D2 that the fuse known from it comprises more differences from that of the present invention (than D1). Further, "In D2 the problem of metal reflow is not referred to. In fact, since D2 by design works with a micro-explosion, the problem of metal reflow occurring with the alloy AlCu cannot arise in the first place, D2 going in a completely different direction. For the above reasons D2 does not present a promising starting point".

811 For D3, it is argued that "D3 mentions the problem of reflow and discloses a layer of epoxy resin, but teaches a quite different solution from that of the present invention. The "upper layer" made of epoxy resin mentioned in par. [003] does not cover the fuse track but is placed between the fuse track and the substrate. Thus D3 leads away from the solution proposed in the present invention of providing a cover layer on the fuse track as a solution to the problem of reducing reflow".

The Examiners' report of paper B 2018 gave an explicit framework for the "Arguments in support of inventive step":

Arguments should support the features of the independent claim. They should be convincing and well-structured. In order to obtain full marks in this section, arguments should have been presented which fully answer the question as to why the skilled person, knowing the teaching of the prior art as a whole, would not arrive at the claimed subject matter.

Such arguments can be structured to consider the following aspects:
"• Would the skilled person arrive at the subject matter of the claim by considering the teaching of the closest prior art on its own?
• Would the skilled person consider combining the teaching of the closest prior art with that of other prior art documents in order to solve the objective technical problem?
• If the skilled person were to combine the teaching of the closest prior art with other items of prior art, would (s)he arrive at the subject matter of the claim?"

This framework should always be in the back of your head when sitting paper B!

In paper B 2019, there were 3 independent claims.

Claim 1 was directed to a cooking process including the steps: providing a heat storage unit (3); concentrating solar radiation (12) onto the heat storage unit (3) to heat it; and cooking food (8) placed on the heat storage unit (3).

Claim 2 was directed to a heat storage unit (3) (suitable) for use in the process of claim 1.

And claim 6 was directed to a solar cooker (1) comprising: a heat storage unit (3) according claim 2.

For claim 1 and for claim 2, different documents were expected to be the closest prior art. In addition, two problem-solution approaches were expected.

For claim 1 the selection of the closest prior art was straight-forward: D1.

For claim 2, the identification of the closest prior art was more challenging. D2 is considered as the appropriate choice of the closest prior art. D2 is considered as the closest prior art since it relates to the same general purpose of cooking and has the most features in common with claim 2. The radiator of D3 is a less promising starting point for the skilled person to obtain the invention, because any modification of the device of D3 would be made by the skilled person with the purpose of obtaining a device of the same type (T570/91, T749/11), i.e. a radiator. D3 leads the skilled person away from using a salt composition with a high melting temperature ([004]) above 115°C in a radiator. The heat storage unit of D1 is an aluminium plate and thus has fewer features in common with the invention as compared to D2.

The differences with the closest prior art assisting on finding the broadest scope of claims.

In mock paper B, novelty objections were raised in respect of a claim directed to an airbag module for protecting a vehicle occupant in a collision comprising: – a control unit; – a gas generator (1) comprising a housing (20) and a gas-generating composition generating gases upon ignition; and – a fabric cushion (2) comprising a pressure regulating valve (3). The client proposes to limit the subject-matter of claim 1 to the subject-matter of former claim 3, with the further restriction that the composition has to have a weight ratio of guanidine borate to ammonium perchlorate between 2:1 and 5:1. Claim 3 teaches a gas-generating composition, comprising guanidine borate, ammonium perchlorate, and either sodium nitrate or potassium sulphate. According to the client, the range of 2:1 to 5:1 is not specifically disclosed in the prior art documents and is linked to a special technical effect.

When checking support in the application as filed, it appears that the range of 2:1 to 5:1 is only directly and unambiguously derivable for the embodiment of guanidine borate, ammonium perchlorate, and potassium sulphate; not with sodium nitrate.

In this mock paper B, there are only two prior art documents, D1 and D2. D1 and D2 both relate airbags. D1 however explicitly relates to airbag modules comprising pyrotechnical powder compositions, whereas D2 only relates to pyrotechnical powder compositions used in airbag modules. Since independent claim 1 relates to an airbag module, and not to a pyrotechnical powder, D1 is considered to be the closest prior art document.

If the amended claim suggested by the client and amended to bring it into conformity with Art. 123(2) EPC is compared with D1, the following differences are found: the gas composition being guanidine borate, ammonium perchlorate, and potassium sulphate and the weight ratio of guanidine borate to ammonium perchlorate being between 2:1 and 5:1.

823 When looking for technical effects, [0014] teaches that "The composition comprising sodium nitrate produces a flame. As an alternative to sodium nitrate, we found that potassium sulphate, a specific member of the family of sulphates, can be added to the composition. The composition with potassium sulphate not only produces large amounts of gas of a lower temperature, but also surprisingly and contrary to all other known additives, prevented the formation of flames during the gas-generating reaction in all the compositions we tested".

824 [0015] teaches "The weight ratio of guanidine borate to ammonium perchlorate usually determines the speed at which gas is generated. Surprisingly, internal research, which tested weight ratios ranging from 1:1 to 10:1, showed that when a weight ratio between 2:1 and 5:1 is used in the presence of potassium sulphate, the gas generation is much faster than the gas generation observed at any other weight ratio".

825 One should realise that the obtention of one of these two technical effects could already bear the invention; that is, could already be used to argue inventive step. This makes that the range of 2:1 to 5:1 can go to a dependent claim and is not needed in claim 1.

8 Claims and Clarity

8.1 Legal basis

EPC Articles and Rules
Art. 69: Extent of protection
Art. 78(1)(c) EPC: Requirements of a European patent application
Art. 82 EPC: Unity of invention
Art. 84: Claims
Rule 43 EPC: Form and content of claims
Rule 49(9) EPC: General provisions governing the presentation of the application documents

Guidelines
F-IV: Claims (Art. 84 and formal requirements)
F-IV, 1: General
F-IV, 2: Form and content of claims
F-IV, 3: Kinds of claim
F-IV, 3.4: Independent and dependent claims
F-IV, 4: Clarity and interpretation of claims
F-IV, 5: Conciseness, number of claims
F-IV, 6: Support in description
F-IV, Annex: Examples concerning essential features
F-V: Unity of invention
F-V, 3.2.5: Markush grouping (alternatives in a single claim)
F-V, 3.2.7: Intermediate and final products
F-V, 5: Dependent claims

Case Law Book
II.A: Claims
II.A.1: Basic principles
II.A.2: Form, content and conciseness of claims
II.A.3: Clarity of claims
II.A.4: Disclaimer
II.A.5: Claims supported by the description
II.A.6: Interpretation of claims
II.A7: Product-by-process claims

Important decisions
See Case Law Book

8.2 Requirements according to Art. 84 EPC

The claims are a mandatory part of European patent application (Art. 78(1)(c) EPC). They define the matter for which protection is sought (Art. 84 EPC). In Art. 84 EPC the three basic requirements are laid down, namely:
- Clarity
- Support by the description
- Conciseness

These requirements have to be met simultaneously. They apply to individual claims and likewise to the (set of) claims as a whole.

The Guidelines, Chapter F-IV, 4 and F-IV, 5 contain extensive information about the requirements of clarity and support, as well as guidance regarding the practice to be followed. In real life, the requirement of conciseness is particularly important in the search stage. In the examination stage, objections of lack of conciseness are raised only in exceptional cases.

8.3 Provisions regarding the form and content of claims

833 The provisions regarding the form and content of claims are laid down *inter alia* in Rule 43 EPC. The main requirements for claims as indicated in Rule 43 EPC and the Guidelines Chapter F-IV, 2.1 to 2.4 may be summarised as follows:

Requirements pertaining to the form and content of claims

834 The matter for which protection is sought must be defined in terms of the technical features (Rule 43(1) EPC). Statements of purpose are permissible and often necessary for reasons of clarity. Non-technical features may be included in claims under certain conditions. References to commercial advantages are excluded. References which attempt to expand the scope of a claim in a vague und undefined manner, such as a reference to the *"spirit of the invention"* are also excluded (Guidelines F-IV, 4.4).

Independent claims have to contain a statement indicating the designation of the subject-matter of the invention (Rule 43(1)(a) EPC).

835 Independent claims must contain all features necessary for the definition of the claimed subject-matter, i.e. all essential features (Rule 43(1)(a), (b) EPC; Guidelines F-IV, 4.5).

836 The subject-matter of a claim in one category may to some extent be defined in terms of features from another category, but only under the condition that the category of the claim remains to be clear (Art. 84 EPC; Guidelines F-IV, 3.8).

837 Product-by-process claims are permissible only when the product cannot be defined properly by its structural or functional features. The product as such must fulfil the requirements for patentability, *i.e.* it must *inter alia* be new and inventive (Guidelines F-IV, 4.12).

838 Independent claims should be formulated in the two part form, if appropriate (Rule 43(1) (a), (b) EPC; Guidelines F-IV, 2.2; 2.3).

839 An independent claim may contain a reference to a claim in another category, or to particular features which belong to another category of claims, provided it is clear to which extent features of the claim referred to are included by the reference (Guidelines F-IV, 3.8).

840 When an application contains more than one independent claim in the same category, the subject-matter of the claimed subject-matter must comply with the requirement of unity of invention (Art. 82 EPC) and, in addition, with Rule 43(2) EPC. If the independent claims do not fall under one of the exceptions a), b) or c) mentioned in Rule 43(2) EPC, multiple independent claims are not permissible.

841 A claim, whether independent or dependent, may refer to alternatives, but the number and presentation of alternatives in a single claim must not make the claim unclear or difficult to construe (Guidelines F-IV, 3.7).

842 Dependent claims have to define particular embodiments of the invention (Rule 43(3) EPC).

843 Dependent claims must contain a reference to the – independent or dependent – previous claim(s) on which they depend (Rule 43(4) EPC).

844 Any dependent claim must include all features of the claim to which it refers back (Rule 43(4) EPC).

845 The claims have to be grouped together in the most appropriate manner (Rule 43(4) EPC; Guidelines F-IV, 3.5; Guidelines F-IV, 4.24).

846 The number of claims has to be reasonable, account being taken of the nature of the invention (Rule 43(5) EPC; Guidelines F-IV, 5).

847 The claims must not contain any references to the specification or the drawings in specifying the technical features, except when absolutely necessary (Rule 43(6) EPC; Guidelines F-IV, 4.17). In particular, expressions such as *"as described in part ... of the description"* or *"as illustrated in figure ... of the drawings"* are to be excluded.

848 When the application contains drawings, the features of the claims should be followed by the corresponding reference signs placed in parentheses (Rule 43(7) EPC; Guidelines F-IV, 4.19). These reference signs do not limit the claims in any way.

849 The claims must not contain any drawings (Rule 49(9) EPC).

850 The claims may contain chemical or mathematical formulae (Rule 49(9) EPC; Guidelines F-IV, 2.4). For reasons of clarity, the symbols and terms must be defined in the respective claims (Art. 84) EPC).

The claims may contain tables, but only if the subject-matter makes the use of tables desirable (Rule 49(9) EPC).

Requirements pertaining to the features of claims

Functional features are permissible, provided that the skilled person has no difficulties in providing some means of performing the function concerned without exercising inventive skill (Guidelines F-IV, 2.1; 6.5).

In general, features which attempt to define the invention in terms of the result to be achieved are not permissible. In exceptional cases they may be acceptable, in particular when the invention either can only be defined in such terms, or cannot otherwise be defined more precisely without unduly restricting the scope of the claims, and if the result can be directly and positively verified by tests or procedures adequately specified in the description or known to the person skilled in the art, so that no undue experimentation is required (Guidelines F.IV, 4.10). In these cases, these terms are called "functional claim language".

Features involving parameters are permissible, in principle, but they have to meet various conditions (Guidelines F-IV, 4.11; 4.18).

Negative limitations in the form of features expressly stating that an item is absent are permissible only if adding positive features to the claim would not define the subject-matter more clearly and concisely (G 1/03; T 4/80), or if positive features would unduly limit the scope of the claim (Guidelines F-IV, 4.20).

8.4 Kinds of claims

For full protection claims in more than one category are often needed. There are only two basic kinds of claim, namely:

Product claims

Product claims are directed to an entity. These claims relate to items having a physical structure, such as an apparatus, a chemical compound, etc.

Process claims

Process claims relate to activities or operations, in which the use of some tangible product for putting the process into practice is implied. For details, see Guidelines F-IV, 3.1.

Use claims relate to the use of an invention in the sense of the technical application thereof (Guidelines F-IV, 2.1). A use claim in a form such as "use of substance X as a catalyst" is construed to be equivalent to a process claim (Guidelines F-IV, 4.16).

Surgical, therapeutical and diagnostic methods when applied to the human or animal body are special categories of processes which are excluded from patentability by virtue of Art. 53(c) EPC. For claims to substances or compositions for use in such methods the provisions of Art. 54(4) EPC and Art. 54(5) EPC are applicable.

Art. 54(4) EPC and Art. 54(5) EPC provide for an exception from the general principle that product claims can only be obtained for (absolutely) novel products. However, this does not mean that product claims for the first and further medical uses need not fulfil all other requirements of patentability, especially the requirement of inventive step.

Where a substance or composition is already known, it may still be patentable under Art. 54(4) EPC for a *"first medical use"*.

Where a substance or composition is already known to have been used in a *"first medical use"*, it may still be patentable under Art. 54(5) EPC for any *"second or further medical use"*.

Claims directed to substances or compositions for a first or further medical use must be drafted in the specific format outlined in Art. 54(4) EPC and Art. 54(5) EPC.

The formulation *"Substance X for use as a medicament"* is permissible, even if X is a known substance, but its use in medicine is not known (first medical use).

Likewise, the formulation *"Substance X for use in the treatment of disease Y"* is permissible, even if X is a known substance and has been used as a medicament, but its use in the treatment of the specific disease Y is not known (second or further medical use).

8.5 Clarity and interpretation of claims

867 The requirements pertaining to the clarity and the interpretation of claims are explained in detail in the Guidelines Chapter F-IV, 4. Further information is provided by the Case Law Book A, in particular in Chapter II.A.1 to 8.

868 The following topics discussed in the Guidelines are particularly important:
F-IV, 4.1: Clarity
F-IV, 4.2: Interpretation
F-IV, 4.3: Inconsistencies
F-IV, 4.5: Essential features
F-IV, 4.6: Relative terms
F-IV, 4.7: Terms such as "about", "approximately" or "substantially"
F-IV, 4.8: Trade marks
F-IV, 4.9: Optional features
F-IV, 4.10: Result to be achieved
F-IV, 4.11: Parameters
F-IV, 4.12: Product-by-process claim
F-IV, 4.13: Interpretation of expressions such as *"Apparatus for ..."*, *"Method for ..."*
F-IV, 4.14: Definition by reference to (use with) another entity
F-IV, 4.15: The expression "in"
F-IV, 4.16: Use claims
F-IV, 4.17: References to the description or drawings
F-IV, 4.18: Methods of and means for measuring parameters referred to in claims
F-IV, 4.19: Reference signs
F-IV, 4.20: Negative limitations (e.g. disclaimers)
F-IV, 4.21: "Comprising" *vs.* "consisting"
F-IV, 4.22: Functional definition of a pathological condition
F-IV, 4.23: Broad claims
F-IV, 4.24: Order of claims

8.6 Support of the claims by the description

869 Art. 84 EPC requires the claims to be supported by the description. This means that there has to be a basis in the description for the subject-matter of every claim. The content of the description, if applicable together with the drawings, determines how broad a claim may be (Guidelines F.IV, 6.1). Most claims are generalisations from one or more particular embodiments or examples of the inventions. The extent to which generalisations are justified depends on the specific information provided by the description. The applicant should be allowed to cover all obvious modifications and equivalents encompassed by the description of the invention (Guidelines F-IV, 6.2). In particular, if it is reasonable to assume that all embodiments covered by a claim produce the technical effects of the invention, then the claim may be regarded as supported by the description, even if it is quite broad. The reason is that all such embodiments solve the technical problem.

870 A claim in broad generic form, which relates to a whole class of chemical compounds or other products, may be acceptable, if there is fair support in the description and there is no reason to suppose, that the invention cannot be worked through the whole of the field claimed (Guidelines F-IV, 6.3).

871 Claims defining the invention by means of functional features may be regarded as supported by the description, if the skilled person is able to recognise on the basis of his common general knowledge, which means can be used for performing the function, and if the skilled person considers that other means are also feasible. One example in the description may be sufficient, depending on the nature of the invention (Guidelines F-IV, 6.5; 2.1; 4.10).

8.7 Independent claims

8.7.1 General principles

872 The claims define the matter for which the applicant seeks protection (Rule 43(1) EPC). By definition, an independent claim is broader in scope than any dependent claim referring

back to it. Therefore, the broadest possible protection is determined by the independent claims.

Any independent claim contains the following mandatory elements:
- A statement indicating the designation of the subject-matter of the invention
- All essential technical features, if applicable in combination with any non-technical features
- Any claim comprises the features explicitly mentioned and, in addition, any implicit features

Definition of essential features

The essential features of a claim are those features, which are necessary for achieving the technical effects underlying the solution of the technical problem with which the invention is concerned (Guidelines F-IV, 4.5.2).

Any features which, even when explicitly mentioned in the context of the invention throughout the application, do not make a contribution to the solution of the problem are non-essential features. Such non-essential features may be included in independent claims, but they may lead to unnecessary limitations of the scope of the claims concerned.

Clarity and conciseness of the wording

The wording of the independent claims should be as clear and concise as possible.

Whenever possible, the subject-matter of a claim should be defined in terms of features belonging to the category of the claim. Thus, a product should be defined by its structural features or in appropriate cases by *"means plus function"* features, and not by process features. A process should be defined in terms of features relating to the actions or operations to be performed, and not by structural features.

If it is possible to define a product reasonably well by the indication of its structural features, a product-by-process claim is not the appropriate form of the claim.

It is sometimes unavoidable to rely on features belonging to another category than the claim. Thus, a device may be defined in terms of a function it is able to perform, or a process may be defined in terms of structural features of an apparatus for carrying out the process. Moreover, it is possible that a particular element of an apparatus can only be defined in terms of the process for its manufacture. In general, such claims are permissible, provided that the following conditions are met simultaneously (Guidelines F-IV, 3.8):

The category of the claim must be beyond any doubt; and the wording of the claim must express unambiguously, which kind of subject-matter is claimed.

Example:

"Catalyst X, when used for carrying out the process Y"

Such a claim raises doubts as to whether a product, *i.e.* a catalyst, or a process using the catalyst is claimed. For this reason, objections under (Rule 43(1) EPC) and Art. 84 EPC arise.

Independent claims containing a reference to another claim or to particular features from another claim

An independent claim may contain a reference to another claim. This does not mean that the claim automatically becomes dependent. The claim referred to may be in the same or a different category. It is possible that the reference to another claim does not relate to all features of the claim referred to, but only to one or more particular features. Another possibility is, that the reference relates to a feature which is replaced by another feature.

Examples:

Claim 1 (independent): Process

Claim 2 (independent):

"2. Apparatus for carrying out the process according to claim 1, ..."

or

Claim 1 (independent: Coffee machine, comprising a boiler, a coffee holder and an upper part.

Claim 2 (independent):

"*2. Cooking device, containing the boiler of the coffee machine according to claim 1, ...*"

or

Claim 1 (independent): Apparatus, containing the element X.

Claim 2 (independent):

"*2. Apparatus according to claim 1, wherein the element X is replaced by the element Y.*"

A claim to a particular product may refer to another interrelated product.

886 **Examples:**
"*2. Plug for use with the socket according to claim 1, ...*"
"*2. Receiver for receiving signals from the transmitter according to claim 1, ...*"

887 Such claims are permissible, provided that they specify the features of the claimed subject-matter in a clear manner.

888 In the absence of any technical features, except those contained in the claim referred to, an objection of lack of clarity and lack of compliance with Rule 43(1) EPC arises, particularly if a change of the claim category is involved (Guidelines F-IV, 3.8).

889 **Examples:**
"*2. Plug for use with the socket according to claim 1.*"
"*2. Receiver for the transmitter according to claim 1.*"
"*2. Apparatus for carrying out the process of Claim 1.*"

8.7.2 Things to avoid when drafting independent claims

890 Certain things should be avoided when drafting claims, because they may give rise to objections. Some selected items are listed below:

891 **Things to avoid ...**
- Inconsistencies
- Relative terms, except when necessary
- Terms like "*about*", "*approximately*", "*essentially*", "*substantially*", etc.
- Trademarks in independent claims, except when absolutely necessary
- Optional features in independent claims
- Features defining the result to be achieved
- Unusual parameters, except when necessary
- Product-by-process claims, except when necessary
- Use claims, except when needed for full protection
  - References to the description or drawings
- References to the "*spirit of the invention*"
- Negative limitations, for example disclaimers, except when necessary

8.8 Combinations of independent claims in different categories

892 A plurality of independent claims in different categories may form a group of separate inventions so linked as to form a single general inventive concept. In this case the subject matter of the invention meets the requirement of unity of invention. Within the limitations defined in Rule 43(2) EPC, independent claims may co-exist in a single application.

893 In general, the case law of the Boards of Appeal and the Guidelines permit the inclusion of any one of the following combinations of independent claims in the same application:

(1) In addition to an independent claim for a given product, an independent claim for a process specially adapted for the manufacture of the product, and an independent claim for a use of the product.
(2) In addition to an independent claim for a given process, an independent claim for an apparatus or means specifically designed for carrying out the process.
(3) In addition to an independent claim for a given product, an independent claim for a process specially adapted for the manufacture of the product and an independent claim for an apparatus or means specifically designed for carrying out the process.

8.9 More than one independent claim in the same category

According to Rule 43(2) EPC an application may contain more than one independent claim in the same category (product, process, apparatus or use) <u>only</u> if the subject-matter of the application involves one of the following:
(a) a plurality of interrelated products,
(b) different uses of a product or apparatus,
(c) alternative solutions to a particular problem, where it is inappropriate to cover these alternatives by a single claim.

In cases where an application discloses simultaneously more than one "*subsequent*" medical indications of a substance or composition, separate claims to the various medical indications are permissible in one application, but only if they meet the requirement of unity of invention (Guidelines G-VI, 7.1).

Rule 43(2) EPC is applied only when the independent claims meet the requirement of unity of invention (Art. 82 EPC). If there is lack of unity, the independent claims defining the separate inventions have to be removed from the set of claims (Guidelines F-V, 2). For full protection, one or more separate applications have to be filed. Separate subject-matter has to be removed from the claims anyway.

8.10 Relevance to Paper B

The claims to be amended form an important part of the answer paper. For single papers A 2017-2019 and 2021, they generated 30 marks. These marks are not given to the claims *per se*, but are allotted to the amendments carried out on the set of amended claim suggested by the client. If the set of claims suggested by the client is uploaded as part of the answer, you lose all these marks. With that set of claims, one can still pass the paper, but I can guarantee that this set suggested by the client is not entirely suitable for the argumentation, motivation and other reasoning expected by the examination committee.

The set of claims to be uploaded has to be in conformity with the provisions of the EPC. Particularly, the claims need to meet the requirements of Art. 123(2) EPC, of clarity, of novelty, of inventive step, of unity of invention, of Rule 43(2) EPC and of any of the other requirements of Art. 52–57 EPC.

In the day-to-day work, claims may be submitted tentatively in order to get a reasoned opinion from the examining division. Such a strategy is not acceptable under the conditions of the examination, where the subject-matter of the claims must be in a form that would result in the receipt of a communication under Rule 71(3) EPC.

8.11 Dependent claims

8.11.1 General principles applicable to dependent claims

Definition

A claim which includes all features of another claim is called "*dependent claim*". According to Rule 43(4) EPC such a claim contains, if possible at the beginning, a reference to a preceding claim, on which it depends.

Form and content of dependent claims

By definition, a dependent claim relates to a particular embodiment of the invention (Rule 43(3) EPC). Therefore, the scope of a dependent claim is narrower than the scope of the claim to which it refers back.

902 There are basically two possibilities for defining a particular embodiment, namely:
– specifying one or more features contained in the claim to which reference is made in the dependent claim; or
– adding one or more features.

903 Both kinds of specification may occur in a dependent claim.

904 It is not permissible to replace one of the features of the claim referred to by different features. A claim having the wording:

"Device according to claim 1, wherein the element X is replaced by an element Y"

is not a dependent claim within the meaning of Rule 43(4) EPC, because it does not include all features of the claim on which it depends. The claim may nevertheless be permissible as an independent claim.

905 Since a dependent claim includes the features of the preceding claims referred to, it is normally not appropriate to use the two-part form of the claim.

Function of dependent claims

906 The main function of dependent claims is to provide a fall-back position in case the independent claims are rejected.

907 Having a good fallback position is important in view of the strict application of the provisions regarding the admissibility of amendments, in particular Art. 123(2) EPC.

908 Any dependent claim should preferably contain at least one non-obvious feature giving rise to a special technical effect in addition to the technical effects produced by the subject-matter of the independent claim to which the dependent claim refers back. Therefore, for dependent claims, the focus should lie on technical features associated with some additional technical advantage. Ideally, such technical effects are surprising to the person skilled in the art.

909 Including trivial features in a dependent claim is useless, because the resulting claim does not provide a good fall-back position. It is even worse, if a dependent claim defines a non-working embodiment. In such a case, it can be concluded that the preceding independent claim, to which reference is made, encompasses non-working embodiments as well and is therefore too broad. Features which are described in the prior art in the same or a similar context as the invention are likely to be trivial.

910 Occasionally, applicants submit several dependent claims defining particular embodiments, which are already claimed in a preceding independent claim in the form of alternatives. Such dependent claims appear to be useless.

References in dependent claims according to Rule 43(4) EPC

911 Any dependent claim refers back, either directly or indirectly, to at least one independent claim.

912 If a dependent claim defines a particular feature, which can be added to more than one previous claim, either independent or dependent, the claim will refer back to more than one claim. Such multiple dependencies are permissible and often appropriate, provided that they are clear. Particular attention is required, whenever the reference contains a juxtaposition of linking words of the *"and/or"* type. This may easily lead to inconsistencies.

913 It has to be borne in mind that a multiple dependency is not construed as disclosing any individual combinations of the claims referred to. If a particular individual combination of claims gives rise to a special technical effect or advantage, it should be claimed in the form of a separate dependent claim containing a reference to the specific combination of claims.

914 It is not excluded that a claim be dependent on more than one independent claim. For example, the following set of claims is permissible:
Claim 1 (independent): *"1. Composition containing the compounds A and B."*
Claim 2 (independent): *"2. Use of the composition according to claim 1 as a herbicide."*
Claim 3 (dependent): *"3. Composition according to claim 1 or use according to claim 2, whereby the composition contains C as a further component."*

915 In general, such complex references lead easily to lack of clarity and should therefore be avoided.

Number and arrangement of the claims

All dependent claims referring back to a single preceding claim, and even more the multiple dependent claims, must be grouped together to the extent and in the most appropriate way possible (Rule 43(4) EPC; Guidelines F-IV, 3.5). As far as the precise order and sequence of the claims is concerned, there exists a large area of discretion.

The claims should be ordered with the broadest independent claim first, followed by any dependent claims referring back to the first independent claim. In the field of Chemistry, there is normally more than a single independent claim, for example a product claim and in addition a process claim. In such cases, the arrangement of the independent and dependent claims should be as simple as possible.

Often it is possible to draft a number of dependent claims all depending on a particular independent claim, and each narrowing down a specific feature of the independent claim. Such claims should be arranged accordingly.

As far as dependent claims referring back to previous claims are concerned, it is important to get the claim dependencies right. It is imperative to ensure that all dependent claims are consistent with themselves and the independent claims. In paper B, the back-referral may attract marks for complying with Art. 123(2) EPC and/or for complying with the clarity requirements.

All claims have to be numbered consecutively in Arabic numerals (Rule 43(5) EPC).

Regarding the number of claims to be drafted, there are no fixed limits, since the number depends on the nature of the invention. Rule 43(5) EPC says that the number of claims must be reasonable. For paper B, generally, the client will make a statement that no further claims are required than those that are in line with his wishes.

8.12 Relevance to Paper B

In paper B, a small number of dependent claims is normally expected. Generally, the letter from the applicant contains statements expressing his wishes. In addition, the set of amended claims suggested by the client provides further guidance for the number of claims expected.

Full points for dependent claims are only awarded if the following conditions are fulfilled:
- The references are consistent
- The references do not lead to a combination of contradicting features
- No aggregations of functionally independent features are included in a single claim
- The claim structure does not only set out the various embodiments one by one, but it covers also other possible combinations of features by appropriate multiple dependencies

8.13 Examples from past papers

Formal matters

An incorrect two-part form of the independent claim generally looses 1 mark from the total marks awarded for the amendments.

For missing or very incomplete reference signs in the claims, generally 1 mark is lost.

In the Examiners' reports of the papers B, it has often been indicated that there is no double penalisation. So when a candidate makes more than one errors or mistakes that are the same, only once 1 or more marks are deducted.

Different categories of claims

In paper B 2019, the set of 6 claims contained 3 independent claims:
1. A cooking process including the steps: providing a heat storage unit (3); concentrating solar radiation (12) onto the heat storage unit (3) to heat it; and cooking food (8) placed on the heat storage unit (3).
2. A heat storage unit (3) for use in the process of claim 1, characterised by: a box (4) having heat-insulating walls and an opening, the box (4) containing a salt composition (6), a light-absorbing plate (5) fitted in the opening and in thermal contact with

the salt composition (6), and a cooking surface (9) in thermal contact with the salt composition (6).
6. A solar cooker (1) comprising: a heat storage unit (3) according to any of claims 2 to 5; and a parabolic mirror (11) for concentrating solar radiation (12) on the light-absorbing plate (5) of the heat storage unit (3).

928 Claim 2 is suitable to be used in the process of claim 1.
Claim 6 comprises the heat storage unit of claim 2.
Clearly, there is no issue with Rule 43(2) EPC, and no arguments were expected, because the Examiner did not raise an objection under that Rule.

929 The issue of unity-of-invention did not play any role either, even not after amending claims 1 and 2 in completely different ways. The Examination Committee for this paper indicated this in the annual meeting between the EQE committees and EQE tutors, "because apparently the Examiner did not see any problems".
For claim 1 and for claim 2, different documents were expected to be the closest prior art.

930 In paper B Electricity/Mechanics 2016, the client proposed to overcome an objection under Rule 43(2) EPC by amending claim 5 to "A warning pole (20) comprising a warning system preferably according to any of the preceding claims".

931 Because of the term "preferably", this claim has two embodiment: an independent claim directed to a warning pole comprising a warning system without any further limitation, which has problems under Art. 123(2) EPC, novelty and inventive step problems; and a dependent claim having the limitations of one or more of the preceding claims.

932 In paper B 2021, there were 3 independent claims:
1. A container (1) for organic refuse, comprising
   a. an upper compartment (3) having a support (3a) for holding the refuse (7) populated with earthworms (8);
   b. a lower compartment (4) for collecting excess moisture (6);
   c. drain holes (5) permitting moisture to drain from the upper to the lower compartment; and
   d. an upwardly opening covering lid (2) which fits over the container (1).
4. A method for producing a fertilizer, the method comprising the following steps
   a. providing a container (1) comprising organic refuse (7) and worms (8);
   b. optionally, adjusting the moisture of the refuse;
   c. composting the refuse with the worms for a time sufficient to convert the refuse into fertilizer, and,
   d. optionally, separating worms from the fertilizer.
6. A calculation method for optimizing processing organic refuse, comprising the steps of
   a. defining a target value TV at time point $tp > 0$ for the amount of the earthworms (8) present in the refuse (7) at said time point tp;
   b. receiving data relating to the moisture of refuse (7) and the amount of earthworms (8) at a plurality of time points tp;
   c. determining if the value for the amount of earthworms (8) present in the refuse (7) at $tp > 0$ is equal to the defined target value TV for the amount of earthworms (8); and
   d. recommending adjusting the amount of moisture added to the refuse (7) at said time point tp, if the value for the amount of earthworms (8) present in the refuse at $tp > 0$ is not equal to the defined target value TV for the amount of earthworms (8).

933 Claims 1 and 4 were held to be anticipated. Claim 1 was not novel over any of D1, D2 and D3. Claim 4 was anticipated by D1 and D3.

934 The client suggests to amend claim 1 by specifying that it now comprises a water spraying device for adjusting the moisture. Particularly, the client suggests to add at the end of claim 1 "wherein the container comprises a water spraying device (13) for adjusting the moisture".

935 The client noticed that in D2 the water spraying device is exclusively used for cleaning. The candidates should realize that the water spraying device of D2 is also suitable for adjusting the moisture, so the suggestion of the client does not solve the novelty issue over D2.

The following wording added to the end of claim 1 does solve the novelty problem: "wherein the container has a water spraying device (13) connected to a water container (14)".

Claim 4, the client suggests, is amended by amending its step a. to providing a container according to claim 1.

This, however, was seen as too limiting.

It was considered sufficient to make step b. in claim 4 an essential step, rather than an optional step; and hence combining claims 4 and 5 as filed. Claim 5 was held not to involve an inventive step, and for that reason new claim 4 needed a further limitation.

One option therefor is limit the covering lid (2) to a non-transparent covering lid; this results to "optimal development" ([013]).

Another option is to use a floating lid (9) with a moisture-absorbing material on its lower surface; this helps to produce the moist, dark conditions preferred by the earthworms.

Essential feature missing

According to the Examiner in the communication of paper B 2019 "Claim 2 lacks an essential feature in the sense of Rule 43(3) EPC and therefore does not satisfy the requirements of Art. 84 EPC. The empty space (7) dimensioned to allow the salt composition to expand upon melting is a feature necessary for the heat storage unit as defined by claim 2 to work". The Examiner apparently deduced this from paragraph [010] stating "The box 4 contains a salt 10 composition 6, which can be chosen from Table 1. The box 4 also comprises an empty space 7 dimensioned to allow the salt composition 6 to expand upon melting".

Because of reasons associated with Art. 123(2) EPC, it was expected that the wording "comprising an empty space 7 dimensioned to allow the salt composition 6 to expand upon melting" was added to claim 2.

[Actually, it would have been logical, if the Examiner would have also raised a clarity objection against claim 1 in paper B 2019. This claim reads: "A cooking process including the steps: providing a heat storage unit (3); concentrating solar radiation (12) onto the heat storage unit (3) to heat it; and cooking food (8) placed on the heat storage unit (3)". According to [005], "Heat storage based on change of phase is advantageous for solar cooking because, during melting, the temperature of the material is kept constant at the melting temperature, thereby avoiding exposure of the solar cooker and especially the food to large temperature variations. The invention concerns solar cooking with heat storage based on this principle". In claim 1 as filed the implementation of this principle, being a melting step (an essential step) was missing. The client in his letter did observe that "The process of claim 1 {as amended} now involves a salt composition. We do not consider it necessary to specify the range of melting temperatures, as long as the process includes melting the salt composition to store the heat of fusion".]

In paper B Chemistry 2015, [014] reads that the fuel particles must have a size of 5 to 80 μm. Outside this range the composition is not suitable for use in airbags. This feature was missing in claim 1, so that the Examiner raised a clarity objection: "This essential feature is missing from claim 1. The requirements of Article 84 EPC are not fulfilled".

"Product for" is "product suitable for"

A good example to see the effect of a for-clause in a product claim was claim 1 in paper B 2021. This claim 1 reads as follows (with the suitable for clauses indicated):

"1. A container (1) [(suitable) for organic refuse], comprising
   a. an upper compartment (3) having a support (3a) [(suitable) for holding the refuse (7) populated with earthworms (8)];
   b. a lower compartment (4) [(suitable) for collecting excess moisture (6)];
   c. drain holes (5) permitting moisture to drain from the upper to the lower compartment; and
   d. an upwardly opening covering lid (2) which fits over the container (1)."

In its letter and its amended claim 1, the client suggested that it would not be necessary to refer to organic refuse in the preamble of claim 1, since the container would be suitable for any type of refuse, so the client deleted it from claim 1. However, since the clause "for organic refuse" only limits the claim to be suitable for this purpose, and since there was no other language available to replace this (be it) small limitation, this clause was to be reintroduced.

943 **Relative terms**

In paper 2018 B, the Examiner raised a clarity objection to claim 5, directed to a fuse, wherein the substrate (12,22) has a smooth surface. The term "smooth" was seen as a relative term. The client suggested to amend this claim to a fuse, wherein the substrate (22) is subjected to a polishing step before providing the fuse track thereon. This suggestion uses however process language in a product claim, so that the suggestion tries to solve one clarity issue with another.

944 The solution to this clarity problem can be found in the description, where it is indicated that "The surface of the substrate should therefore be quite smooth. An average surface roughness Ra equal to 5 µm or less is thus preferred. To reduce roughness, the surface of the substrate may be subjected to a polishing step prior to forming the fuse track thereon". Here, the surface smoothness is coupled to an average surface roughness Ra parameter that can be obtained by subjecting the surface to a polishing step and, hence, is entirely in line with the wish of the client.

945 The only question that remains is whether the average surface roughness Ra parameter is a usual or an unusual parameter. This question is answered by D1, which states that "The average surface roughness Ra is a well-known parameter defined in accordance with the International Standards Organization (ISO)".

946 The amended claim should hence be directed to a fuse, wherein the substrate (22) has an average surface roughness Ra equal to 5 µm or less.

947 Claim 2 in paper B Chemistry 2013 refers to "lower alkyl", twice. In the communication, it is noted that this claim lacks clarity in respect of that term, as the claim does not define the number of possible C atoms. This objection can be overcome on the basis of [008], reading ""Alkyl" is taken to mean a saturated hydrocarbon group containing only C and H atoms. "Lower alkyl" is taken to mean an alkyl group containing from 1 to 4 C atoms (C1-C4 alkyl)".

948 **Process language in a product claim**

In paper 2018 B, the client suggests to amend claim 5 to a fuse, wherein the substrate (22) is subjected to a polishing step before providing the fuse track thereon. This suggestion uses process language in a product claim and hence introduces a clarity issue. In the description, it is described that "An average surface roughness Ra equal to 5 µm or less is thus preferred. To reduce roughness, the surface of the substrate may be subjected to a polishing step prior to forming the fuse track thereon". According to D1 in paper B 2018 "The average surface roughness Ra is a well-known parameter defined in accordance with the International Standards Organization (ISO)".

949 Also in Mock paper B, such issues came up. For as far relevant, the claims in that paper read as follows:
1. An airbag module for protecting a vehicle occupant in a collision comprising:
   – (…);
   – a gas generator (1) comprising a housing (20) and a gas-generating composition generating gases upon ignition; and
   – (…).
3. The airbag module according to claim 1 or 2 wherein a gas is generated by a composition comprising (…), the gas-generating composition being present inside the housing (20).

950 In its communication, the Examiner noted that "The subject-matter of claims 1 and 3 is unclear. The features "generating gases upon ignition" (claim 1) and "a gas is generated by a composition" (claim 3) are process steps, whereas the claims refer to a product. This is not allowable under Article 84 EPC, because all features of an apparatus claim have to be device features if possible".

It was expected that a candidate would argue that in claim 1, the expression "generating gases upon ignition" is not a process step, but a further description of the product feature "gas-generating composition"; and in claim 3, it was easy to replace the phrase "a gas is generated by a composition comprising" by "a gas-generating composition comprising".

Parameters in claims

In paper B Chemistry 2014, a clarity objection was raised to an average pore size parameter. Claim 2, directed to a process, wherein the support is porous, the pores having an average pore size of 0.05 to 2 µm, was said to violate Art. 84 EPC as the average pore size is not clearly defined. As is well-known, there are various standard methods for determining pore sizes, which give different results. The application does not disclose a method for determining the average pore size.

The client observes that the average pore size of the support material was, of course, determined by nitrogen adsorption, using client's internal standard method for calculation. The client thinks this is clear.

This is (of course) not the case, and the only solution is to delete claim 2.

The Examiner raised a clarity objection in paper B 2018 to a claim wherein the relative term "smooth" was used for a surface. The solution for this objection was to replace the term "smooth" by the surface having "an average surface roughness Ra equal to 5 µm or less". This surface roughness parameter was according to D1 in paper B 2018 a "well-known parameter defined in accordance with the International Standards Organization (ISO)". In this light, this parameter may be used in a claim.

In the same paper B 2018, the client suggests to amend claim 1 by introducing that "the fuse has a quality score of at least 60". According to the description of the invention "A quality score (Q) was determined according to our in-house protocol, namely by counting the number of "good" fuses. We define a "good" fuse as one where metal reflow was minimal. Thus a high quality score (Q) indicates a low degree of metal reflow". An in-house protocol, which is only defined in the patent application using relative terms like "good" fuses and "minimal" metal reflow, is unsuitable to use the quality score Q parameter in the claim.

When studying the data in Table 2 of the patent application, you could see that only when AlCu is used as metal for the fuse track, having an amount of copper of 10, 15, and 20 %, one obtains fuses having a quality score above 60. The question then is, can these individual values be generalized? The answer is "yes". In paragraph [011] of the description, it is observed that ", it can be seen that a 5 quality score (Q) greater than 60 is obtained if the metal of the fuse track is AlCu alloy having a content of Cu in the range 10-20% by weight and a cover layer made of epoxy resin is provided. A fuse with a quality score (Q) greater than 60 provides protection for high-sensitivity electronic components against dangerous overload currents", hence there is support for generalizing the data to a range of 10-20 wt.%, be it that then an epoxy resin cover layer must also be present. This is supported by paragraph [008] teaching that "The fuse 21 differs structurally from the fuse 11 of Fig. 2 in that a cover layer 25 made of epoxy resin is provided to cover the fuse track 23. When an overload current passes through the fuse 21, the AlCu fuse track 23 heats up, melts, and ruptures, thereby forming a gap. Some of the heat is transferred to the cover layer 25 which then softens and flows into the gap. With the material of the cover layer 25 present in the gap, the metal of the fuse track 23 cannot flow back into the gap. Metal reflow of the fuse track 23 is thereby reduced. The amount of Cu in the AlCu alloy is 10-20 % by weight". Again, a range of 10-20 wt. % Cu in the AlCu alloy is described together with a cover layer of epoxy resin.

"Result-to-be-achieved" and functional claim language

In paper B Chemistry 2016, claim 1 of the application as filed was directed to a "composition containing at least one cyclohexylurea derivative, by which at least 50 % of dogs and cats are kept away from an object over a one-year period". In its Communication, the Examiner held that this claim lacked clarity, "as the compounds are defined by the result to be achieved and the skilled person does not know which structural features are crucial to the result or which compounds fall under the term "derivatives"".

959   This clarity objection could be overcome by introducing in claim 1 the structural formula for the cyclohexylurea derivatives that give the indicated effect.

960 **Problem with antecedent in a higher ranked claim**

The Examiner in paper B 2018 raises a clarity objection to claim 4, claiming a fuse, wherein the upper layer is made of epoxy resin. Perhaps you would expect a clarity objection to the relative term "upper", but this was not the case. The objection was that in the previous claims, there was "no precedence" to any "upper layer". At the end the issue could be solved by replacing "upper layer" by "cover layer", which term was also used in the claims as originally filed, but that was not objected to.

961   The Examiner in paper B Electricity/Mechanics 2016 objects to claim 3. The "LCD screen" od dependent claim 3 was not defined in any of the preceding claims. This objection could easily be overcome by replacing the term "LCD screen" by "the first display means" as supported by Fig. 1 and [008].

962   In paper B Electricity/Mechanics 2015, claims 2 and 4 read as follows:
2. Ski (1) according to claim 1 further comprising a switch (4) connected to the radio transmitter (5), the switch (4) comprising an actuator (4a) moveable between a first position in which the radio transmitter (5) is inactive and a second position in which the radio transmitter (5) is active.
4. Ski according to claim 2 or 3 comprising a switch (10) arranged to deactivate the radio transmitter (5).

The Examiner raised a clarity objection, because it is not clear whether or not the switch claimed is the same as that defined in claim 2.

From [009] of the application it becomes clear that switch (10) is "a further switch (10)".

963 **Amending dependency**

Original claim 3 in paper B 2018 only depended on claim 2. Claim 3 was directed to the "fuse according to claim 2, (…) wherein the fuse track has a neck portion". Claim 2 read as follows: "Fuse according to claim 1, wherein the fuse track is made of AlCu alloy having 15 % by weight Cu". The intention of this paper was that claim 1 was amended to require that the AlCu alloy has an amount of 10–20 % by weight of copper. The client requested to give him "the broadest possible scope of protection" and in the light of paragraph [008] teaching for the second embodiment "The amount of Cu in the AlCu alloy is 1–20 % by weight. The fuse track 23 comprises an optional neck portion 23a", it was expected that claim 3 was amended to also refer to amended claim 1.

964 **Negative claim feature**

In Mock paper B, claim 1 was directed to an airbag module, *inter alia* comprising a fabric cushion (2). In its letter, the client not only suggested a claim, wherein the fabric cushion (2) is made of fabric coated with a polyamide resin, but also indicated that it wished a further dependent claim to cover fabrics without coating.

965   Not only is such a wording ("without coating") a negative claim feature, but the support in the description for these terms was rather doubtful. What came closest as support was paragraph [0011]: "The fabric cushion of the airbag can be made of polyester and can be coated with a polyamide resin. As compared to uncoated fabrics, a polyamide resin coating, for example Nylon, will give the fabric a better resistance to flames". This is no direct and unambiguous teaching of a fabric cushion made of uncoated fabric. It was expected not to add a claim wherein uncoated fabrics were used, but to realise that such embodiments would be within the scope of claim 1, which just refers to fabric in general.

966   Paper B 2012 Electricity/Mechanics is a well used example paper in CEIPI seminars. It contains a claim directed to a self-cooling barrel (30) (…) wherein there is no zeolite arranged at the bottom of the barrel (30).

967   According to the communication, this claim is not clear. "The negative limitation "there is no zeolite arranged at the bottom of the barrel" is not admissible because it can be more clearly defined in terms of an alternative positive feature without unduly limiting the scope of the claim" (see Guidelines F-IV, 4.19).

This clarity objection could be overcome by taking the following wording from the description of the application: "the zeolite is arranged only at the side of the barrel".

Ambiguous terms

An interesting situation dealing with multiple terms which were held to be ambiguous by the Examiner occurred in paper B Chemistry 2016. This is interesting, because the clarity issues needed to be dealt with in different ways.

Claim 4 of the application as filed was directed to the "use of a polymer matrix containing a dog or cat repellent to prepare a paint or a ready-to-spray dispersion". The Examiner considered this claim unclear, "because the features "dog or cat repellent", "polymer matrix", "paint" and "ready-to-spray dispersion" are ambiguous terms.

Claim 1 of that application as filed was directed to a "composition containing at least one cyclohexylurea derivative, by which at least 50 % of dogs and cats are kept away from an object over a one-year period". This claim was held unclear, because the compounds are defined by the result to be achieved (*vide supra*).

This clarity objection could be overcome by introducing in claim 1 the structural formula for the cyclohexylurea derivatives that give the indicated effect. With this amendment in claim 1, the feature "dog or cat repellent" becomes superfluous and could be deleted from claim 1. However, in the expected use claim 5, based upon the original use claim 4, this feature was maintained. According to the Examiners' Report, "the expression "dog and cat repellent" is now clearly defined by the reference to the specific cyclohexylurea derivatives of claims 1 to 3".

For the terms "polymer matrix" and "paint", the Examiners' Report observes that "it should be argued" that these terms are clear from the description with appropriate references. For example "with regard to the term "paint", reference should be made to paragraph [08], wherein a definition of the general term "paint" is provided and an example is given; it is thus not necessary to specify the compounds of the paint."

As a personal note, I add that for the term "polymer matrix" it could additionally be argued that said term is also used in both prior art references Document D1 and Document D2.

As to the feature "ready-to-spray dispersion", it is noted in the section directed to "Clarity" in the Examiners' Report that this term "is deleted from the claims". This statement should be presented in the response to the communication: "The clarity objection in respect of the terms "ready-to-spray dispersion" is overcome, because these terms were deleted from the claims".

The expression "in"

The client suggested the following claim in paper B 2013 Electricity/Mechanics: "In a bottle, a closure according to any previous claim, wherein the bottle (21) has an internal parabolic surface (16)".

This introduces a clarity problem. The solution came from reformulating this claim to "A system of a bottle and a closure (…)".

Unity of invention

In paper B Chemistry 2016, claim 1 of the application as filed was directed to a "composition containing at least one cyclohexylurea derivative, by which at least 50 % of dogs and cats are kept away from an object over a one-year period" and claim 4 was directed to the "use of a polymer matrix containing a dog or cat repellent to prepare a paint or a ready-to-spray dispersion".

The Communication posed that the application lacks unity (*a posteriori*) "because cyclohexylurea derivatives with a dog-repellent rate of more than 50 % over a one-year period are known from D1. Accordingly, the following inventions are not interlinked: Invention group 1 (claims 1 to 3): each of the individual compounds alternatively possible in general formula (I) is a separate invention; Invention 2 (claim 4): use according to claim 4. The search report was drawn up for all inventions. The applicant is asked to choose one invention and delete the others. It may be possible to file one or more divisional applications for the other inventions".

980 It was clear from the client's letter that the client "wish(es) to limit (itself) to paints and ready-to-spray dispersions containing particular cyclohexylurea derivatives". In addition, the client instructs to "delete inventions where necessary".

981 It was necessary to discuss why the amendments to the claims obviate the objections raised against unity of invention. Mentioning that the unity objections are overcome by amending the claims was worth 4 marks. The application relates to one group of inventions only that is linked by the following general inventive concept: paint comprising polymer matrix comprising the cyclohexylurea derivatives of formula (I). Identifying the concept and explaining that the concept is new and inventive over D1 and D2 was worth 4 marks. The claims have been fully searched.

982 **Rule 43(2) EPC**

In paper B Electricity/Mechanics 2016, the set of claims as filed contained the following two independent claims:
1. Warning system for a driveway crossing (3,13), comprising:
   – a control unit (5),
   – a pavement sensor (7, 8, 17) connected to the control unit (5) and configured to detect pedestrians on a pavement (2, 12) approaching the driveway crossing (3, 13), and
   – a first display means (6, 16) connected to the control unit (5), the control unit (5) being configured so that the first display means (6, 16) gives a warning signal to the driver of a vehicle in the driveway (1, 11) in response to the output of the pavement sensor (7, 8, 17); and
5. Warning pole (20) comprising a sensor and a first display means connected to the sensor.

983 The Examiner objected that "Claims 1 and 5 are both independent apparatus claims. Therefore, the requirements of Art. 84 EPC in conjunction with Rule 43(2) EPC are not met".

984 This objection can be overcome by amending claim 5 in such a way that it comprises the warning system of claim 1.

985 The client in paper B Electricity/Mechanics 2015 suggests to have two independent claims, one directed to a ski and one directed to a ski binding, but otherwise with the same features. In its communication, the Examiner already pointed to Rule 43(2) EPC.

986 It could be easily argued that in this case, the two independent claims are allowable, because these form two alternative solutions corresponding to the implementation of the inventive idea into two alternative types of ski bindings (Rule 43(2)(c) EPC), while also unity-of-invention is given.

9 Amendments and correction

9.1 Legal basis

EPC Articles and Rules
Art. 123 EPC: Amendments
Rule 137: Amendment of the European patent application
Rule 139 EPC: Correction of errors in documents filed with the European Patent Office

Guidelines
H-IV, 2: Allowability of amendments – Art. 123(2)
H-V, 3: Amendments in claims
H-V, 4: Disclaimers not disclosed in the application as originally filed
H-VI, 2: Correction of errors in documents filed with the EPO

Case Law Book
II.E: Amendments
II.E.1.1: General principles
II.E.1.2: Content of the application as filed: Parts of the application which determine the disclosure of the invention
II.E.1.3: Standard for assessing compliance with Article 123(2) EPC
II.E.1.3.1: Gold standard: directly and unambiguously derivable
II.E.1.3.7: Novelty test
II.E.1.3.8: Non-technical subject-matter
II.E.1.4: Removal or replacement of features from a claim
II.E.1.4.4: The essentiality or three-point test
II.E.1.5: Ranges of parameters – setting upper and lower limits
II.E.1.6: Combination of features pertaining to separate embodiments or lists
II.E.1.7: Disclaimer
II.E.1.8: Generalisations
II.E.1.9: Intermediate generalisations
II.E.1.12: Errors in the disclosure
II.E.1.13: Disclosure in drawings

Further reference
C-Book, Chapter 7, p. 149–167: Added Subject-matter

Important decisions and references

Gold standard   G 2/10

An amendment is regarded as introducing subject-matter which extends beyond the content of the application as filed, and therefore unallowable, if the overall change in the content of the application (whether by way of addition, alteration or excision) results in the skilled person being presented with information which is not directly and unambiguously derivable from that previously presented by the application, even when account is taken of matter which is implicit to a person skilled in the art.

Replacement or removal of a feature   H-V, 3.1 and 3.4; T 331/87

The requirements of Art. 123(2) are only met if the replacement or removal of a feature lies within the limits of what a skilled person would derive directly and unambiguously, using common general knowledge and seen objectively and relative to the date of filing (or the date of priority according to Art. 89), from the whole of the application documents (G 3/89, G 11/91 and G 2/10).

If the amendment by replacing or removing a feature from a claim fails to pass the following test by at least one criterion, it necessarily contravenes the requirements of Art. 123(2):
(i) the replaced or removed feature was not explained as essential in the originally filed disclosure;

(ii) the skilled person would directly and unambiguously recognise that the feature is not, as such, indispensable for the function of the invention in the light of the technical problem the invention serves to solve; and

(iii) the skilled person would recognise that the replacement or removal requires no modification of one or more features to compensate for the change (it does not in itself alter the invention).

994 However, even if the above criteria are met, it must still be ensured that the amendment by replacing or removing a feature from a claim satisfies the requirements of Art. 123(2) as they also have been set out in G 3/89 and G 11/91, referred to in G 2/10 as "the gold standard".

995 Deletion of a statement regarding use or intended purpose in an independent claim for a product is not allowable under Art. 123(2) EPC if there is in the description no mention that the product can be used in some other way, or if the statement of purpose indeed amounts to a functional limitation.

996 **Adding subject-matter from cross-referenced document** T 689/90; T 737/90

Features can only be taken from a cross-referenced document ("incorporated by reference"), if all the following conditions are fulfilled:
- there is no doubt for the skilled reader that protection was sought for that subject-matter
- the features help to achieve the invention's aim and thus contribute to the solution of the problem
- the features belong implicitly clearly to the description of the invention
- the features were precisely defined and identifiable within the total technical information content of the reference document.

997 Moreover, documents not available to the public on the date of filing of the application can only be considered if:
- if a copy of the document was available to the EPO, or to the receiving Office if the application is a Euro-PCT application which was not filed at the EPO as the receiving Office, on or before of filing of the application; and
- the document was made available to the public no later than on the date of publication of the application under Art. 93 EPC (e.g. by being present in the application dossier and therefore made public under Art. 128(4) EPC).

998 **Abstract and priority document no basis for amendments** G 3/89; G 11/91

The abstract is only for documentation and information purposes and does not form part of the application. Neither does the priority document form part of the application as originally filed (except for the exception of Rule 56(3) EPC).

999 **Taking subject-matter from drawings** H-V,6; T 169/83
T 191/93; T 170/87; T 523/88; T 398/92

Subject-matter may be taken from a drawing, but only if the structure and function of these features are clearly, unmistakably and fully derivable for the skilled person from that drawing.

They should not be at odds with other parts of the disclosure and should be taken up in their entirety (no selection of certain features).

A negative feature (such as "no internal fittings") cannot be derived from schematic drawings not showing that feature.

1000 Measurements cannot be taken from drawings (unless the drawing is mentioned as being true to scale).

1001 **Intermediate generalisation/isolation of only certain features** H-V, 3.2.1

For an amendment, it is normally not admissible under Art. 123(2) EPC to extract isolated features from a set of features that have originally been disclosed in combination for that embodiment, if the feature is related or inextricably linked to the other features of that combination. Neither is this allowable if the overall disclosure does not justify the generalising isolation of the feature and its introduction into the claim. The same can apply to features taken from the drawings (see T 191/93).

Undisclosed disclaimers — G 1/03; G 2/03; G 1/16

A disclaimer which excludes subject-matter that is not directly and unambiguously disclosed in the application as filed is allowable under Art. 123(2) EPC only if certain conditions are met.

An undisclosed disclaimer may be allowable if its purpose is:
- to restore novelty by delimiting a claim against state of the art under Art. 54(3) EPC;
- to restore novelty by delimiting a claim against an accidental anticipation under Art. 54(2) EPC; an anticipation is accidental if it is so unrelated to and remote from the claimed invention that the person skilled in the art would never have taken it into consideration when making the invention; and
- to disclaim subject-matter which, under Art. 52 EPC to Art. 57 EPC, is excluded from patentability for non-technical reasons.

However, a disclaimer should not remove more than is necessary either to restore novelty or disclaim subject-matter excluded from patentability for non-technical reasons.

Further, a disclaimer that is or becomes relevant for the assessment of inventive step or sufficiency of disclosure adds subject-matter contrary to Art. 123(2) EPC.

Moreover, a claim containing a disclaimer must meet the requirements of clarity and conciseness of Art. 84 EPC.

Disclosed disclaimers — G 2/10; G 1/16

An amendment involving a disclaimer consisting of features that were originally disclosed in the application as filed may conflict with Art. 123(2) EPC if the skilled person would, by the amendment, be presented with new information by what now remains in the claim. If what remains in the claim would not be directly and unambiguously (or at least implicitly) derivable for the skilled person, Art. 123(2) EPC is violated. An example is when what remains results in the singling out of compounds or sub-classes of compounds or other "intermediate generalisations" that were not specifically mentioned or implicitly disclosed.

Correction of errors — G 3/89; G 11/91; H-VI, 2.2.1

Correction of errors under Rule 139 EPC forms a special case involving an amendment, which has to fulfil the following additional requirements:
- it must be obvious that an error has occurred
- it must be obvious what the correction should be
  both only taking account of the original application documents.

Correction of translation errors — A-VII,7; H-VI, 2

Art. 70(2) EPC states that if a European patent application has been filed in a language of a contracting state that is not an official language of the EPO, that text will be "the application as originally filed". Corrections bringing the application in conformity with the originally filed text are allowable throughout the entire proceedings.

This also applies to PCT applications filed in a language that is not an official language of the EPO.

9.2 Relevance to paper B

One of the most important parts of paper B is the amendment of the claims. The claim may not be amended in such a way that these contain subject-matter which extends beyond the content of the application as filed. So, while amending the claims suggested by the client, care is needed not to violate Art. 123(2) EPC and there are marks associated with these amendments. In addition, the amendments must be motivated in that support in the application as originally filed must be indicated. For the arguments in respect of Art. 123(2) EPC normally about 20–25 marks are available; a substantial part of the marks available.

9.3 Judging added subject-matter

1012 ### 9.3.1 The gold standard

An amendment should be regarded as introducing subject-matter which extends beyond the content of the application as originally filed, and is therefore unallowable, if the skilled person is presented with new information which is not directly and unambiguously derivable for the skilled person using common general knowledge, from the originally filed application, taking into account matter which is implicit (not merely obvious) to a person skilled in the art.

1013 Exact wording is not necessary in the application as originally filed, but the skilled person should not be confronted with new information. If the exact wording used in the claim that you amended for paper B is not the same as the wording present in the application as originally filed, you should clearly argue why the wording of that claim is directly and unambiguously derivable from the application as filed. If in this argumentation "common general knowledge" plays a role, this knowledge either should be known to everyone, or the exam paper should contain information, supporting this. It would however be much safer to use the exact wording of the patent application coming with paper B.

1014 ### 9.3.2 The "Novelty test" and the "Modified novelty test" or "Disclosure test"

In the past, it was not uncommon to use the "novelty test" for judging added subject-matter. According to this test, one compares the amended application with the original application and checks whether there has been matter added. If the added matter brings novelty over the original disclosure, then this added matter violates Art. 123(2) EPC.

1015 This test works fine when, for example, a completely new feature has been added to the application as filed, or when a species is introduced of an originally disclosed genus.

1016 When, however, the matter added is a generalisation of what was originally applied, the test does not lead to a novelty objection, whereas a generalisation usually involves unallowable added subject-matter.

1017 The novelty test hence does not always lead to correct conclusions.

1018 To take this flaw into account, in the modified novelty test or disclosure test, it is determined what the new information added is, and whether that information is novel over the originally filed application. By way of example, if "copper" is described in the application as originally filed and by amendment is generalised to "metal", the novelty test concludes that the added matter is not novel over the originally filed application; the modified novelty test however notes that the new information is "any metal except copper" and this new information is novel over the originally filed patent application.

1019 ### 9.3.3 Removing or replacing features (Essentiality test or Three-Point test)

If the amendment by replacing or removing a feature from a claim fails to pass the following test by at least one criterion, it necessarily contravenes the requirements of Art. 123(2) EPC, when
(i) the replaced or removed feature was not explained as essential in the originally filed disclosure;
(ii) the skilled person would directly and unambiguously recognise that the feature is not, as such, indispensable for the function of the invention in the light of the technical problem the invention serves to solve (in this context special care needs to be taken in cases where the technical problem is reformulated during the proceedings, see H-V, 2.4 and G-VII,11 of the Guidelines); and
(iii) the skilled person would recognise that the replacement or removal requires no modification of one or more features to compensate for the change (it does not in itself alter the invention).

1020 However, even if the above criteria are met, it must still be ensured that the amendment by replacing or removing a feature from a claim satisfies the requirements of Art. 123(2) EPC as they also have been set out in G 3/89 and G 11/91, referred to in G 2/10 as "the gold standard".

9.3.4 Unallowable intermediate generalisation 1021

An intermediate generalization occurs when an amendment to a claim adds a feature to that claim, which feature has been disclosed in the original application with one or more other features. When it can be derived from the original application that there is a functional and/or structural relationship between the feature added to the claim and the one or more other features, this amounts to an unallowable amendment to isolate the feature in question.

When a feature is taken from a particular embodiment, for example from one of the working examples, and added to the claim, it has to be established that: 1022
- the feature is not related or inextricably linked to the other features of that embodiment and
- the overall disclosure justifies the generalising isolation of the feature and its introduction into the claim.

These conditions are to be understood as an aid to assessing, in the particular case of an intermediate generalisation, if the amendment fulfils the requirements of Art. 123(2) EPC. In any case it has to be ensured that the skilled person is not presented with information which is not directly and unambiguously derivable from the originally filed application, even when account is taken of matter which is implicit to a person skilled in the art using the common general knowledge. 1023

9.4 Disclaimers

9.4.1 Undisclosed disclaimers

The Enlarged Board of Appeal has clarified the framework for the allowability of disclaimers which were not directly and unambiguously derivable from the application documents as originally filed (see the decisions G 1/03, G 2/03 and G 1/16. 1024

Such so-called "undisclosed disclaimers" are allowed to limit the scope of a claim to: 1025
(i) restore novelty over a **disclosure under Art. 54(3);**
(ii) restore novelty over an **accidental anticipation** under Art. 54(2). "An anticipation is accidental if it is so unrelated to and remote from the claimed invention that the person skilled in the art would never have taken it into consideration when making the invention". The status of "accidental" is to be ascertained without looking at the available further state of the art. A related document does not become an accidental anticipation merely because there are other disclosures even more closely related. The fact that a document is not considered to be the closest prior art is insufficient for achieving the status of "accidental". An accidental disclosure has nothing to do with the teaching of the claimed invention, since it is not relevant for examining inventive step. For example, this is the case when the same compounds serve as starting materials in entirely different reactions yielding different end products. A prior art, the teaching of which leads away from the invention, however, does not constitute an accidental anticipation; the fact that the novelty destroying disclosure is a comparative example is also insufficient for achieving the status of "accidental";
(iii) remove subject-matter which, under Art. 52 to Art. 57, is excluded from patentability for **non-technical reasons**. For example, the insertion of "non-human" in order to satisfy the requirements of Art. 53(a) is allowable.

These criteria may however not provide a technical contribution to the subject-matter disclosed in the application as filed. That is, the undisclosed disclaimer may not qualitatively change the original technical teaching in the sense that the applicant's (or proprietor's) position with regard to other requirements for patentability is improved. In particular, it may not be or become relevant for the assessment of inventive step or for the question of sufficiency of disclosure. 1026

In addition, the disclaimer may not remove more than necessary either to restore novelty or to disclaim subject-matter excluded from patentability for non-technical reasons. 1027

The Guidelines (Part H, Ch. V, 4.1) give the following examples: 1028

An undisclosed disclaimer is, in particular, **not** allowable if:
(i) it is made in order to exclude **non-working embodiments** or remedy **insufficient disclosure**;

(ii) it makes a technical contribution.
(iii) the limitation is relevant for assessing inventive step;
(iv) the disclaimer, which would otherwise be allowable on the basis of a conflicting application alone (Art. 54(3)), renders the invention novel or inventive over a separate prior art document under Art. 54(2), which is a **not accidental** anticipation of the claimed invention;
(v) the disclaimer based on a conflicting application also serves another purpose, e.g. it removes a deficiency under Art. 83.

1029 Finally, Art. 84 has to apply equally to the claim *per se* and to the disclaimer itself.

1030 ### 9.4.2 Disclosed disclaimers

With its decision G 2/10, the Enlarged Board of Appeal clarified the situation, where a disclaimer is used to cut out features that were originally disclosed as part of the invention (disclosed disclaimer). Such features may be the subject of a disclaimer on the condition that what remains in the claim must be derivable for the skilled person, directly and unambiguously (i.e. at least implicitly), from the original application. If not, that disclosed disclaimer violates Art. 123(2) EPC.

1031 Whether or not a disclosed disclaimer is allowable depends on the circumstances of the case. If for instance a claim remains, wherein a compound is singled out, or wherein an unallowable intermediate generalization results, the disclosed disclaimer is not allowed. Neither will the disclosed disclaimer likely be allowed, if by its disclaiming, all working embodiments illustrating the effect of the invention would become useless.

9.5 Corrections of errors

1032 During the examination procedure, an applicant may correct any error in the translation filed at any time. Thereto, the translation must be brought into conformity with the application as filed in the original language.

1033 Further, there may be linguistic errors, errors of transcription and other mistakes made in application documents. Under Rule 139, an applicant may request a correction. For the correction to be allowable in the description, drawings or claims of an application, both the error and the correction must be such that it is immediately evident:
– that an error has occurred; and
– what the correction should be.

9.6 Examples from previous papers

Removal of a feature from an independent claim as filed

1034 In Mock paper B, it was suggested by the client to remove the valve from claim 1 that referred to a fabric cushion, being part of an airbag module, comprising a pressure relating valve. However, in the description, it is noted that "the presence of a pressure regulating valve is essential when large amounts of gases are generated by the gas generator" ([0002]); "As seen in Figures 2 (a) – (c), the fabric cushion 2 always comprises a pressure regulating valve 3, i.e. a device that regulates the pressure inside the fabric cushion 2 by regulating the flow of gas exiting the fabric cushion" ([0008]); and, while discussing Figure 3 "If, due to the magnitude of the impact, the pressure surpasses a certain threshold, the valve will allow gas to be liberated from inside the cushion". Working without a valve would introduce new matter and this removal would not meet the essentiality or three-point test.

1035 In paper B 2021, claim 1 is directed to a container (1) for organic refuse, comprising
a. an upper compartment (3) having a support (3a) for holding the refuse (7) populated with earthworms (8);
b. a lower compartment (4) for collecting excess moisture (6);
c. drain holes (5) permitting moisture to drain from the upper to the lower compartment; and
d. an upwardly opening covering lid (2) which fits over the container (1).

1036 In the client's opinion, the lower compartment and the drain holes are both optional and are not essential to the container. They can therefore be omitted. The client further notes that the skilled person knows that excess moisture can alternatively be removed by other means such as a water absorbent material.

In [018] of the patent application of paper B 2021, it is stated that "The lower compartment (4) may be removable, allowing the upper compartment (3) to be placed directly on soil, so that the excess moisture drains into the soil".

Indeed, the lower compartment is thus not essential.

After a little re-writing, claim 1 can be broadened to a container (1) for organic refuse, comprising

a. ~~an upper~~ compartment (3) having a support (3a) for holding the refuse (7) populated with earthworms (8);

c. drain holes (5) permitting moisture to drain from the ~~upper to the lower~~ compartment having a support (3a) for holding the refuse (7) populated with earthworms (8);

b. an optional removable ~~lower~~ compartment (4) for collecting excess moisture (6) from the drain holes (5);
and

d. an upwardly opening covering lid (2) which fits over the container (1).

The optional removable compartment could also go to a new dependent claim.

Allowable intermediate generalisation

The client in paper B 2019 proposed "a limitation of the melting temperatures (…) to overcome the objections against claim 2. Furthermore, after further tests we have abandoned the use of the salt composition A ($MgCl_2 \cdot 6H_2O$). The material with the lowest melting temperature that we plan to use in commercial products is the salt composition B. The range of melting temperatures from 120°C to 350°C of claim 2 should exclude salt composition A but include salt composition B (melting temperature of 130°C) and the remaining salt compositions".

For the suggested lower limit of 120°C, there is no support in the application as originally filed, from which the following part is copied:

"[006] (…) Salt compositions particularly suitable for cooking in accordance with the invention have a melting temperature from 110°C, sufficiently above the boiling temperature of water, to 350°C. Examples of suitable salt compositions are listed in Table 1:

Table 1

	Chemical formula	Name	Melting temp. (°C)
A	$MgCl_2 \cdot 6H_2O$	Magnesium chloride hexahydrate	115
B	$LiNO_3$ (33 %) - KNO_3 (67 %)	Lithium nitrate (33 %) - Potassium nitrate (67 %)	130
C	$AlCl_3$	Aluminium chloride	192
D	$LiNO_3$	Lithium nitrate	252
E	$NaNO_3$	Sodium nitrate	307
F	KNO_3	Potassium nitrate	334
G	LiCl (58 %) - KCl (42 %)	Lithium chloride (58 %) - Potassium chloride (42 %)	348

[007] Referring to standard chemical databases, other suitable salt compositions can be found that have melting temperatures identical or close to those indicated in Table 1."

The intended solution was to limit the range of melting temperatures to 130°C-350°C. This restriction complies with the client's indication that the material with the lowest melting temperature for use in commercial products has a melting temperature of 130°C. This restriction is allowed under Art. 123(2) EPC because it is obtained from the range 110°C–350°C ([006]) in combination with the value 130°C of composition B of Table 1. The test to be applied is whether the isolated value 130°C is not so closely associated with the other features of the example, *i.e.* the particular salt composition B, in order to determine the effect of this example (T 201/83, Case Law Book E-II 1.3.2). In this case the test is passed because the application discloses ([007]) that other salts are known having the same melting temperatures of those of Table 1, and would thus have the same effect. The temperatures of Table 1 are thus not inextricably associated to the respective salts. This amendment merely represents a quantitative reduction of the original range to a value already envisaged in the application, without a new technical effect or new information being presented to the skilled person.

1044   This is a school example of an allowable intermediate generalisation.

10 Drafting the letter in response to the communication

In addition to the set of amended claims, a response to the official communication is to be prepared when sitting paper B.

In the words of Rule 24(3) IPREE, the response shall be in the form of a letter to the EPO, wherein the candidates are expected to respond to all points raised in the official communication. In their reply, candidates shall identify clearly all amendments made in the claims and their basis in the application as filed, and provide additional explanations where necessary. Candidates shall also set out their arguments in support of the patentability of the independent claim(s).

The description shall not, however, be amended.

From the response, it must be clear that it is directed to the EPO Examiner. It is not necessary to provide all address details, and to be overly polite. Just a plain formal letter suffices. Neither is it necessary to request Oral Proceedings. What you upload as your answer paper should either result in a communication, wherein the Examiner only invites you to file a description that is brought into conformity with the amended claims, or in a communication under Rule 71(3) EPC. A suitable response can just start with "It is requested to grant a European patent on the basis of the attached set of claims".

Or said in the words of an Examiners' report (B 2007 Chemistry) "As in previous years some candidates apparently spent considerable time in including things such as the date, the address of the EPO or requests for oral proceedings. Candidates may find it a better use of their time to concentrate on substantive issues first. Few, if any, marks are available for including matters such as the address of the EPO".

To maximize the possibilities to collect marks, it is of the utmost importance to work in a structured way. That is, deal with each type of objection in a separate section and work claim-by-claim.

At least the following types of objections are generally expected to be answered: support in the application as originally filed under Art. 123(2) EPC; clarity of the claims; novelty, wherein each independent claim is discussed in view of all references cited and this is advisably done by using one paragraph per piece of prior art; inventive step, wherein each independent claim is discussed using the problem-solution approach in all its steps; often unity-of-invention and/or Rule 43(2) EPC; and optionally any other objection based on any of the Articles 52–57 EPC or any other issue that was raised in the communication.

Most candidates start with a section dealing with support in the application as originally filed under Art. 123(2) EPC. According to Art. 123(2) EPC, the European patent application or European patent may not be amended in such a way that it contains subject-matter which extends beyond the content of the application as filed. In paper B, the arguments showing that the amendments meet the requirements of Art. 123(2) EPC attract a high number of marks, generally 20 marks and even more. This means that you should elaborate quite a bit on this requirement.

In the Guidelines Part H, Ch. IV, 2.1, the underlying idea and basic principle of Art. 123(2) EPC are sketched.

The underlying idea of Art. 123(2) is that an applicant is not allowed to improve its position by adding subject-matter not disclosed in the application as filed, which would give him an unwarranted advantage and could be damaging to the legal security of third parties relying on the content of the original application (see G 1/93).

An amendment is regarded as introducing subject-matter which extends beyond the content of the application as filed, and therefore unallowable, if the overall change in the content of the application (whether by way of addition, alteration or excision) results in the skilled person being presented with information which is not directly and unambiguously derivable from that previously presented by the application, even when account is taken of matter which is implicit to a person skilled in the art (see G 2/10).

The so-called "gold standard" according to G 2/10 (also called "relevant disclosure test" in G 1/16) hence is that a document discloses subject-matter (implicitly or explicitly) if the skilled person directly and unambiguously derives that subject-matter from the document, using common general knowledge and seen objectively and relative to the relevant date. In other words, the disclosure content of a document is the information that the skilled person derives – explicitly or implicitly – directly and unambiguously from the document as a whole.

1057 For discussing your set of amended claims, it is wise to check your set of claims with the set of claims as originally filed and to address each change or amendment in the letter to be drafted. It is suggested to work claim-by-claim and amendment-by-amendment. I suggest to deal with any claim and any amendment in a new paragraph.

1058 To collect all marks, it is important to give all the support for an amendment that you can find. This encompasses to refer explicitly to, for example, original claim 1, if that claim is amended ("Amended claim 1 is based on original claim 1, with the following amendments …).

1059 Particular attention is to be paid, when of a feature is removed from the claim. In such a case, this amendment necessarily contravenes the requirements of Art. 123(2) EPC, if the removal fails to pass at least one criterion of the essentiallity test or three-point test described in Part H, Ch. V, 3.1 of the Guidelines. But, even if the removal meets these three criteria, it must still be ensured that the amendment satisfies the gold standard. From your letter, it must be clear that this double requirement (meeting the essentiality test and meeting the gold standard) has been met.

1060 And when a removal is allowable, it is essential that you check whether this removal affects the dependency of the other claims. Not only may this be an issue under Art. 123(2) EPC, but in addition or alternatively it may also be an issue under the section clarity of the claims. As already indicated, it is advised not to make arguments in respect of different objections in one and the same paragraph or section, but to raise issues on support in the section on Art. 123(2) EPC and to raise issues on clarity in the section on Art. 84 EPC.

1061 It is good custom to end a section, in this case the section on Art. 123(2) EPC with the statement: "It is concluded that the requirements of Art. 123(2) EPC have been met.

1062 After discussing support in the application as originally filed, it generally makes sense to discuss any potential clarity issues.

1063 Any clarity objections raised by the Examiner in his communication, must be dealt with as well. Even if you decide to delete the claim in which a clarity issue was observed, it is advised to explicitly observe this in the letter. (Mostly, however, it was expected that that claim was to be amended.) When an amendment is made to overcome a clarity objection, the response to the communication should explain this.

1064 Often, there are issues associated with the dependency of the claims in paper. A removal of a feature from an independent or a dependent claim, or the deletion of a claim may make that there is no antecedent basis anymore in the claim to which reference was made in a particular dependent claim, so that the dependency was amended. This has to be observed and explained in the letter to the Examiner.

1065 Again, finalise the section on clarity with the statement that the set of claims as amended meets the requirements of Art. 84 EPC.

1066 In a next session, the novelty may be discussed.

1067 A claim is novel relative to a particular piece of prior art, if it contains at least one feature that is not directly and unambiguously derivable from that particular piece of prior art.

1068 So, when discussing novelty, it is advisable to discuss the novelty of an independent claim relative to each piece of prior art in a separate paragraph.

1069 If you have decided to draft your independent claim in the two-part form differentiating it from the closest prior art, then the differences between closest prior art and that independent claim have to be the features in the characterizing part. You may observe this, but it is better to explicitly indicate in the letter to the Examiner which claim features bring novelty over the closest prior art.

1070 If there are two or more differences between closest prior art and an independent claim, it would in principle be sufficient to just refer to one of these differences. However, because the differences need to be given in the problem-solution approach anyway, while discussing inventive step, it makes sense to refer to the two or more differences.

1071 Also the differences between each other piece of prior art and an independent claim need to be given. For the discussion on novelty, it now suffices to refer just to one difference. However, I myself prefer to give all differences, if there is no discussion on the terms used.

1072 Use for the novelty discussion over each prior art reference a separate paragraph.

When an independent claim is novel over a particular piece of prior art, normally it is not required to discuss the claims dependent on that independent claim. However, always check the specific claim wording of the dependent claims. 1073

The section on novelty preferably is closed while concluding that "hence, all claims meet the requirement of novelty". 1074

The next issue to be discussed is the matter of inventive step. For this issue, the number of marks is generally even higher than for the discussion of Art. 123(2) EPC. 1075

In principle, this discussion is to be carried out for each independent claim. And just like I indicated for the discussion on novelty, if an independent claim meets the requirement of inventive step, normally also the claims depending on that independent claim involve an inventive step. 1076

In paper B, this discussion always uses the problem-solution approach as set out in the Guidelines Part G, Ch. VII, 5. The problem-solution approach has three main stages: (i) determining the "closest prior art"; (ii) establishing the "objective technical problem" to be solved; and (iii) considering whether or not the claimed invention, starting from the closest prior art and the objective technical problem, would have been obvious to the skilled person. 1077

For the response to be uploaded as part of the answer to paper B, each step of problem-solution approach must be taken, indicated and motivated. 1078

This starts with the determination of the closest prior art. 1079

The closest prior art is that piece of prior art which in one single reference discloses the combination of features which constitutes the most promising starting point for a development leading to the invention. In selecting the closest prior art, the first consideration is that it must be directed to a similar purpose or effect as the invention or at least belong to the same or a closely related technical field as the claimed invention. 1080

This first consideration makes clear why in the methodology of paper B, the technical field and the technical effect, purpose or (dis)advantages are collected; not only for the patent application, but also for the documents forming the prior art. 1081

In practice, the closest prior art is generally that which corresponds to a similar use and requires the minimum of structural and functional modifications to arrive at the claimed invention. This latter part, however, is a secondary consideration. Such a secondary consideration may play a role in the determination of the closest prior art, if the first consideration is not sufficient. That is, if on the basis of the first consideration there is more than one candidate, then it may be needed to argue why the other candidates should not be the closest prior art. 1082

This is reflected in the marking. Normally, one gets at least one mark for an explicit statement that a particular piece of prior art forms the closest prior art; and one gets additional marks for providing arguments why that particular piece of prior art is the closest prior art, and one gets marks for providing arguments why each of the other pieces of prior art do not form the closest prior art. 1083

Once you have selected the closest prior art for a particular independent claim, you have to determine what the difference is. The difference between the independent claim and the closest prior art is expressed in features of the independent claim that are not directly and unambiguously derivable from the closest prior art. 1084

If the independent claim is in a correct two-part form, the difference is formed by the features following "characterised in that". However, in the discussion on novelty, the differentiating features are identified as well. This being the case, one still gets at least one mark by explicitly stating what the difference is between the independent claim and the closest prior art reference. 1085

Subsequently, the technical effect(s) associated with the difference(s) is (are) sought and, again, explicitly mentioned in the letter. 1086

Subsequently, one has to establish in an objective way the technical problem to be solved relative to the closest prior art. In the context of the problem-solution approach, the technical problem means the aim and task of modifying or adapting the closest prior art to provide the technical effect(s) that the invention provides over the closest prior art. The technical problem thus defined is often referred to as the "objective technical problem". 1087

Based on the technical effects associated with the differences between the closest prior art and the independent claim, you may define the objective technical problem as follows: 1088 to provide the technical effect(s) [not using these words, but actually representing the technical effects!] in the product or process described in the closest prior art.

1089   Subsequently, it is always good to check whether this problem is indeed solved by the features that distinguish independent claim 1 from the closest prior art.

1090   Now that we have the closest prior art and the objective technical problem, the question is whether there is any teaching in the prior art as a whole that would (not simply could, but actually would) have prompted the skilled person, faced with the objective technical problem, to modify or adapt the closest prior art while taking account of that teaching, thereby arriving at something falling within the terms of the claims, and thus achieving what the invention achieves.

1091   In paper B, one starts with providing arguments, why the closest prior art taken per se would not bring the skilled person to the claimed subject-matter.

1092   If this hurdle is taken, arguments are provided why the closest prior art in combination with another prior art document would not bring the skilled person to the claimed subject-matter.

1093   At this stage, there can be two types of arguments. The first type of argument is to find and give arguments why a skilled person starting from the closest prior art would never have turned to the second piece of prior art.

1094   The second type of argument is to find arguments as to why, when the skilled person starting from the closest prior art would turn to the second piece of prior art, he still would not come to the claimed invention.

1095   These first and second types of arguments are checked for all other pieces of prior art, separately.

1096   Normally (partial problems excluded; see thereto the chapter of this book on Inventive Step), it is not convincing when a combination of the closest prior art with two or more other documents are needed to contest inventive step. However, if you have time, you may wish to provide an argument as to why a combination of three documents would still not bring you to the claimed invention.

1097   This section ends again with the statement that hence the claimed subject-matter involves an inventive step.

1098   The above-discussed concepts essentially always are present in paper B. But also other objections could have been raised, such as unity-of-invention problems, issues under Rule 43(2) EPC and/or issues under other grounds of Articles 52–57 EPC. For paper B 2017, these issues did not play a role. For paper B 2021, there were arguments to made as to why the amended claims would overcome an objection under Art. 52(2)(c) EPC. Moreover, a detailed reaction was needed to address the third party observations.

1099   What needs further to be borne in mind is that you do not sign the letter in your own name. The answer paper must be anonymous.

1100   In Appendix 3 to this book, an example of the response and a set of claims is given in the form of the CEIPI model solution.

Appendix 1 – Paper B 2017

EN
EUROPEAN QUALIFYING EXAMINATION 2017
Paper B

This paper comprises:
- Description of the Application   2017/B/EN/1–3
- Claims   2017/B/EN/4
- Drawings of the Application   2017/B/EN/5
- Communication   2017/B/EN/6–7
- Document D1   2017/B/EN/8
- Drawings Document D1   2017/B/EN/9
- Document D2   2017/B/EN/10
- Drawing Document D2   2017/B/EN/11
- Document D3   2017/B/EN/12
- Drawing Document D3   2017/B/EN/13
- Client's Letter   2017/B/EN/14
- Draft set of claims   2017/B/EN/15

Description of the Application

[01] The present application relates to monitoring at least one vital sign of the human body by optical means. The four vital signs, pulse, body temperature, blood pressure and blood oxygen saturation, have to be monitored regularly for controlling the medical status of a patient in hospital. Monitoring vital signs at home will play a more and more important role in remote medicine. D1 discloses monitoring vital signs by attaching sensors to the human body with a clip. This has the drawback that the clip is uncomfortable and that for long-term measurements the attachment is not reliable, because the clip can move. Therefore, the aim of this invention is to provide a reliable and comfortable system for long-term remote monitoring of the vital signs of patients, such as small children and babies.

[02] The invention concerns a system comprising means for attaching an optical sensor and a motion sensor to the human body. The attaching means comprises means for transmitting output signals from the sensors to an evaluation means for calculating at least one vital sign from the output signals. The inventive idea is that the attaching means is a garment, such as a sock or a wristband, and that the evaluation means is configured to correct the output signal from the optical sensor based on the output signal of the motion sensor, and vice-versa. It is not important for the invention how the signals are transmitted to the evaluation means.

[03] Figs. 1–3 show systems according to first, second and third embodiments of the invention. The invention will be described below with reference to the drawings.

[04] Fig. 1 shows a system for remotely monitoring vital signs. The system comprises a sock 1 for attaching an optical sensor 2 and a motion sensor 3 to a human body 10. The sock 1 comprises transmitting means 4 for transmitting the output signals of sensors 2 and 3 to evaluation means 5. The transmitting means 4 may be any kind of transmitting means, such as a serial port for a cable, or wireless transmitting means, such as a wireless local network emitter.

[05] The evaluation means 5 is configured to receive and process the transmitted signals and may be a computer, a software application called App, or a smart phone, such as a *jPhone*. The vital signs are calculated from the output signals of the sensors and may be outputted as an audio signal or displayed on a screen 6 of the evaluation means 5.

[06] The optical sensor 2 comprises a light source 2a and a light detector 2b. The light source 2a emits a light beam 7a towards the human body 10 and the light detector 2b measures the light 7b having passed through the human body, i.e. not absorbed by the human body. 2a and 2b are part of an optical pulse oximeter as described in D1.

[07] Accommodating an optical sensor into a garment adds electrical noise to the output signal of the optical sensor 2. A sock 1 worn by a baby moves frequently, which adds further noise to the output signal from the optical sensor 2. This further reduces the

quality of the output signal. In order to overcome this drawback, in the first embodiment, the motion sensor 3 is placed next to, preferably between, the light source 2a and the light detector 2b. However, motion sensor 3, light source 2a and light detector 2b may be placed at any position in the garment 1. The relative position of these components to each other is not important. The output signal of the motion sensor 3 is also transmitted by the transmitting means 4 to the evaluation means 5.

[08] In the evaluation means 5 the output signal from the optical sensor 2 is corrected based on the output signal from the motion sensor 3 such that noise is reduced. This leads to better signal quality, thereby preventing false measurements.

Example for correcting the signal: A quick movement of the foot causes an erroneous peak to occur in the output signal of the optical sensor 2 and simultaneously, a peak in the output signal of the motion sensor 3. The evaluation means 5 uses the output signal from the motion sensor 3 to remove the erroneous peak in the output signal of the optical sensor 2. Vice versa the output signal from the motion sensor 3, which may be used for directly measuring a patient's pulse, may be corrected by the output signal of sensor 2. The relative position of the motion sensor 3 with respect to the optical sensor 2 is not important for correcting the signals.

[09] The evaluation means 5 is configured to calculate from the corrected signals the vital signs as is described in more detail in D1. The sock 1 may be replaced by a wristband 11 as shown in Fig. 2. However, any garment may be used. The garment may be at least partially made of *Optitex*™, which is a material comprising 50–60 % cotton, 30–40 % polyurethane and 10–20 % polyethylene glycol in % by weight. The remaining technical features, such as the transmitting means 14, light source 12a, light detector 12b and motion sensor 13, are identical to the first embodiment.

[10] Fig. 3 shows a system for use while doing sport such as running or cycling. The system comprises a headband 21 for goggles 20. The goggles 20 protect the eyes from foreign objects and water. The optical sensor 22, i.e. light source 22a and light detector 22b, and the motion sensor 23 are attached to the ear 27 by means of the headband 21. The headband 21 is a garment and may be made of *Optitex*™ which provides reliable, secure and comfortable attachment of the sensors to the ear.

[11] Accordingly, Fig. 3 shows a system for monitoring the vital signs of the human body, the system comprising the headband 21 for attaching the optical sensor 22 and the motion sensor 23 to the human body. The headband 21 comprises, in addition to the sensors 22 and 23, transmitting means 24 for transmitting the output signals from the sensors. The system further comprises an evaluation means 25 for receiving the output signals and calculating therefrom at least one of the vital signs. The evaluation means 25 is configured to correct the output signal from the sensor 22 based on the output signal of sensor 23, and vice-versa.

[12] In this embodiment it is essential that the vital signs are not displayed on the screen of the evaluation means 25, because the screen is used for other purposes, such as displaying a map. Instead the vital signs may be output as an audio signal, e.g. to an earphone 26 attached to the headband 21. The transmitting means 24 may be a wireless transmitting means or any other kind of transmitting means, such as described for the other embodiments.

Claims

1. System for monitoring at least one vital sign of a human body, the system comprising:
   - holding means (1, 11, 21) for holding an optical sensor (2, 12, 22) and a motion sensor (3, 13, 23) close to the human body (10, 27), the holding means (1, 11, 21) comprising in addition to the sensors (2, 12, 22, 3, 13, 23) transmitting means (4, 14, 24) for transmitting output signals from the sensors (2, 12, 22, 3, 13, 23),
   - evaluation means (5, 25) for receiving the output signals and calculating from the output signals the at least one vital sign,

   characterised in that the evaluation means (5, 25) is configured to correct the output signal from the optical sensor (2, 12, 22) based on the output signal of the motion sensor (3, 13, 23) or to correct the output signal from the motion sensor (3, 13, 23) based on the output signal of the optical sensor and in that the transmitting means (4, 14, 24) is a wireless transmitting means.

2. System according to claim 1, wherein the at least one vital sign is pulse, body temperature, blood pressure and/or blood oxygen saturation.
3. System according to claim 1 or 2, wherein the wireless transmitting means (4, 14, 24) is a wireless local network emitter.
4. System according to any of claims 1 to 3, further comprising a screen (6) and configured to display the at least one vital sign on the screen.
5. System according to any of claims 1 to 4, wherein the holding means is an attaching means (1, 11, 21) such as a sock (1), a wristband (11) or a glove.
6. System according to any of claims 1 to 5, wherein the attaching means (1, 11, 21) is at least partly made of Optitex™.

Drawings of the Application

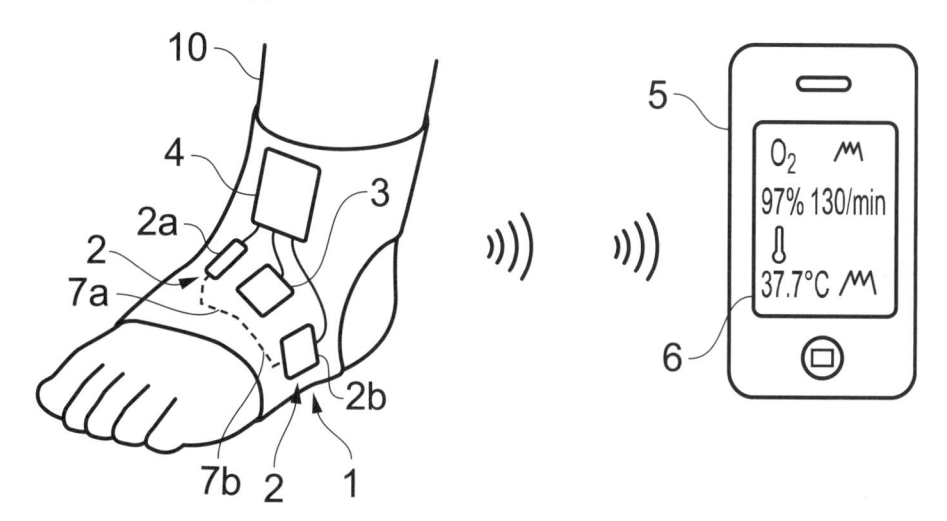

FIG. 1

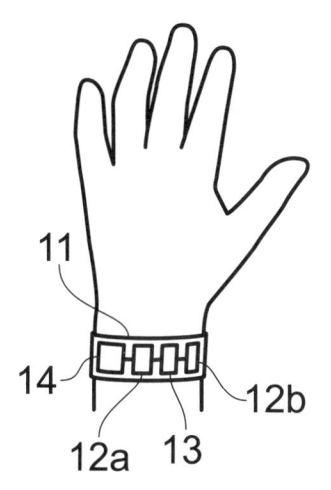

FIG. 2

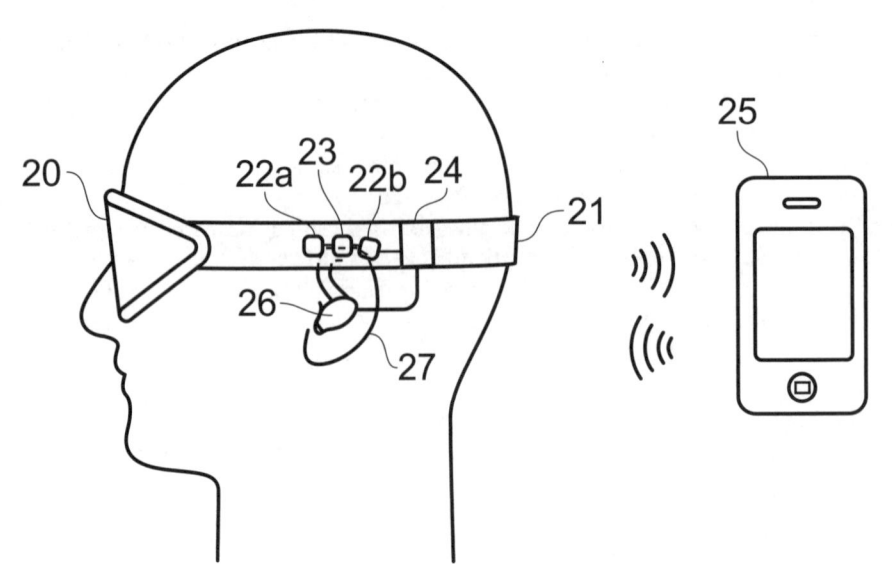

FIG. 3

Communication

1. The examination is based on the application as originally filed. Documents D1-D3 are prior art according to **Art. 54(2) EPC**.
2. **Art. 54(1) and (2) EPC (Novelty)**
   The subject-matter of **claims 1–4** is *not novel* within the meaning of **Art. 54(1) and (2) EPC**, because it is known from D2:
2.1 Claim 1: D2 discloses in paragraph [01] a system for monitoring at least one vital sign of a human body, the system comprising holding means (support for the camera (2), cf. par. [01]) for holding an optical sensor (camera sensor) and a motion sensor (motion sensor in the camera) "close" to the human body (cf. point 3.1 below), the holding means comprising a transmitting means for transmitting output signals from the sensors to evaluation means (smart phone), the evaluation means being configured to correct the output signal from the optical sensor based on the output signal of the motion sensor (SMOOTHY App, cf. par. [02]). The evaluation means calculates a vital sign (pulse, cf. par. [01]). The transmitting means is a wireless transmitting means (cf. par. [02]).
2.2 Claim 2: D2 further discloses in par. [01] measuring the pulse.
2.3 Claim 3: D2 further discloses in par. [02] a wireless local network emitter.
2.4 Claim 4: D2 further discloses in par. [01] as display means a screen.
3. **Art. 84 EPC (Clarity)**
3.1 Claim 1: The expression "[holding] ... **close** to the human body" is a relative term and thus unclear. An unclear term cannot be used by the applicant to distinguish the invention from the prior art (Guidelines F-IV, 4.6).
3.2 Claim 5: The technical feature **"glove" is only mentioned in the claims and not in the description**. According to **Art. 84 EPC** it is required that the **claims are supported by the description**.
3.3 Claim 6: Optitex™ is a **Trademark**. The definition of a composition by a trademark may change and therefore is unclear under **Art. 84 EPC** (cf. Guidelines F-IV, 4.8).
4. If the applicant wishes to maintain the application, **new claims** should be filed which take the above objections into account.
5. Care should further be taken that the **dependency** of the amended **dependent claims** is correct.
6. In order to facilitate the examination as to whether the new claims contain subject matter which extends beyond the content of the application as originally filed, the applicant is requested to indicate precisely where in the application documents any **amendments** proposed find a **basis (Art. 123(2) EPC and Rule 137(4) EPC). This also applies to the deletion of features.**

7. Care should be taken to ensure that the new claims comply with the requirements of the EPC in respect of **clarity, novelty, inventive step** and, if relevant, **unity** (**Art. 84, 54, 56 and 82 EPC**).
8. In the letter of reply, the **problem and solution approach** should be followed. In particular, the **difference between the independent claim** and the **prior art (D1-D3)** should be indicated. The **technical problem** underlying the invention in view of the **closest prior art** and the **solution** to this problem should be readily derivable from the reply of the applicant.

Document D1: From text book "Medical Technology"

[01] Described is an optical pulse oximeter for measuring the pulse and the oxygen saturation in the blood.

[02] As shown in the figures the optical pulse oximeter typically utilizes a first LED (lightemitting diode) 221 and a second LED 222 facing an optical sensor 207 on both sides of a part of a patient's body, usually a fingertip or an earlobe. The first LED 221 emits red light and the second LED 222 emits infrared light. Absorption of light at these wavelengths differs significantly between blood loaded with oxygen and blood lacking oxygen. Oxygenated haemoglobin absorbs more infrared light and allows more red light to pass through. Deoxygenated haemoglobin allows more infrared light to pass through and absorbs more red light. The LEDs flash about thirty times per second.

[03] The optical sensor 207 measures the intensity of the light that passes through, i.e. is not absorbed. The measurement fluctuates in time because the amount of arterial blood pulses with the heartbeat frequency. An evaluation means 205 calculates the oxygen saturation in the blood as well as the pulse from the ratio of the red light measurement to the infrared light measurement. The intensity of the infrared signal measured by the optical sensor 207 is proportional to the body temperature. From the blood oxygen saturation, pulse and body temperature, the blood pressure can be calculated. The calculated values are displayed on screen 206.

[04] The LEDs 221, 222 and the optical sensor 207 are integrated into a clip 201 which is attached to a finger 210. The clip 201 is connected to the evaluation means 205 by means of a cable 204. In order to achieve better accuracy and reliability of the pulse measurement, the pulse can be measured independently from the optical pulse oximeter by means of a sensor 203, such as a pressure sensor or a motion sensor, which could also be integrated into the clip. Preferably a pressure sensor is used, because a motion sensor, which is reliable enough to measure the pulse, is typically large and heavy and therefore uncomfortable for the patient. The evaluation means 205 comprises simple, but fast software. This allows quick signal processing, but no further software can be installed in the evaluation means 205.

Drawings Document D1

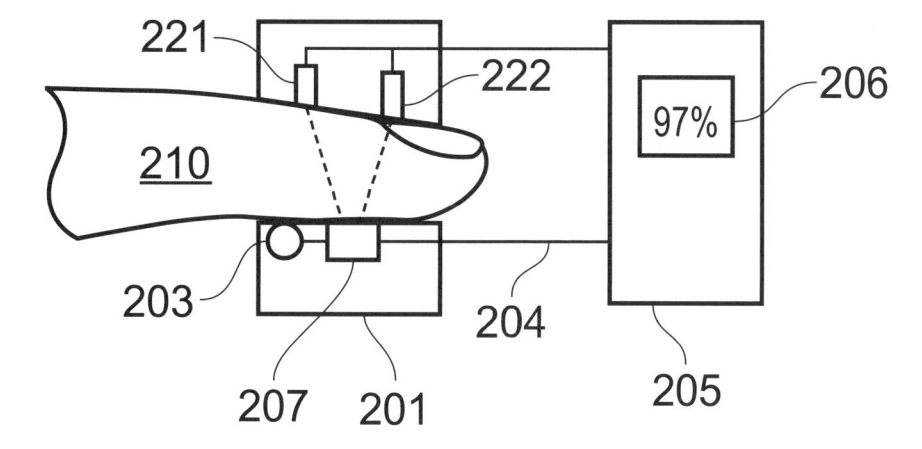

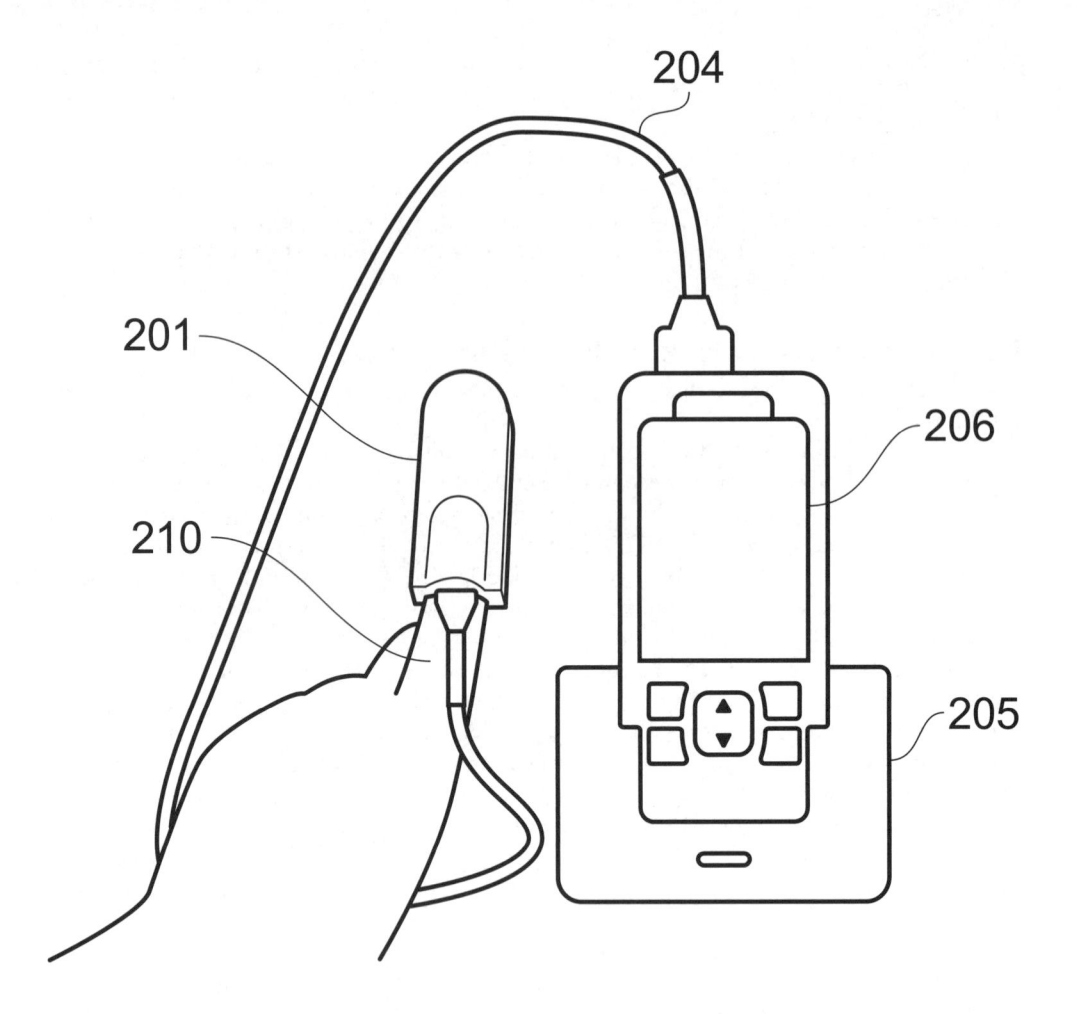

Document D2: Advertisement from the magazine "Smart phone & Co"

[01] Now there is the latest gadget for your *jPhone*: a *jPhone* babyphone! With the *Wittings Smart Baby Monitor WSBW 4.0* you don't just simply monitor your child (also at night, thanks to a built-in infra-red image sensor), but you can directly interact with your child, e.g. by sending soothing music. Even better, the *WSBW 4.0* not only transmits sound and images, but also monitors the current room temperature and the relative humidity of the air. The camera 1 detects small changes in the colour of the skin to measure the pulse of your baby and to display the pulse on a screen. The camera is mounted on a support 2 holding the camera close to the baby, but out of reach of the baby such that the camera cannot be damaged. The camera is movable about two axes. The infra-red sensor is used to automatically adjust the position of the camera 1 when your baby moves.

[02] The *Wittings Smart Baby Monitor* exchanges all data with your smart phone via wireless local network or any other wireless connection. Many *jPhone* apps are available for the *WSBW 4.0*. The *SMOOTHY* App installed in your *jPhone* 3 determines the motion of the camera 1 using a motion sensor in the camera. The *SMOOTHY* App corrects the sound and image signals from the camera on the basis of the motion data from the motion sensor in the camera, thereby reducing undesired noise from the signals. This achieves even better sound and picture quality.

[03] The *Wittings Smart Baby Monitor* is available for 130 Euros from October 2014 at www.arctic.com. *SMOOTHY* App: 1 Euro.

Drawing Document D2

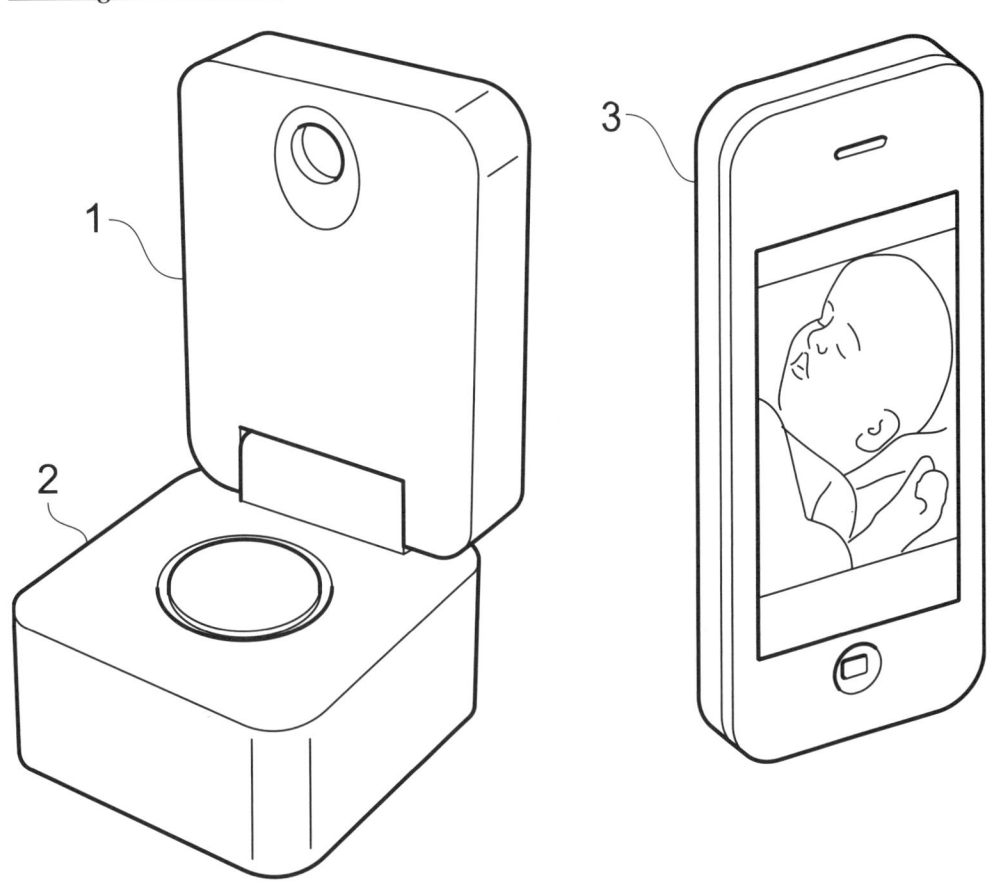

Document D3: Technical Disclosure from "Brooker, Phils & Siems"

[01] Disclosed is a sock, comprising an electrical sensor for electrocardiography. Electrocardiography is the recording of the electrical activity of the heart. The electrical activity of the heart is detected by electrical sensors in contact with the skin of a human body.

[02] The figure shows a sock 301 comprising an electrical sensor 309 and a cable 304 that can be connected to an evaluation means 305 for processing the data from the sensor. The sock 301 is pulled over a patient's foot 310 such that the electrical sensor is in contact with the foot. The electrical signal from the electrical sensor 309 is evaluated and displayed by the evaluation means 305.

[03] The sock 301 is a reliable, secure and comfortable means for attaching the electrical sensor 309 to the human body. The sock 301 is at least partially made of a material comprising 50–60 % cotton, 30–40 % polyurethane and 10–20 % polyethylene – glycol in % by weight. This material unfortunately allows measurements only with electrical sensors, because for any other type of sensor, e.g. optical sensor, the signal to noise ratio would be too low for measuring vital signs of the human body. Therefore, this material is not suitable for recording vital signs.

[04] Instead of a sock another kind of garment may be used, such as a glove, a wristband or a headband. A glove in particular is a reliable and comfortable means for attaching sensors to the human body.

Drawing Document D3

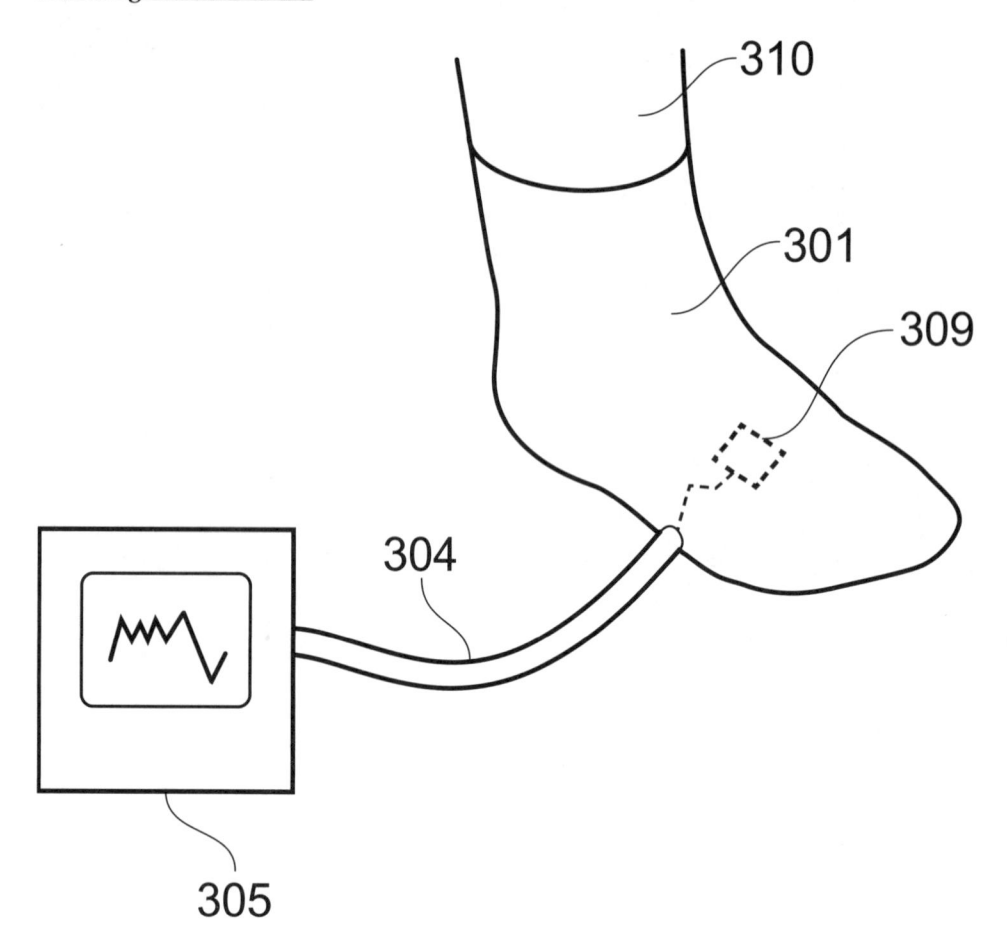

Dear Ms. Evita Lee-Tea,

[01] Our invention has the advantage that the vital signs can be remotely monitored with a reliable, secure and comfortable attachment of the sensors in combination with a high signal quality, which is achieved by noise reduction through correcting the sensor output signals.

[02] We propose filing the enclosed draft set of claims together with your reply to the official communication. We are convinced that the subject-matter of amended claim 1 is novel and inventive. Please make any amendments to the proposed set of claims you consider to be necessary for the claims to fulfil the requirements of the EPC, whilst giving us the broadest possible scope of protection for our invention.

[03] Claim 1 has been restricted by including the features of dependent claim 5. Claim 1 is drafted in the two-part form with respect to D1, because D2 and D3 are from remote technical fields. We have moved the wireless transmission from claim 1 to amended dependent claim 2, because for some applications this kind of transmission is not suitable. We do not want to have a dependent claim related to the subject matter of original claim 2. We only want to protect a system, where the attaching means is (any kind of) a garment. Please amend the claims accordingly, if possible.

[04] The third embodiment is enjoying unexpected success in the sports article market. To cover this embodiment, we replaced the erroneous word "glove" in amended claim 1 by "headband for goggles". It is very important for us to have protection for this embodiment. Inspired by the erroneous word "glove" and by the teaching of D3 we intend to

produce a glove comprising optical and motion sensors according to our inventive idea. If possible, please protect the option that the garment is a glove. In view of the comment of the examiner in section 3.2 you may have to provide corresponding reasoning. Otherwise we do not want you to add further dependent claims.

Regards
B. Aby

Enclosure: Draft set of claims

1. System for monitoring at least one vital sign of a human body, the system comprising:
   – ~~holding~~ attaching means (1, 11, 21) for ~~holding~~ attaching an optical sensor (2, 12, 22) and a motion sensor (3, 13, 23) ~~close~~ to the human body (10, 27), the ~~holding~~ attaching means (1, 11, 21) comprising in addition to the sensors (2, 12, 22, 3, 13, 23) transmitting means (4, 14, 24) for transmitting output signals from the sensors (2, 12, 22, 3, 13, 23),
   – evaluation means (5, 25) for receiving the output signals and calculating from the output signals the at least one vital sign,
   characterised in that <u>the attaching means (1, 11, 21) is one of a sock (1), a wristband (11) or a headband (21) for goggles (20) and in that</u> the evaluation means (5, 25) is configured to correct the output signal from the optical sensor (2, 12, 22) based on the output signal of the motion sensor (3, 13, 23) or to correct the output signal from the motion sensor (3, 13, 23) based on the output signal of the optical sensor ~~and wherein the transmitting means is a wireless transmitting means (4, 14, 24)~~.

2. System according to claim 1, wherein the ~~at least one vital sign is pulse, body temperature, blood pressure and/or blood oxygen saturation~~ <u>output signals are transmitted by wireless transmitting means (4, 14, 24)</u>.

3. System according to claim 1 or 2, wherein the wireless transmitting means (4, 14, 24) is a wireless local network emitter.

4. System according to any of claims 1 to 3, further comprising a screen (6) and configured to display the at least one vital sign on the screen.

~~5. System according to any of claims 1 to 4, wherein the holding means is an attaching means such as a sock (1), a wristband (11) or a glove.~~

5. ~~6.~~ System according to any of claims 1 to ~~5~~ <u>4</u>, wherein the attaching means (1, 11, 21) is at least partly made of Optitex™.

Appendix 2 – Examiners' Report Paper B 2017

1. General considerations

It is noted that any references in this text to the Guidelines for Examination at the European Patent Office (GL) refer to the version valid at the date of the examination.

1.1 Introduction

The paper relates to a <u>system for remotely monitoring at least one vital sign of the human body</u>: pulse rate, body temperature, blood pressure and blood oxygen saturation. The four vital signs have to be monitored regularly for controlling the medical status of a patient in hospital. Monitoring vital signs at home will play a more and more important role in remote medicine. Parents wish to monitor the health status of their small children remotely and continuously. Therefore, the aim of the invention is to provide a reliable and comfortable system for long-term remote monitoring of the vital signs of a person, which is also suitable for small children and babies.

1.2 The invention as presented in the application as filed

The invention as initially claimed concerns a system for monitoring a human body, the system comprising holding means for holding an optical sensor and a motion sensor close to the human body, the holding means further comprising transmitting means for transmitting output signals of the sensors, the system further comprising evaluation means for receiving the output signals and calculating vital signs from the output signals, wherein the evaluation means is configured to combine and correct the output signals of the sensor and wherein the transmitting means is a wireless transmitting means.

1.3 The prior art

Three documents are cited against the application. Only D2 is novelty destroying for claims 1–4 of the application as originally filed.

<u>Document D1 is from the same technical field</u> and discloses a <u>pulse oximeter</u> as it is usually used in a medical environment. D1 discloses recording vital signs by attaching sensors to the human body with a clip. This has the drawback that for long-term measurements the attachment is not reliable or comfortable for the patient. The pulse oximeter comprises in addition to the optical sensors a motion sensor. D1 is silent about correcting the output signals of the sensors. Apart from the clip D1 does not disclose or teach any other means for attaching the sensors to the human body.

Document D2 discloses a <u>baby monitor</u>, which is an advanced camera with additional functions. The monitor allows not only to monitor sound and images, but also to monitor the pulse rate of a baby. The camera transmits the data by means of a wireless connection and corrects the data by combining the signals of the camera with the data of a motion sensor. <u>D2 takes away the novelty of original claim 1</u>.

<u>Document D3 is from a similar technical field and</u> discloses a sock for attaching <u>electrical medical sensors</u> in a secure, comfortably and reliable manner. D3 is silent about optical sensors, motion sensor, wireless data transmission and correcting sensor signals. The application discusses only the disclosure of D1 in the description.

1.4 The communication

Novelty objections are raised by the examiner in the communication against claims 1–4 on the basis of document D2.

Finally observations under Article 84 EPC are raised against claims 1, 5 and 6. It is noted that the technical feature "glove" is only mentioned in the claims and not in the description, wherein it is required that the claims are supported by the description. It is further noted that Optitex™ is a trademark and its composition is not further specified as required under Guidelines F-IV, 4.8.

1.5 The letter from the applicant

The client proposes a set of claims addressing only the objections raised by the examiner for claims 1–4. In this set of claims, claim 1 is limited to one of a sock, a wristband or a headband for attaching the sensors to the human body. The client in the letter also stresses that the third embodiment of the application is enjoying unexpected success in the sports article market. To cover this embodiment, he replaced the erroneous word "glove" in original claim 5, serving as basis for amending claim 1, by "headband for goggles".

The feature stating that a wireless transmitting means is used for transmitting the sensor output was deleted, because this kind of transmission is not suitable for some applications. In addition, the client states that he would like to protect a system comprising any kind of garment for attaching the sensors to the human body. He asks for the claims to be amended accordingly, if possible. The client stresses that, inspired by the erroneous word "glove" and by the teaching of D3, he intends to produce a glove comprising optical and motion sensors according to the inventive idea.

Therefore, it was expected from the candidates that a system comprising any kind of garment is protected by the independent claim. It was further expected to claim both the glove and headband for goggles as specific examples of a garment in the dependent claims.

The client does not address the observations under Art. 84 EPC. Therefore, it was expected from the candidates that the objection against missing support in the description for claiming a glove is discussed and that the trademark Optitex is specified by its composition in the corresponding dependent claim. In addition, the relative term "close to" had to be addressed.

The amendments proposed by the client add subject-matter, contrary to the requirements of Art. 123(2) EPC. The proposed amendment to claim 1 unallowably adds subject-matter in combination with unchanged claim 4. There is no basis in paragraphs [10]–[12], where the third embodiment is described, that the headband for goggles is claimed together with a screen for displaying the at least one of the vital signs, such as a display of a smart phone or a computer. Therefore, candidates had to amend claim 1 or claim 4 in order to overcome this violation of Art. 123(2) EPC or to provide a reasoning that such a combination of features has support in the application as originally field.

1.6 The draft set of claims

The client introduced the following deficiencies in the dependent claims of the draft set of claims:

In new dependent claim 2 the signal transmission is formulated as a method step (The "signals are transmitted by wireless transmitting means (4, 14, 24)"). Consequently, the candidates were expected to reformulate this feature as a structural feature as it was originally formulated in claim 1.

In new claim 3 the dependency was incorrect, because in claim 1 the feature of the wireless transmitting means was deleted, thus making a reference back to claim 1 unclear. New claim 4 has no basis in the description in so far as claim 4 refers back to "headband for goggles", as discussed above.

New claim 5 does not overcome the objection of the examiner under Art. 84 EPC (trademark).

1.7 The challenges of the paper

The main challenges of the paper were to:
a) Amend the client's draft claim set according to the wishes of the client to fulfil the requirements of the EPC.
b) Write a reasoned letter of reply
   – explaining the basis for the amendments of the claims,
   – arguing for supporting the deletion of a feature in claim 1,
   – arguing for support of original claim 4
c) Addressing all the clarity objections raised by the examiner in his communication.
d) Arguing that the subject matter of the amended independent claim is new and involves an inventive step in the light of D1-D3.

1.8 The marking scheme

Answer papers are marked on a scale of 0 to 100 marks:

Appropriate amendments to the draft set of claims: Max. **30 marks**, min. **0 marks**.

This year again not the claim set as a whole, but the amendments carried out received marks. However, from the marks awarded for the amendments, marks were deducted for unnecessary limitations or non-compliance e.g. with Art. 123(2) EPC or 84 EPC. The overall number of marks per claim could not be negative.

As in the previous years the number of available marks corresponds to the difficulties of each challenge or the complexity of the expected amendment. Therefore, more difficult challenges may receive more marks than easier challenges. This year, as in some previous years, a considerable number of challenges/expected amendments have been in the dependent claims such that for dependent claims an important part of the marks for the claim set was available.

For the argumentation max. 70 marks and min. 0 marks have been available. Unless otherwise stated, the individual marks referred to in the various sections of this document apply to the example set of claims. This year the expected amendments required a detailed reasoning, such that one third of the available marks for the letter of reply was available for this section. Again one third of all marks was available for a reasoning in support of inventive step.

Although the marking scheme is divided into separate sections such as the marks awarded for amendments to the claims and marks awarded for argumentation, the answer paper as a whole was considered and the scheme reflects this. Candidates who have provided very good arguments for the claims they have submitted can receive good marks for argumentation even if the claims receive few marks. Reasoning supporting novelty and inventive step based on an un-amended draft set of claims was this year almost the same as for the example claim set.

No marks were available for formulating a letter to the client setting out the reasons why the client's suggested claims were further amended.

2. Example set of claims

A suitable wording for the amended claims is as follows:

1. System for monitoring at least one vital sign of a human body, the system comprising:
   - <u>attaching means</u> ~~holding means~~ (1, 11, 21) for <u>attaching</u> ~~holding~~ an optical sensor (2, 12, 22) and a motion sensor (3, 13, 23) close to the human body 810, 27), the <u>attaching means</u> ~~holding means~~ (1, 11, 21) comprising in addition to the sensors (2, 12, 22, 3, 123, 23) transmitting means (4, 14, 24) for transmitting output signals from the sensors (2, 12, 22, 3, 13, 23),
   - evaluation means (5, 25) for receiving the output signals and calculating from the output signals the at least one vital sign,
   characterised in that
   - <u>the attaching means (1, 11, 21) is a garment and in that</u>
   - the evaluation means (5, 25) is configured to correct the output signal from the optical sensor (2, 12, 22) based on the output signal of the motion sensor (3, 13, 23) or to correct the output signal from the motion sensor (3, 13, 23) based on the output signal of the optical sensor ~~and in that the transmitting means (4, 14, 24) is a wireless transmitting means.~~

   [Original claim 2 deleted]
2. <u>System according to claim 1 wherein the transmitting means (4, 14, 24) is a wireless transmitting means (4, 14, 24).</u>
3. System according to claim 1 or 2 wherein the wireless transmitting means (4, 14, 24) is a wireless local network emitter.
4. System according to any of claims 1 to 3, further comprising a screen (6) and configured to display the at least one vital sign on the screen.
5. System according to any of claims 1 to 4, wherein <u>the garment is</u> ~~the holding means is an attaching means (1, 11, 21) such as~~ a sock (1) or a wristband (11) ~~or a glove~~.
6. <u>System according to claim 1 to 4, wherein the garment is a glove.</u>
7. <u>System according to any of claims 1 to 3, wherein the garment is a headband (21) for goggles (20).</u>

8. ~~6.~~ System according to any of claims 1 to ~~5~~ 7, wherein the attaching means (1, 11, 21) is at least partly made of ~~Optitex™~~ a material comprising 50–60 % cotton, 30–40 % polyurethane and 10–20 % polyethylene glycol in % by weight.

(For convenience, here is a set of claims where the amendments are shown vis à vis the client's draft set of claims.:
1. System for monitoring at least one vital sign of a human body, the system comprising:
   – attaching means (1, 11, 21) for attaching an optical sensor (2, 12, 22) and a motion sensor (3, 13, 23) to the human body (10, 27), the attaching means (1, 11, 21) comprising in addition to the sensors (2, 12, 22, 3, 13, 23) transmitting means (4, 14, 24) for transmitting output signals from the sensors (2, 12, 22, 3, 13, 23),
   – evaluation means (5, 25) for receiving the output signals and calculating from the output signals the at least one vital sign,
   characterised in that the attaching means (1, 11, 21) is ~~one of a sock (1), a wristband (11) or a headband (21) for goggles (20)~~ a garment and in that the evaluation means (5, 25) is configured to correct the output signal from the optical sensor (2, 12, 22) based on the output signal of the motion sensor (3, 13, 23) or to correct the output signal from the motion sensor (3, 13, 23) based on the output signal of the optical sensor.
2. System according to claim 1 wherein ~~the output signals are transmitted by~~ the transmitting means (4, 14, 24) is a wireless transmitting means (4, 14, 24).
3. System according to claim 1 ~~or 2~~ wherein the wireless transmitting means (4, 14, 24) is a wireless local network emitter.
4. System according to any of claims 1 to 3, further comprising a screen (6) and configured to display the at least one vital sign on the screen.
5. System according to any of claims 1 to 4, wherein the garment is a sock (1) or a wristband (11);
6. System according to claim 1 to 4, wherein the garment is a glove.
7. System according to any of claims 1 to 3, wherein the garment is a headband (21) for goggles (20).
8. ~~6.~~ System according to any of claims 1 to ~~4~~ 7, wherein the attaching means (1, 11, 21) at least partly made of ~~Optitex™~~ a material comprising 50–60 % cotton, 30–40 % polyurethane and 10–20 % polyethylene glycol in % by weight.)

3. Expected amendments to the claims

The draft set of claims submitted by the client contains features, which result in claims, which are considered not to be consistent with the EPC. Marks were awarded for making amendments to the draft claim set appropriate for bringing it into accordance with the EPC.

No marks were awarded for merely filing the claim set provided by the client or for the formulation of additional (dependent) claims.

Apart from the claims explicitly requested by the client, drafting additional claims was not expected. The client had stated in the last sentence of his letter after all his very specific wishes, that "otherwise we do not want you to add further dependent claims". It was clear from the context and the structure of his letter that this relates only to subject matter other than the garment being a sock, a wristband, a glove or a headband.

It is noted that full marks were awarded for amendments that differ from those of the example claim set, provided their scope is comparable. This was considered on a case-by-case basis. Marking of the dependent claims was adapted accordingly.

3.1 The independent claim (6 marks)

The expected solution for claim 1 was generalising the feature "one of a sock, a glove or a headband for goggles" to "garment". Basis for this generalisation can be found in the description for all embodiments. The last but one sentence of paragraph [02] states that the attaching means may be a garment. Paragraph [07] states that the sock is a garment and paragraph [09] discloses that instead of a sock and a wristband any kind of garment can be used. In paragraph [10] the headband for goggles is defined as garment. Replacing "sock, wristband and headband for goggles" by "garment" was awarded with **5 marks, 1 mark** was awarded for replacing the feature "holding ... close to" by "attaching ... to".

3.2 The dependent claims (24 marks)

3.2.1 Wireless transmitting means

In **claim 2 (3 marks)** a structural feature like "the transmitting means (4, 14, 24) is a wireless transmitting means" was expected. The expected reformulation was disclosed in original claim 1. **3 marks** were available for replacing the feature related to a method by a structural feature.

3.2.2 Local network emitter

Claim 3 (3 marks) had to be made dependent exclusively upon claim 2, because the "wireless transmitting means" has no antecedent in claim 1. **3 marks** were available for correcting the dependency of claim 3.

3.2.3 Screen

Claim 4 could remain unchanged, if claim 1 was amended as suggested.

3.2.4 Sock, wristband

The client has included the features "sock, wristband and headband for goggles" into claim 1 of the draft set of claims, because he was not sure whether a generalisation by "garment" was authorised. If the features "sock, wristband and headband for goggles" are replaced by the more general term "garment", it was expected from the candidates to resume these features in the dependent claims.

4 marks were available for a dependent claim related to a sock and a wristband.

In the example set of claims several dependent claims have been formulated. However, other solutions are possible, provided that the whole set of claims is clear and the dependencies are correct: e.g. instead of separate dependent **claim 5 and claim 6** one single claim could be formulated in line with original claim 5: "<u>System according to any of claims 1 to 4, wherein the garment is a sock (1), a wristband (11) or a glove</u>". (9 marks)

3.2.5 Glove

5 marks were available for maintaining "glove". The option "glove" was originally disclosed only in the claims and only in combination with wireless transmitting means. However, paragraph [02] provides a sufficient basis under Art. 123(2) EPC to omit the feature "wireless transmitting means" from this embodiment (see also the GL F-IV, 6.3).

The feature "glove" was apparently erroneously claimed instead of "goggles" in the original application. This is clear from the client's letter, paragraph [04]. Although no explicit support is provided in the description (cf. communication, section 3.2), it is very important for the client to have protection for this embodiment. Inspired by the (erroneous) word "glove" and by the teaching of D3, he intends to produce a glove comprising optical and motion sensors according to the invention (client's letter, paragraph [04]).

A glove is
- originally disclosed by the claims,
- not in contradiction to the description,
- in alignment with the invention and
- an alternative attaching means known by the prior art (D3, paragraph [04]).

In order to make the claims consistent with the description, the statement of invention in paragraph [02] of the description could at any time be replaced by a reference to the set of claims.

3.2.6 Headband for goggles

Claim 7 **(6 marks)**. The headband for goggles had to be claimed in a separate dependent claim, because it could be argued that this embodiment is – in contrast to the sock, wristband and glove – not disclosed in combination with a screen as claimed in claim 4. A suitable solution in this exceptional case was to formulate a **new claim 7** directed to the headband and not dependent upon claim 4. **3 marks** were available for a dependent claim directed to the headband for goggles, **3 marks** were available for the correct dependency of such a claim. If however "headband for goggles" was claimed in combination with a screen, reasoning was expected in the letter of reply that such a combination has a basis in the application as originally filed. Up to 3 marks were available for such a set of claims.

3.2.7 Optitex

Claim 8 **(3 marks)**. In claim 5 of the draft set of claims the lack of clarity related to the trade mark Optitex™ could be overcome by replacing Optitex™ by "a material comprising 50–60 % cotton, 30–40 % Polyurethane and 10–20 % Polyethylene Glycol in % by weight".

This definition can be found in paragraph [09] of the description. In view of new dependent claims the claim had to be renumbered to **new claim 8** according to the example set of claims. **3 marks** were available for claiming the composition of Optitex™ instead of the expression "Optitex™", for deleting Optitex™ and the correct dependency of this claim, i.e. all other claims.

4. Claims differing from the example claims

Note: The overall number of marks per claim cannot be negative.

4.1 Deductions for too "narrow" claims

Where an independent claim of an answer paper differs from that of the example solution and results in a claim which is considered to be inappropriate for protecting the client's invention, e.g. because it does not give the applicant the broadest possible protection for his invention, marks have been deducted. Marks were also deducted for an independent claim not corresponding to the applicant's wish (see below).

Sometimes, candidates have drafted very narrow independent claims. Such claims are much easier to argue for novelty and inventive step. Such claims often also go against the client's wishes. Therefore, in general fewer marks were awarded in the inventive step argument section for very limited independent claims.

Examples:

- Adding to claim 1 the feature that the motion sensor is placed next to or between the optical sensor(s).
- Candidates having an independent claim comprising the composition of Optitex in most cases could not achieve more than 20 out of 32 marks for reasoning in favour of inventive step.

4.1.1 Independent claim

For an independent claim of an answer paper having one or more additional features that are considered to limit the claim unnecessarily, **3 marks** per unnecessarily limiting feature were deducted from the total marks awarded for the claim. However for severe limitations that result in a claim of minimum use for the client **6 marks** were deducted.

Examples:

- Claiming one or more of sock, wristband or headband, instead of garment. However, only 1–2 marks may have been deducted (cf F-IV,4.9), if these features were claimed as optional features/examples for garment ("such as ..."), especially, if these examples have rendered features in the dependent claims unclear.
- Adding the composition of Optitex™: 6 marks were deducted
- Claiming that the evaluation means (5, 25) is configured to correct the output signals from the optical sensors (2, 12, 22) based on the output signal of the motion sensor (3, 13, 23) <u>and</u> to correct the output signal from the motion sensor (3, 13, 23) based on the output signal of the optical sensor, or to omit one of the two options: 3 marks were deducted.

4.1.2 Dependent claims

For a dependent claim of an answer paper having one or more additional features that are considered to limit the claim unnecessarily, **2 marks** per unnecessarily limiting feature per claim were deducted from the total marks awarded for the claims.

Examples:

- Claiming wireless transmitting means only in combination with wireless local network emitter or combining other dependent claims.
- Unnecessarily excluding other claims in the dependency.
- Headbands for goggles in combination with an earphone or transmitter of audio signals.

4.2 Deductions for non-compliance with the EPC

Claim sets which have been amended so that they differ from the client's draft set of claims, but which result in claims which do not fulfil the requirements of the EPC, for example because they result in an unclear or non-inventive claim, have not received full marks.

Examples:

- Keeping "sock, wristband or headband for goggles",
- Deletion of technical features in the independent claim of the draft set of claims leading to lack of novelty/ inventive step,
- Addition of technical features from the description leading to unallowable intermediate generalisation or unclear back-references.

4.2.1 Independent claim

For an independent claim of an answer paper not fulfilling the requirements of the EPC, for example due to lack of novelty or inventive step **6 marks** were deducted, for added subject matter or lack of clarity, up to **3 marks** per issue were deducted from the total marks awarded for the claim.

Examples:

- The features "garment" or "correcting the signals" are omitted in the independent claim. Omitting "garment" in the claim, but maintaining all the other features as suggested in the example set of claims would define a system not solving the technical problem reported by the application (paragraph [01]) vis-à-vis D1 of providing a comfortable and reliable way of monitoring vital signs. Moreover, since D2 suggests that the output of an optical sensor as a function of the output of a motion sensor be corrected to reduce noise, a system obtained by adding in D1 the signal correction would be obvious over a combination of D1 and D2.
- An independent claim as proposed above but omitting the feature related to the signal correction would be unallowable under Art. 123(2) EPC because this feature is in original claim 1 and is essential for the invention. Such a claim would arguably not be inventive in view of a combination of the teachings of D1 and D3.
- The client explicitly requests a claim comprising garment and suggests a claim with the specific examples of the garment. Any claim omitting features from the suggested claim would be against the explicit wish of the client. Up to 6 marks were deducted for an independent claim not being in line with the wishes of the client.

4.2.2 Dependent claims

For a dependent claim of an answer paper not fulfilling the requirements of the EPC, for example due to added subject matter or lack of clarity, **2 marks** per issue were deducted from the total marks awarded for the claim.

Examples:

- Unclear back-references to the independent claim,
- Wrong dependencies,
- Addition of technical features from the description leading to unallowable intermediate generalisation.
- No marks were deducted for adding to the claim related to the goggles the literal wording from the description "wherein the evaluation means 25 is configured to correct the output signal from the sensor 22 based on the output signal of sensor 23, and <u>vice-versa</u>" (see below).

4.3 Formal matters

For an answer paper having an independent claim according to the example solution it is considered appropriate to use the <u>two-part form</u> with respect to one of D1-D3. **1 mark** was deducted if the two-part form was not correct with respect to any of these documents. **1 mark** was not deducted, if the document chosen is not the document being considered the closest prior art in the example solution. **1 mark** was deducted, if the claims did not comprise reference signs.

Example:

- D1 is considered to represent the closest prior art. D1 discloses all the technical features of the draft independent claim except that the attaching means is a garment and that the sensor signals are corrected.
- D2 discloses all the technical features of the draft independent claim except that attaching means attach the sensors to the human body and that the attaching means is a garment.

4.4 Solutions not based on the client's draft claim set

The client provides a draft claim set that he proposes for filing. He asks for any necessary amendments for fulfilling the requirements of the EPC, whilst giving him the broadest possible protection. Answer papers which have claim sets not based on client's wishes are not considered to be in the interest of the client and such claims may therefore receive less marks or no marks.

For dependent claims in addition to the dependent claims of the expected solution, **no marks** were available, because it was the explicit request of the client not to add new, i.e. further dependent claims. However, new dependent claims are not considered new if they claim the originally claimed subject-matter or subject-matter claimed in the client's draft claim set in a different way.

For amendments to the description **no marks** were available.

5. Letter of reply to the EPO (up to 70 marks available)

5.1 General remark

It was necessary to provide arguments demonstrating that the objections raised by the examiner have been overcome, providing a basis for all the amendments made and explaining why the subject-matter is both novel and inventive.

It is noted that the examples for sections of a letter of reply given in the following are, unless otherwise stated, appropriate for the example claim set. For an answer paper having a different claim set, the letter of reply may differ and the answer paper is considered accordingly.

No marks were available for
a <u>letter to the applicant</u>
a <u>letter to the marker</u>

All the necessary information should be contained in the letter of reply to the examining division.

A total of 70 marks was available for the arguments. The arguments were assessed on the basis of the actual set of claims submitted. Thus for example, if additional claims are formulated, a full basis needs to be provided for all the claims. If additional independent claims are submitted, novelty and inventive step arguments for these claims are expected, the total amount of marks for arguments staying the same.

5.2 Basis for the amendments (24 marks)

A full basis had to be provided for all amendments. In order to obtain full marks it is necessary to identify all the amendments made in the set of claims filed as compared to the original set of claims. The basis needs to be provided irrespective of whether or not the amendment was proposed in the client's letter or is a further amendment to the draft set of claims. Amendments proposed by the client but not being in the set of claims submitted should not be discussed.

Arguments needed to be provided if features have been combined from different parts of the application. Similarly, if the wording used in the application was modified, if a feature was taken from an example or if features were deleted from a claim, detailed arguments needed to be provided in support of these amendments.

5.2.1 Claim 1 (12 marks)

12 marks were available for indicating and explaining a basis for claim 1. For the example claim 1, these marks were awarded according to the following scheme:

2 marks were available for appropriately stating claims 1 and 5 as basis for new claim 1 and explaining that based on the original disclosure of claim 1 "holding ...close to the human body" was replaced by "attaching ... to the human body". Further basis for the new wording of claim 1 is paragraph [02], first sentence. A statement addressing the clarity objections of the examiner is discussed below in section 5.3.1.

2 marks were awarded for indicating paragraph [02] as general basis for adding the feature that the attaching means is a garment.

2 marks were given, if additionally the paragraphs [07], [09] and [10] as further basis for claim 1 were mentioned:

Paragraph [07] discloses for the first embodiment the general statements "Accommodating an optical sensor into a garment". For the second embodiment paragraph [09] discloses clearly the use of any garment instead of a sock or a wristband: "The sock 1 may be replaced by a wristband 11 as shown in the embodiment in Fig. 2. However, any garment may be used". As to the third embodiment paragraph [10] discloses "The headband 21 is a garment and may be made of Optitex™ which provides reliable, secure and comfortable attachment of the sensors to the ear".

GL H-V,3.2.1 (intermediate generalisation) requires that, *"when a feature is taken from a particular embodiment and added to the claim, it has to be established that the feature is not related or inextricably linked to the other features of that embodiment and that the <u>overall disclosure justifies the generalising</u> isolation of the feature and its introduction into the claim"*. As the general term "garment" is mentioned for all embodiments, the requirements of GL H-V,3.2.1 are fulfilled.

Therefore, the description not only provides a basis for generalizing the specific examples of sock, wristband and headband to "garment", but mentions for each of the three examples the more general term "garment". The detailed description of the embodiments reflects the broad scope of the claims, because specific features are given only as optional examples. Consequently, generalizing the features sock, wristband and headband to garment is not an unallowable intermediate generalization.

6 marks were available for a reasoning supporting the deletion of "wireless transmitting means" using the essentiality test (GL H-V,3.1).

<u>Example:</u>

New claim 1 is based on original claim 1 and 5 and paragraphs [02], [07], [09] and [10] of the description. Based on the original disclosure of claim 5 and paragraph [02], first sentence, "holding ...close to the human body" was replaced by "attaching ... to the human body". The general term garment is disclosed for all three embodiments ([07], [09] and [10]). From paragraph [02] and [07], it is clear that any garment can be used instead of sock, wristband and headband. Par [09] directly and unambiguously teaches that instead

of the specific examples for the attaching means any garment can be used. As the general term "garment" is mentioned for all embodiments as well as in the general description of the invention in paragraph [02], the requirements of GL H-V,3.2.1 are fulfilled. Adding garment to claim 1 therefore is not an unallowable intermediate generalisation. (**6 marks**)
The feature "wireless transmitting means" was deleted from original claim 1. The gist of the invention lies in the design of the attaching means and the correction of the sensor signals. Therefore, the feature "wireless transmitting means" is not essential for the inventive idea. Paragraphs [02], [04], [09] and [12] make clear that any kind of transmitting means can be used, such as a serial port for a cable for instance. From the same passages the skilled person learns that a wireless transmission is not indispensable for the invention, because wireless transmission is just one option out of several possibilities. Carrying out the inventive idea is independent from the transmitting means. Wireless transmitting means can be replaced without any technical difficulty e.g. by a serial port for a cable and there is no need to modify the remaining features to compensate for the change. (**6 marks**)

5.2.2   Claim 2 – wireless transmitting means (2 marks)

1 mark was available for indicating and explaining a basis for claim 2, i.e. for stating that the claim is based on the feature, which was removed from original claim 1.

5.2.3   Claim 3 – local network emitter (2 marks)

1 mark was available for indicating that claim 3 corresponds to original claim 3. **1 additional mark** was available for indicating that only the dependency was changed.

5.2.4   Claim 5 and 6 – sock, wristband, glove (2 marks)

1 mark was available for indicating that claims 5 and 6 (sock, wristband, glove) correspond to the original claim 5. **1 mark** was available for referring to the reasoning as provided under section 5.2.1, where it is argued that the feature "wireless transmitting means" is not essential for the inventive concept and thus can also be isolated from the embodiment "glove".

5.2.5   Claim 7 – Headband for goggles (marks)

1 mark was available for indicating that claim 7 (headband for goggles) corresponds to paragraph [11] of the description. **3 marks** were available for arguments supporting this: Paragraph [11] discloses that the evaluation means is configured to correct the output signals from the optical sensors based on the output signal of the motion sensor <u>and vice versa</u>, i.e. the option "or to correct the output signal from the motion sensor based on the output signal of the optical sensor" is not explicitly disclosed as an alternative option. Here, arguments should be provided that this expression has to be seen in the light of the statement of invention in paragraph [02] and the original version of the independent claim. From both disclosures in combination the skilled person directly and unambiguously understands that with the term "and vice versa" the second alternative option of correcting the signal is meant and that both ways of correcting the signal are alternative options.

Example:

Claim 7 is based on paragraph [11] of the description. This paragraph corresponds almost literally to the claim wording of present claim 1. The only difference is that "attaching means" is replaced by "headband for goggles" and that "the evaluation means is configured to correct the output signals from the optical sensors based on the output signal of the motion sensor <u>and vice versa</u>". The option "or to correct the output signal from the motion sensor based on the output signal of the optical sensor" is here not explicitly disclosed as an alternative option. However, this expression has to be seen in the light of the statement of invention in paragraph [02] in combination with the original version of the independent claim, where the two alternative options of correcting the signal are explicitly claimed. Therefore, in view of the general description of the invention in paragraph [02] and the formulation of independent claim 1 it is clear that with "and vice versa" the second alternative option of correcting the signal is meant and that both ways of correcting the signal are alternative options.

Furthermore, the wireless transmitting means is an optional feature. Therefore, new claim 7 does not represent an unallowable intermediate generalisation. (4 marks)

Note: For this embodiment only an ear plug is disclosed as output means. Therefore, this claim cannot be dependent upon claim 4.

5.2.6   Claim 8 – Optitex (3 marks)

1 mark was available for indicating that claim 8 corresponds to original claim 6. The term Optitex™ was replaced by the material composition as disclosed in paragraph [09].
(2 marks)

Further arguments as to why the claim is now clear were expected and are discussed under "clarity" (see next section).

5.3   Clarity (8 marks)

In the letter of reply it needs to be explained how the clarity objections raised in the communication have been overcome.

5.3.1   "close to human body" (claim 1) (2 marks)

Replacing "holding …close to the human body" by "attaching … to the human body" as originally disclosed in claim 5 and in paragraph [02] overcomes the objections in section 3.1 of the examiners' communication. **(2 marks)**

5.3.2   Glove supported by the description (claim 6) (4 marks)

Apparently the word "goggles" was erroneously replaced by "glove" in original claim 5. "Glove" is not mentioned in the description. This has been noted in the examiner's communication. It has not been objected as lacking clarity, but it is clear from the examiner's statement that a reasoning is expected, as to how the example of a glove is supported by the inventive idea and by the description as required by GL F-IV,6.3. GL F-IV,6.3 requires that "*as a general rule, a claim should be regarded as supported by the description unless there are well-founded reasons for believing that the skilled person would be unable, on the basis of the information given in the application as filed, to extend the particular teaching of the description to the whole of the field claimed by using routine methods of experimentation or analysis*".

4 marks have been available for the reasoning supporting the maintenance of "glove" in the claims.

Example:

"Glove" is mentioned in original claim 5, but is not mentioned in the description as originally filed. "Glove" is not in contradiction to the disclosure and to the teaching of the description. Therefore, no lack of clarity under Art. 84 EPC arises. For all three embodiments the description (cf. paragraphs [07], [09] and [10]) discloses that any garment can be used instead of the examples described in more detail in the description. A glove is furthermore in alignment with "garment" as stated in paragraph [02].

As illustrated by the last paragraph of D3, it is common knowledge for the skilled person that instead of a sock and a wristband a glove may be used as attaching means for attaching a medical sensor to the human body.

The description therefore fulfils the requirements of GL F-IV,6.3 concerning support under Art. 84 EPC, i.e.: "*as a general rule, a claim should be regarded as supported by the description unless there are well-founded reasons for believing that the skilled person would be unable, on the basis of the information given in the application as filed, to extend the particular teaching of the description to the whole of the field claimed by using routine methods of experimentation or analysis*".

If the examiner is of the opinion that the embodiment of the glove is to be mentioned in the description, it can always be added to the description based on original claim 5 without violating Art. 123(2) EPC. (4 marks)

5.3.3 Trademark Optitex™ (claim 8) (2 marks)

2 marks were available for reasoning that Optitex™ was replaced by "material comprising 50–60 % cotton, 30–40 % polyurethane and 10–20 % polyethylene glycol in % by weight." This feature clearly specifies the composition of the claimed material and is not objectionable under Art. 84 EPC.

5.4 Novelty (6 marks)

Novelty of the claims also had to be discussed. It is sufficient to mention a single technical feature rendering claim 1 novel with respect to D1, D2 and D3.

Examples:

(1) Claim 1 is novel with respect to D1, because D1 does not disclose a garment for attaching the sensors to the human body. D1 does not disclose means for correcting the sensor signals (**2 marks**)
(2) D2 does not disclose attaching means for attaching a garment to the human body (**2 marks**).
(3) D3 does not disclose a motion sensor. D3 further does not disclose means for correcting the sensor signals (**2 marks**).

5.5 Inventive step argumentation for the independent claim (up to 32 marks)

It is appropriate to provide arguments, which are structured to follow the problem solution approach (see Guidelines G-VII 5).

5.5.1 Identifying the closest prior art (7 marks)

In selecting the closest prior art, the first consideration is that it should be directed to a similar purpose or effect as the invention, or at least belong to the same or a closely related technical field as the claimed invention.

5.5.1.1 Stating the closest prior art (1 mark)

For stating an item of prior art as being the closest prior art in a consistent manner with the two-part form of the independent claim, **1 mark** was available.

For claims such as the example claims presented herein above, D1 is considered to represent the closest prior art according to GL-VII,5.3, since it addresses the same field as that of the invention and is the best starting point for the most convincing problem-solution-approach in favour of inventive step; for a clear statement to this effect, **1 mark** is available.

D2 is not a suitable starting point for assessing inventive step, because it is not in the same technical field. This is true even if D2 has many technical features in common. D3 could *prima facie* also be a suitable starting point. However, it has fewer features in common than D1.

5.5.1.2 Arguments justifying the choice of closest prior art (6 marks)

Discussing D1 (**2 marks**), discussing D2 (**2 marks**) and discussing D3 (**2 marks**).

Example for the example independent claim:

Closest prior art is D1, because D1 is the only available document in the field of the invention. D1 mentions indirectly in the last paragraph the underlying purpose of the invention, i.e. attaching the optical and motion sensor to the human body in a comfortable and reliable manner. Therefore, D1 is the closest of the available prior art (**2 marks**). D2 has as many features in common as D1, but is in a remote technical field with respect to the invention, i.e. in the field of baby phones and remotely monitoring the behaviour of babies. The system in D2 is not adapted for monitoring the vital signs of a human body in a reliable manner as required in the medical sector. This however is a key feature of the invention (**2 marks**).

D3 could also be a suitable starting point. However, it has fewer features in common than D1 and is silent about a motion sensor, which is of fundamental importance for the invention. (**2 marks**).

5.5.2 Formulation of the objective technical problem (7 marks)

The next stage is to establish in an objective way the technical problem to be solved. This requires the steps of:
(1) identifying, in terms of features, the difference between the claimed invention and the closest prior art, i.e. the distinguishing features of the claimed invention (**1 mark**);
(2) stating the technical effects or the advantages of the difference (**3 marks**); and
(3) formulating a problem which is solved by these technical effects (**3 marks**).

Example:

The subject-matter of claim 1 differs from D1 by the features of the characterising portion, i.e. in that the attaching means is a garment and in that the evaluation means is configured to correct the output signal from the optical sensor based on the output signal of the motion sensor or vice versa (**1 mark**).

The **technical effect** of a garment as the attaching means is that sensors required for pulse oximetry are attached in a secure, comfortable and reliable manner to the human body for remotely monitoring the vital signs of the human body. An undesirable side effect of accommodating an optical sensor into a garment is that noise is added to the output signal of the optical sensor 2 (paragraph [07]). Therefore, in the evaluation means the signal of the optical sensor has to be combined with the signal of the motion sensor and corrected such that the noise is reduced (paragraph [08]). In addition to improving the attachment of the sensors therefore also the signal to noise ratio must be improved. This also overcomes the prejudice mentioned in D3 that a garment may not be used for attaching an optical/motion sensor to the human body for monitoring vital signs. The advantage of the invention is that the vital signs can be monitored in a remote position over a long period. The patient is able to wear the sensors attached to his body in a comfortable manner. This allows medical staff a secure and reliable monitoring of vital signs of a patient on a long-term scale (see paragraphs [01] and [10]).

In contrast to the system disclosed in D1, long-term observation is possible. The system described in D1 is designed only for short-term observation.

Contrary to D2, the invention has the advantage that the four vital signs (pulse, body temperature, blood pressure and blood oxygen saturation) can be monitored. These vital signs can be monitored only if the sensors are attached to the human body.

With respect to D3, the invention has also the advantage that the four vital signs can be monitored by means of an optical/motion sensor. In addition, the signal to noise ratio is improved for the sensor signals. (**3 marks**).

Citing the advantages provided by the client in paragraph [01] of his letter attracts **2 marks**: The *invention has the advantage that the vital signs can be remotely monitored with a reliable, secure and comfortable attachment of the sensors in combination with a high signal quality, which is achieved by noise reduction through correcting the sensor output signals.*

The **objective technical problem** may therefore be formulated as:
Providing a reliable and comfortable system for long-term remote monitoring of the vital signs of a person, including small children and babies, in combination with a high signal quality (paragraph [01] of the description and paragraph [01] of the client's letter) (**3 marks**).

Other convincing argumentation could also achieve full **7 marks**. Marks were redistributed accordingly between the formulation of the effect/advantages of the invention and the formulation of the problem, as long as they are consistent overall.

5.5.3 Arguments in support of inventive step (18 marks)

Arguments should support the features of the independent claim. They should be convincing and well structured. In order to obtain full marks in this section, arguments which fully answer the question as to why the skilled person, knowing the teaching of the prior

art as a whole, would not arrive at the claimed subject matter had to be presented. Such arguments can be structured to consider the following aspects:
- Would the skilled person arrive at the subject matter of the claim by considering the teaching of the closest prior art on its own?
- Would the skilled person consider combining the teaching of the closest prior art with that of other prior art documents in order to solve the objective technical problem?
- If the skilled person were to combine the teaching of the closest prior art with other items of prior art, would they arrive at the subject matter of the claim?

Example:

5.5.3.1 *Considering D1 on its own* (4 marks)

In the last paragraph of D1 the attachment of the sensors is addressed. D1 discloses only a clip for attaching the sensors. D1 does not provide any teaching for using garment as attaching means. In D1 the motion sensor is too large and heavy for being integrated into garment. In D1 the pulse is measured separately and independently. This teaches away from combining the different sensor signals. Apparently, a special motion sensor was developed or the author of D1 was not aware of such a sensor. Therefore, the skilled person faced with the teaching of D1 had no suitable sensor at hand, which could be integrated into a sock, a wristband or a headband for suitably carrying out the invention. Even if the skilled person had had such a motion sensor, he would still have been faced with the problem of suitable attaching means and noise reduction. The general knowledge of a person skilled in the medical area does not provide any solution to these problems.

5.5.3.2 *Considering D1 + D2* (6 marks)

D2 is not concerned with the problem of providing a way of attaching a sensor to a body in a comfortable and reliable way. To the contrary, the camera of D2 has to be kept at a distance from the body. Therefore, the skilled person has no motivation to look in D2 for a solution to the technical problem. Furthermore, D2 neither discloses nor remotely suggests a sensor attached to a body by means of a garment, because the camera of D2 is too large to be integrated in a garment and would presumably not function properly if in contact with the human body. Therefore, even if the skilled person would look in D2 for a feature of interest in D1, he would not find any suggestion of implementing a garment in D1.

Accordingly, the signal correction algorithm of D2 is not directed to the reduction of noise introduced by implementing the sensors in a garment. It is also noted that no further software can be integrated in the electronics of D1 ([04]), so that the implementation in D1 of the correction algorithm of D2 would require an extensive modification of the electronics of D1. The skilled person would not attempt to overcome these technical difficulties in absence of a clear suggestion in D2 that the modification would solve the technical problem.

5.5.3.3 *Considering D1 + D3* (8 marks)

In the event that the skilled person is pointed to D3 to solve the problem, he would see that D3 teaches using garment for attaching <u>electrical</u> sensors. In D3 none of pulse, body temperature, blood pressure and blood oxygen saturation is measured. D3 does not teach to integrate optical and motions sensors into a garment. To the contrary, D3 teaches (paragraph [03]) that the integration of optical sensors such as in D1 in the garment disclosed by D3 creates additional noise representing additional technical difficulties, leading the skilled person away from the combination of D1 and D3. The garment of D3 and the optical sensor of D1 are therefore presented to the skilled person as incompatible features (Guidelines G-VII 6 (i)).

The skilled person might try to override this drawback by looking for another material for the garment, but he does not find in D3 any suggestion of a correction algorithm based on the output of a motion sensor.

For this technical drawback neither D1 nor D3 suggests a possible solution. As discussed above, even the algorithm disclosed for the SMOOTHY App is not suitable for improving the signal to noise ratio for an optical sensor and a motion sensor. Therefore, even if the skilled person combines D1 and D3, (s)he would still be faced with the problem of increased noise on the sensor signals.

5.5.3.4 *Considering D1 + D2 + D3*

To arrive at the invention, the skilled person should implement in D1 the correction algorithm of D2 and the garment of D3, even overriding the contrary indications given by D3. In any event, the fact that more than one document must be combined with the closest prior art is an indication of inventive step (Guidelines G VII 6, paragraph 1) since the invention is not a mere aggregation of features, rather there is a functional interaction (Guidelines G-VII 7, paragraph 1) between the correction algorithm and the garment (see paragraph [07] of the application). It would therefore not be correct to argue that each of these features is an obvious solution to a respective independent technical problem. Therefore, in the unlikely case, where the skilled person tried to combine the teachings of D1, D2 and D3 (s)he would encounter the technical difficulties mentioned above.

Consequently the subject-matter of claim 1 is inventive in view of the available prior art D1-D3.

All the other claims are dependent on claim 1 and therefore also relate to inventive subject matter. It is concluded that the invention defined in claim 1 involves an inventive step.

It was not expected that candidates provide all the above-listed arguments. With a convincing reasoning comprising many of the above-listed arguments full marks could be achieved. On the other hand the above-listed arguments are not exhaustive and other convincing arguments may attract marks.

The distribution given above (4, 6 and 8 marks) is only indicative for a possible distribution. The available 18 marks have been distributed as a whole for discussing inventive step with respect to D1-D3.

Candidates starting their reasoning from D2 and D3 as closest prior art could in most cases not attract more than 20 marks and 26 marks, respectively, out of available 32 marks, because their reasoning in support of inventive step was less convincing. In the case of very limited independent claims, e.g. comprising the composition of Optitex™, in most cases not more than 20 marks out of 32 marks were achieved, because the reasoning was less complex and less convincing.

Examination Committee I: Paper B – Marking Details – Candidate No

Category		Max. possible	Marks Marker 1	Marker 2
Claims	Claims	30		
Arguments	Amendments	24		
Arguments	Clarity	8		
Arguments	Novelty	6		
Arguments	Inventive step	32		
Total				

Appendix 3

CEIPI – Model Solution according to the Examiners' Report
Paper B2017

To:
European Patent Office
80298 München
Germany

1. It is requested to grant a European patent on the basis of annexed claims 1 to 7.
2. **Disclosure Article 123 (2) EPC**
2.1 The new independent claim 1 has been based on the combination of features of the original claims 1 and 5, with the following additional amendments:
    - The attaching means (1, 11, 21) has been specified as (suitable) for attaching ... "to" the human body, instead of "close to". Basis for this amendment can be found in paragraph [02], first sentence, of the original description.
    - The attaching means (1, 11, 21) has been specified as a garment. Basis for this amendment can also be found in paragraph [02], now third sentence. It has to be noted in this respect, that all specific examples of attaching means given in the original description have been defined as "a garment". See, for instance, paragraphs [07] (sock 1 = garment), [09] (sock 1, wristband 11, "any garment may be used") and [10] ("headband 21 is a garment"). It will further be clear that a glove, only disclosed in original claim 5, is also a garment.
    - The feature "that the transmitting means (4, 14, 24) is a wireless transmitting means" has been deleted from original claim 1. As clearly stated in paragraph [02], last sentence, it is not important for the invention how the signals are transmitted to the evaluation means. For the specific embodiments of the attaching means disclosed this is further supported by paragraphs [04], last sentence (sock 1 – "transmitting means 4 may be any kind of transmitting means"), [09] (wristband 11 – transmitting means 14 is identical to the first embodiment), and [12] (headband 21 – transmitting means 24 may be as described for the other embodiments). Even for an attachment means in the form of a glove, only disclosed in original claim 5 in connection with a wireless transmitting means, it will be clear that such a transmitting means is not essential and can be generalised. It can thus be concluded that, on the basis of what a skilled person would derive directly and unambiguously, using common general knowledge, and seen objectively and relative to the date of filing, from the whole of the documents as filed, the above feature concerning the wireless transmitting means can be deleted from the independent claim. Thus, the requirements of the Guidelines, H-V, 3.1, have been fulfilled.

    Summarising, no subject-matter has been added when formulating the new claim 1.
2.2 The new dependent claim 2 is based on the feature removed from original claim 1.
2.3 The new dependent claim 3 is identical to original dependent claim 3, with its dependency changed in view of new claim 2.
2.4 Dependent claim 4 corresponds to original claim 4.
2.5 The dependent claim 5 corresponds to original claim 5. Concerning the allowability of claiming a glove without a wireless transmitting means reference is made to Section 2.1 above.
2.6 New dependent claim 6 has been based on paragraphs [10] and [11] and claims a headband for goggles as an embodiment which was originally disclosed, but not explicitly claimed before. The last sentence of paragraph [11] describing this embodiment does not explicitly disclose the two alternative options of correcting the output signals (and vice versa vs. or in claim 1). However, in view of the general description of the invention in paragraph [02], penultimate sentence, and the formulation of independent claim 1 it will be clear to the skilled person that both ways of correcting the signals are alternative options.
2.7 New dependent claim 7 corresponds to original claim 6, except that the term Optitex™ was replaced by the material composition as disclosed in paragraph [09].

2.8 On the basis of the explanations set out above, it can be concluded that the subject matter of claims 1 to 7 fulfils the requirements of Article 123(2) EPC.

3. Clarity – Article 84 EPC

3.1 Under point 3.1 of the Office Communication the objection is raised that the expression "holding ... close to the human body" is a relative term and thus unclear. This objection was overcome by the formulation "attaching ... to the human body" in new independent claim 1.

3.2 Point 3.2 of the Office Communication raises the objection that the feature "glove" is only mentioned in the original claims and not in the description. It is submitted that the skilled person would recognise directly and unambiguously, from the whole of the documents filed, that a glove constitutes a garment suitable for carrying out the invention. In this respect, reference can also be made to prior art document D3, paragraph [04]. The requirements of the Guidelines, F-IV, 6.3, have thus been fulfilled.

3.3 In view of the objection raised in point 3.3 of the Office Communication, the term Optitex™ has been replaced by its material composition as disclosed in paragraph [09].

3.4 It is submitted that the claims are now clear within the meaning of Article 84 EPC.

4. Novelty – Article 54 EPC

4.1 According to the independent claim 1 the attaching means for attaching sensors to the human body is a garment.

4.2 Document D1 discloses an optical pulse oximeter for measuring the pulse and the oxygen saturation in the blood, i.e. a system for monitoring at least one vital sign of a human body. However, the attaching means used is a clip (201). There is no mentioning of a garment as attaching means.

4.3 Document D2 discloses a system comprising a camera which is mounted on a support holding the camera close to e.g. a baby. Although the system is able to monitor at least one vital sign of a human body, there is no mention at all of an attachment means.

4.4 Document D3 discloses a sock (i.e. a garment), comprising an electrical sensor for electrocardiography. There is neither a mention of a motion sensor nor of a correction means as according to independent claim 1.

4.5 Therefore, the conclusion is that none of the prior art disclosures D1, D2 and D3 reveals the combination of all the features set out in new independent claim 1. Thus, the subject-matter of claim 1 is novel within the meaning of Article 54 EPC.

5. Inventive Step – Article 56 EPC

5.1 As already stated in Section 4.2 above, document D1 describes, similar to claim 1, a system for monitoring at least one vital sign of a human body. It further discloses an optical sensor, a motion sensor and evaluation means. These sensors are attached to the human body by means of a clip (201). The document thus relates to the same technical field as the invention.

Document D2 is not concerned with the attachment of an optical sensor and a motion sensor to the human body. In the document it is even stated that the camera comprising the sensors should be mounted out of reach of the human body (i.e. the baby) to be monitored (paragraph [01] of D2). The document thus relates to a technical field different from that of the invention, which is monitoring vital body signs for controlling the medical status of a patient.

Document D3, like document D1, also relates to the same technical field as the invention. However, it only discloses electrical sensors for recording the electrical activity of the heart. It teaches away from the use of other types of sensors, such as an optical sensor. Furthermore, it fails to mention a motion sensor, which is of fundamental importance for the invention.

The invention, document D1 and document D3 all relate to a system for monitoring at least one vital sign of a human body. However, the invention as claimed in claim 1 has more features in common with document D1 than with document D3. It is therefore concluded that document D1 represents the closest prior art for the subject matter of independent claim 1. The two-part form of the claims according to Rule 43 (1) EPC has thus been based on the disclosure of document D1.

5.2 The subject-matter of independent claim 1 differs from the disclosure of document D1 by the features of the characterising portion, namely in that
- the attaching means is a garment, and in that
- the evaluation means is configured to correct the output signal from the optical sensor based on the output signal of the motion sensor or to correct the output signal from the motion sensor based on the output signal of the optical sensor.

5.3 The distinguishing features set out above give rise to the following technical effects:
- the attaching means in the form of a garment provides reliable, secure and comfortable attachment of the sensors to the human body (see also paragraphs [01] and [10] of the description);
- at the same time the configuration of the evaluation means as claimed overcomes the drawback of using a garment as an attaching means, namely that accommodating an optical sensor or a motion sensor into the garment adds electrical noise to the output signal of the sensor (see paragraphs [07] and [08] of the description, and see also paragraph [03] of document D3).

As a result vital signs of a human body can be monitored long-term and remotely, in a comfortable manner for the patient and with high signal quality.

5.4 The objective technical problem underlying the invention is thus to provide a reliable and comfortable system for long-term remote monitoring of the vital signs of patients, including small children and babies, with sensors attached to the patient's body, in combination with a high signal quality (see also paragraphs [01] and [08] of the description).

5.5 The solution as claimed in claim 1 is not obvious for the following reasons:

5.5.1 Regarding document D1 taken in isolation, and considering the objective technical problem as defined above, it is to be noted that a skilled person does not find any pointer to the solution according to the invention.

Document D1 uses a clip (201) as an attaching means. There is a brief reference to the patient's comfort (paragraph [04]), but only in order to suggest the use of a pressure sensor instead of a large and heavy motion sensor. It does not provide any teaching for using a garment for that purpose.

Document D1 uses an optical sensor (207) for measuring pulse and the oxygen saturation in the blood. It further mentions that, in order to achieve better accuracy and reliability of the pulse measurement, a motion sensor or preferably a pressure sensor could be integrated into the clip (201) (paragraph [04]). There is no disclosure of any evaluation means combining the signals coming from the different sensors. There is even a suggestion to use fast, but simple software, thus teaching away from any, presumably more complicated, signal-correction means.

5.5.2 Document D2 is not concerned with the problem of providing a way of attaching sensors to a body in a comfortable and reliable way. On the contrary, the camera in document D2 is mounted close to the child to be monitored, but out of its reach. Therefore, the skilled person has no motivation to look in document D2 for a solution to the technical problem.

In the unlikely event that a skilled person would combine the teachings of documents D1 and D2, he would not find any suggestion of implementing a garment as the attaching means in document D1. Furthermore, the correction algorithm disclosed in document D2 (paragraph [02]) is not directed to the reduction of electrical noise caused by accommodating sensors in a garment: it aims at improving sound and picture quality of the camera which is mounted remote from the child to be monitored. It is further noted that document D1 indicates that no further software should be installed in the evaluation means (205) disclosed there (paragraph [04], last sentence).

5.5.3 Starting from document D1 and considering the objective technical problem defined above, the skilled person would probably consider document D3, since it belongs to the same technical field as the invention. Document D3 suggests using a sock (301), glove, wristband or headband (i.e. a garment) as a reliable, secure and comfortable means for attaching <u>electrical</u> sensors to the human body (paragraphs [03] and [04]). However, the document actively discourages the skilled person from using such garments for measurements with other types of sensor, e.g. optical sensors, since the signal to noise ratio would be too low for measuring vital signs of the human body.

Even if the skilled person would combine the teachings of documents D1 and D3, none of these documents suggests a solution to the signal quality problem caused by using a garment for attaching other types of sensors than electrical sensors for electrocardiography.

In the unlikely case where the skilled person would try to combine the teachings of documents D1, D3 <u>and</u> D2, he would encounter the technical difficulties mentioned in view of document D2's correction algorithm in Section 5.5.2 above. Consequently, he would not be led towards the combination of features of present claim 1.

5.6 In summary, the conclusion is that the subject-matter of independent claim 1 involves an inventive step having regard to the prior art. Thus, claim 1 is in conformity with Article 56 EPC.

5.7 Dependent claims 2 to 7 define advantageous embodiments of the system according to independent claim 1. They fulfil the requirements of novelty and inventive step by virtue of the novelty and inventive step of the subject-matter of claim 1.

Annex: New claims 1 to 7
Evita Lee-Tea
Authorised Representative

New Claims 1 to 7

1. System for monitoring at least one vital sign of a human body *(10)*, the system comprising:
   - *attaching* means (1, 11, 21) for *attaching* an optical sensor (2, 12, 22) and a motion sensor (3, 13, 23) to the human body (10), the *attaching* means (1, 11, 21) comprising in addition to the sensors (2, 12, 22, 3, 13, 23) transmitting means (4, 14, 24) for transmitting output signals from the sensors (2, 12, 22, 3, 13, 23),
   - evaluation means (5, 25) for receiving the output signals and calculating from the output signals the at least one vital sign,

   <u>characterised in that</u>

   the attaching means (1, 11, 21) is a garment, and in that

   the evaluation means (5, 25) is configured to correct the output signal from the optical sensor (2, 12, 22) based on the output signal of the motion sensor (3, 13, 23) or to correct the output signal from the motion sensor (3, 13, 23) based on the output signal of the optical sensor (2, 12, 22).

2. *System according to claim 1, wherein the transmitting means (4, 14, 24) is a wireless transmitting means.*

3. System according to claim 2, wherein the wireless transmitting means (4, 14, 24) is a wireless local network emitter.

4. System according to any claims 1 to 3, further comprising a screen (6) and configured to display the at least one vital sign on the screen.

5. System according to any of claims 1 to 4, wherein the *garment* is a sock (1), a wristband (11) or a glove.

6. *System according to any of claims 1 to 3, wherein the garment is a headband (21) for goggles (20).*

7. System according to any of claims 1 to 6, wherein the attaching means (1, 11, 21) is at least partly made of *a material comprising 50–60 % cotton, 30–40 % polyurethane and 10–20 % polyethylene glycol in % by weight.*

Index

2021 EQE 138

A

Alternative solutions 894
Alternatives 826, 841, 894, 910
Amended description 153
Amendments 987
Analysis
– in-depth 82, 173, 181
– preliminary 79, 81, 173, 181
Anonymity 126, 172

C

Case Law of the Boards of Appeal 50, 68, 108, 113, 120, 128, 491, 569, 576, 598, 600, 624, 673, 685, 689, 698, 708, 724, 729, 735, 741, 747, 758, 777, 779, 826, 867, 893, 987
Checklist
– final check 87, 173, 557, 570
– response to communication 87
Choice of paper 122
Claimed subject-matter 663, 746, 773, 835, 840, 886
Claims
– categories of 839
– checking 173, 570
– clarity of 826
– combination of independent claims 892
– containing a reference 884, 911
– drafting 890
– drafting of dependent 173, 570
– drafting of independent 173, 570
– interpretation 867
– multiple dependent 916
– parameters in 683, 692, 719, 739, 741, 747, 853, 867, 999
– preamble of 652
– process 858
– product 857
– product-by-process 491, 692, 826, 837, 867, 891
– reference signs 848, 867
– Swiss type 629
– two-part 905
– use 859, 867, 891
Clarity 4, 44, 152, 570, 683, 826, 830, 832, 834, 850, 867, 876, 888, 915, 999
Closest prior art 758, 779, 786, 806
– determination of 779
Commentaries on the EPC 60
Computer implemented invention 624, 655, 671
Content of the examination 69, 129, 147

Correction of errors 987, 988, 1008
Correction of translation errors 1009
Corrections 987
Cosmetic treatment 634

D

Delimitation of subject-matter 640
Disclosed disclaimer 1007, 1030, 1031
Disclosure 488
– generic 590
– implicit 707
– in the letter from the client 288
– in the state of the art 598, 600, 612, 613, 678, 680, 687, 702, 704, 710, 714, 725, 794, 991, 996
– oral 607, 608, 611, 612, 617
– written 608, 615
Disclosure test 1018
Draft the letter in response to the communication 86
Draft the set of amended claims 83
Drafting the response to the communication 5
Duration of paper B 15, 148

E

eEQE 157
EQE
– examination syllabus 120, 128, 569
– Instructions to the candidates 12, 97
– marking 106, 130, 565, 570
– online forum 75
Essentiality test 385
European patent application
– filing 8, 469, 488, 611, 758
Examination Committees 6, 12, 58, 106, 112, 130, 156, 566
Examination Compendium 58, 110, 115, 133, 565
Examination Secretariat 30, 110, 115, 124
Examiners report 58, 110, 131, 465, 481, 565, 570
Exceptions to patentability 624, 634, 657

F

Fall-back positions 151, 570, 906, 909
Features
– distinguishing 677, 696, 784, 786, 792, 806
– essential 826, 835, 867, 874
– functional 837, 852, 871
– identical 587
– implicit 598, 685, 707, 750, 873
– incorporated by reference 595

- inherent 681, 998
- intrinsic 681, 998
- mandatory 318, 321
- means plus function 877
- negative limitations 855, 867, 891
- non-limiting 585
- non-technical 636, 637, 655, 662, 785, 787, 834, 873
- optional 318, 321, 867, 891, 922
- specific 587, 590, 595, 918
- technical 323, 624, 636, 642, 662, 677, 699, 785, 787, 791, 797, 834, 847, 873, 888, 908

Find the objections 80

G

General instructions 47, 141
Generalisation 869
Gold standard 386, 994, 1012, 1020, 1056, 1059
Grades 112, 134
Guidelines for Examination in the EPO 39, 50, 68, 73, 141, 151, 152, 491, 569, 575, 598, 600, 624, 659, 673, 698, 718, 724, 758, 777, 787, 801, 826, 832, 833, 858, 867, 893, 987

I

Implementing provisions to the EQE 12, 55, 97, 98, 128, 560, 770
Inconsistencies 486, 867, 891, 912
Industrial application 625, 646, 656, 667
Information on the schedule for the EQE 2021 examination papers 21
Instructions to candidates 12, 35, 47, 55, 97, 98, 136, 137, 141, 560, 564
Intermediate generalization 1021, 1031
Interpretation 32, 73, 481, 577, 661, 826, 867
- principles of 826, 867
Invention
- non patentable 4, 624
- patentable 4, 624, 641
Inventive step 4, 151, 152, 570, 758
- analogy process 762, 767, 803
- closest prior art 758, 778, 786, 787, 793, 806
- indications of 795, 798
IPREE 12, 55, 98, 106, 110, 120, 128, 464, 468, 469, 560, 564, 569, 615, 620, 638, 770, 772, 774, 804, 805

L

Language 30, 40, 49, 117, 119, 130, 131, 143, 144, 316
Legal texts 32
- Case Law of the Boards of Appeal 50
- European Patent Convention 32
- Guidelines for Examination in the EPO 39

- Official Journal of the EPO 37, 128, 141, 560, 563
- Regulation on the EQE 12, 54, 97, 98, 100, 560, 564, 569

Letter in response to the communication 493

M

Marking 26
Marking sheet 106, 107, 112, 132, 133
Markush group 727, 826
Medical indication 652, 665, 895
- second / further 628
Medical use 649, 652, 861
- first 649, 861, 863
- second / further 624, 650, 718, 863, 866
Methodology 3, 88, 92
- checking the claims 570
- detailed 173
- determining the subject-matter to be claimed 173, 570
- drafting the dependent claims 173, 570
- drafting the independent claims 173, 570
- drafting the introductory part 894
- drafting the supplementary note 464
- final check 87, 173, 557, 570
- keywords 317, 318
- overall 76
- overview 31, 61, 68, 76, 173, 175
- strategy 1, 97, 559, 899
Model solution of Paper B 2017 6
Modified novelty test 1018
Multiple dependencies of claims 912, 920
Multiple selections 747

N

Negative limitations 855, 867, 891
Non-inventions 624, 640, 642, 653, 663
Novelty 4, 151, 152, 489, 569, 570, 590, 600, 637, 666, 673, 770, 773, 784, 803, 806, 898
- analysis of 698
- distinguishing features 677, 696, 784, 786, 792, 806
- test 750
Novelty conferred by an invention 697, 732
Novelty test 1014
Number of dependent claims 918, 922

O

Obviousness 758, 767, 803
Overlapping ranges 727, 741
Overview of the components 78
Overview of the components of your paper B 174

P

Paper B
- content of 146, 174

Parameters 683, 684, 692, 719, 727, 739, 743, 749, 867, 891, 999

Partial problems 765, 792

Preparation of a reply to an official letter 102

Prior public use 606, 612, 619, 620, 794

Problem and solution approach 758, 773

Process 491, 619, 620, 647, 684, 685, 708, 723, 727, 748, 762, 767, 782, 803, 805, 826, 867, 877, 879, 881, 885, 889, 893, 894, 917
- biological 657
- microbiological 647, 657

Product 491, 605, 606, 619, 620, 624, 634, 647, 657, 660, 673, 681, 685, 692, 708, 709, 716, 719, 720, 723, 727, 748, 762, 767, 803, 805, 837, 857, 858, 861, 870, 877, 878, 882, 885, 893, 894, 903, 917, 998
- final 734, 826
- intermediate 826
- interrelated 885, 894
- product-by-process 491, 692, 826, 837, 867, 878, 891

Protection 470, 624, 642, 662, 677, 699, 826, 830, 834, 856, 872, 891, 896
- broadest possible 151, 152, 638

R

REE 12, 55, 98, 100, 560, 564

Reference signs 848, 867

Reference to claims 689, 802, 839, 841, 884, 900, 902, 909, 911, 923

Reference to documents 613, 704

Reference to the description 867, 891

Regulation of the EQE 12, 54, 97, 98, 100, 123, 128, 560, 569, 770

Regulation on the EQE 97, 98, 99, 127, 564, 569

Relative terms 867, 891, 943

Requirements (Art. 52–57 EPC) 84

Response to an official communication 13

Response to the official communication 1045

Result to be achieved 853, 891

Rule 22 IPREE 47

Rule 24 of the Implementing provisions 12

Rule 24(1) IPREE 15

Rule 43(2) EPC 152, 476, 477, 479, 840, 892, 894, 896

S

Selection inventions 674, 724, 759, 798

Selection of chemical substances 729

Selection of sub-ranges 734, 745

Separate applications 469, 474, 896

Single list principle 731

State of the Art 4, 73, 81, 150, 175, 178, 181, 318, 321, 323, 575, 577, 587, 595, 598, 600, 629, 649, 651, 673, 677, 684, 686, 695, 698, 699, 701, 705, 710, 713, 720, 722, 723, 725, 727, 729, 735, 741, 743, 744, 751, 758, 762, 767, 772, 774, 777, 793
- oral disclosure 607, 608, 611, 612, 617
- prior public use 606, 612, 619, 794
- written disclosure 608, 615

Study materials 31
- Commentaries on the EPC 60
- EQE online forum 75
- Guides for preparing for the EQE 70

Subject-matter to be claimed 173, 323, 570

Supplementary note 85, 87, 144, 154, 173, 463, 464, 467, 468, 473, 476, 479, 480, 483, 486, 489, 490, 491, 493, 558, 570

Supplementary notes 154

Support in the application as originally filed 4

Support of the claims 689, 714, 826, 830, 832, 869, 987

Swiss-type claims 630

T

Technical field 13, 104, 105, 145, 146, 321, 570, 582, 647, 649, 721, 726, 775, 780, 782, 895

Technical problem 81, 323, 642, 665, 758, 772, 777, 778, 780, 783, 786, 793, 806, 869, 874

Third party observation 17, 22, 27, 176, 622

Three-point test 385

Trademarks 867, 891

Two lists principle 732, 740

U

Uncommon parameter 722

Undisclosed disclaimer 1003, 1025, 1026, 1028

Unity of invention 44, 152, 155
- single general inventive concept 892

Use 606, 607, 612, 619, 628, 649, 657, 673, 716, 859, 867, 881, 882, 891, 893, 894

Wolters Kluwer

Praxiserprobte Inhalte auch zu Spezialthemen

Mit dem Modul Heymanns Patentanwälte auf dem neuesten Stand:

- 75 und mehr hochrelevante Titel zu Patent-, Marken-, Design- und Wettbewerbsrecht
- Mit den führenden Standardkommentaren *Schulte*, PatentG, und *Singer/Stauder/Luginbühl*, EPÜ
- Für Ausbildung, Anmeldeverfahren oder gerichtliche Auseinandersetzungen
- Zeitschrift MarkenR inkl. Archiv

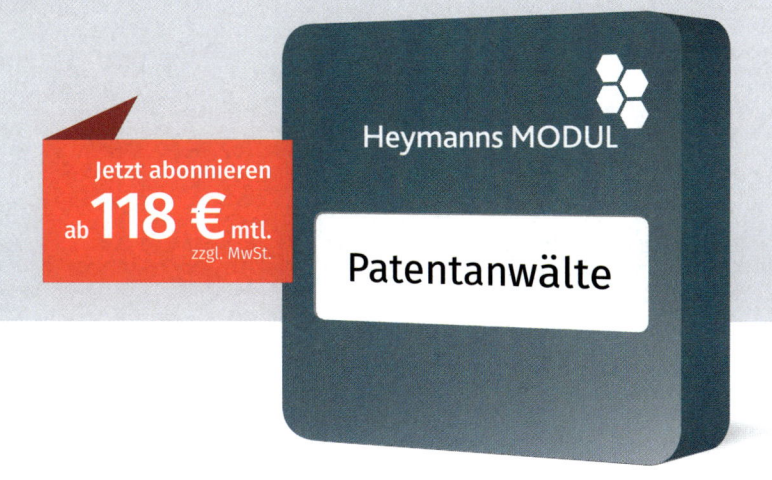

Jetzt abonnieren ab 118 € mtl. zzgl. MwSt.

Heymanns MODUL — Patentanwälte

Profitieren Sie von den Vorteilen eines Abonnements: stets aktuelle Inhalte und komfortable Tools, die Ihre Recherche erleichtern.
Mit Wolters Kluwer Recherche haben Sie außerdem Zugriff auf unsere kostenlose Rechtsprechungs- und Gesetzesdatenbank.

wolterskluwer-online.de

ALLES, WAS EXPERTEN BEWEGT.